S0-BZZ-314

# *Religion and Resistance Politics in South Africa*

# Religion and Resistance Politics in South Africa

## LYN S. GRAYBILL

Westport, Connecticut
London

**Library of Congress Cataloging-in-Publication Data**

Graybill, Lyn S.
    Religion and resistance politics in South Africa / Lyn S. Graybill.
      p.    cm.
    Bibliographical references and index.
    ISBN 0–275–95141–3 (alk. paper)
    1. Religion and politics—South Africa.  2. South Africa—Politics
and government—20th century.  3. Blacks—South Africa—Politics and
government.  4. Nationalism—South Africa.  I. Title.
    BR1450.G73   1995
    322′.1′0968—dc20      95–13895

British Library Cataloguing in Publication Data is available.

Copyright © 1995 by Lyn S. Graybill

All rights reserved. No portion of this book may be
reproduced, by any process or technique, without the
express written consent of the publisher.

BR
1450
.G73
1995

Library of Congress Catalog Card Number: 95–13895
ISBN: 0–275–95141–3

First published in 1995

Praeger Publishers, 88 Post Road West, Westport, CT 06881
An imprint of Greenwood Publishing Group, Inc.

Printed in the United States of America

The paper used in this book complies with the
Permanent Paper Standard issued by the National
Information Standards Organization (Z39.48–1984).

10 9 8 7 6 5 4 3 2 1

**Copyright Acknowledgments**

The author and publisher are grateful for permission to reprint excerpts from the following copy-
righted materials:

Albert Luthuli. *Let My People Go*. London: HarperCollins Publishers Limited, 1962; Albert Luthuli.
*The Road to Freedom is Via the Cross*. London: The African National Congress, n.d.; Basil Moore,
ed. *Black Theology: The South African Voice*. London: C. Hurst & Co., 1973; *I Write What I Like: A
Collection of His Writings: By Steve Biko* by Aelred Stubbs, editor. Copyright © 1978 by The
Bowerdean Press. Copyright © 1987 by Father Aelred Stubbs, C.R. Reprinted by permission of
HarperCollins Publishers, Inc.; Mangaliso Robert Sobukwe. *Speeches of Mangaliso Subukwe, 1949–
1959*. Johannesburg: Pan Africanist Congress of Azania Headquarters; Desmond Tutu. *Crying in the
Wilderness*. London: Mowbray, 1982.

Every reasonable effort has been made to trace the owners of copyright materials in this book, but in
some instances this has proven impossible. The author and publisher will be glad to receive information leading to more complete acknowledgments in subsequent printings of the book and in the
meantime extend their apologies for any omissions.

# Contents

# Acknowledgments

I wish to thank several individuals for their assistance and advice while researching and writing this book. First and foremost, I am grateful to Kenneth Thompson, director of the White Burkett Miller Center of Public Affairs, whose work in the realm of values and politics remains unsurpassed, and whose friendship has sustained me over the years. In addition, I am indebted to Robert Fatton whose seminar on South African Politics at the University of Virginia challenged me to study further the dynamics of protest in that country. Finally, I would be remiss not to mention David Holmes, professor of Religion at the College of William and Mary, who taught all his students to take notice of the vital link between faith and action.

Work on this book was supported by the Woodrow Wilson Department of Government and Foreign Affairs at the University of Virginia, and by the Institute for the Study of World Politics. I am grateful to both.

Writing this book would have been impossible without the forbearance of my husband, Jamie Aliperti, and the patience of my children, Pia and Britt. Finally, I dedicate this book to my parents in appreciation for a lifetime of love and encouragement.

# Introduction

In 1981 the Study Commission on U.S. Policy Toward Southern Africa produced what was generally considered a definitive study on South African politics and society.[1] In this exhaustive study, however, religion was covered in a mere page and a half. Given its thorough treatment of a multitude of other subjects, including trade unions, political parties, and the press, and given the use to which this study would be put in helping to develop U.S. foreign policy toward South Africa over the next decade, this omission is especially egregious. Unfortunately, the Commission's oversight is not the exception but the rule in analyses of South African politics. Since the report was written, most scholars continue to pay insufficient attention to the impact of religion on political development. In the South African context, this oversight is especially unfortunate since the South African is above all else a "religious animal."[2]

Not only census figures[3] but also official pronouncements overwhelmingly support the designation of South Africa as a Christian state. One cannot read a political document published by the South African government without being struck by the numerous references to God. Prime ministers have been known to respond publicly to synodical resolutions, and these resolutions have led to debates in Parliament, with each side attempting to show the consistency of its position with Scripture. What this suggests is that the role of religion is not insignificant. De Gruchy's statement that theology "is . . . not pushed to the edges of life but operates at the very pulse of South African culture"[4] is no exaggeration.

A review of South African history reveals how central religion has been to political life in that nation. The relationship between the Dutch Reformed Church and the National Party has been recognized, with the Dutch Reformed Church sometimes referred to as "The National Party at Prayer." The linkages between the Dutch Reformed Church and the government are ample; many prime ministers and members of Parliament have served as ministers or church leaders of that denomination.[5] Indeed, the Dutch Reformed churchmen have boasted that it was their church, and not the National Party, that first laid down the principles and framework of apartheid. The thesis that Calvinism helped to foster *Afrikaner* nationalism is recognized in the academic literature; Moodie, de Klerk, and Templin have demonstrated how theology has buttressed, rationalized, and promoted Afrikaner nationalism.[6] According to these scholars, the Calvinism that developed during the Great Trek—the nineteenth-century exodus of Boers from the Cape to escape British rule—held that God had divided mankind into distinct nations. Furthermore, it taught that God had chosen the Afrikaner nation as the elect, as His instrument in Southern Africa to fulfill a divine mission. The doctrine of separation in time legitimized the political policy of apartheid, and the idea of election sanctified beliefs in racial superiority.

Both popularly and among intellectuals there is less appreciation of Christianity's role in the development of *African* nationalism. Popularly, it is assumed that communism is the most salient ideology that has shaped black political resistance. One need only turn to Ronald Reagan's explanations of "constructive engagement" to see that the main threat envisaged to South Africa both externally and internally has been communism. As recently as 1986, even as it was passing the Anti-Apartheid Act, the U.S. Congress expressed its concern that the African National Congress (ANC) was "infiltrated by communists" and urged the ANC to make known its "commitment to a free and democratic South Africa not captive to the Communist Party and ideology."[7]

In the academic literature, studies that deal with the impact of Christianity on black nationalism are few in number. Among the best are Walshe's history of the ANC,[8] which looks at the ideological influences on that organization; Gerhart's work,[9] which traces the role of various philosophies on the evolution of the ANC's Youth League, the Pan-Africanist Congress (PAC), and the Black Consciousness Movement (BCM); and Motlhabi's studies,[10] which examine the Christian legacy on the African National Congress, Pan-Africanist Congress, Black Consciousness Movement, United Democratic Front (UDF), and National Forum (NF). Though indebted to these, especially the latter two, this study's perspective is narrower than Gerhart's, focusing solely on Christian influences and unlike Motlhabi, makes no attempt to judge which organization's strategy was the more moral.

The conventional wisdom is that religion's impact on African political activity, if any, has been negative—preaching patience, encouraging forbearance, teaching obedience to the state, and urging dialogue rather than revolt. Religion is viewed as having hampered African assertiveness, the degree of piety corresponding to the level of passivity within the African population. However, the Marxist critique that religion is an ideology of the oppressing class used to mystify the oppressed is an oversimplification. At no time did black South Africans accept the condition of oppression as an expression of the will of God. Counter-theologies arose in opposition to the theology of the oppressors, which enabled

Africans to pierce the myth of racial inferiority and see themselves as equal before God.

Even the South African government recognizes that Christian theology can be put to the service of radical politics. The Schlebush and Eloff Commissions, appointed to investigate the Christian Institute and the South African Council of Churches (SACC), respectively, determined that Christian theology was capable of launching a "dangerous and subversive attack . . . on the existing political, social, and economic order in the Republic."[11] The banning of the Christian Institute can be understood in the context of the government's fear of a militant black Christian-based political opposition. More recently, at the height of the sustained resistance of the 1980s, it was liturgies, Bible studies, and worship resources linking the political aspirations of Africans to Christian teaching that were confiscated by the security police.[12]

Admittedly, in the early days of the ANC, religion did play a somewhat moderating role. The ANC stressed modest goals: the right for representation in government as junior partners and the removal of certain discriminatory laws that assaulted the dignity of the black man. The white brother, it was believed, could be petitioned on the basis of a shared Christian morality to play fairly. Other tactics were prohibited: one could not justify illegal methods against a God-ordained state nor employ violent means against a neighbor one was enjoined to love.

By the time of the Defiance Campaign in 1952, the point at which this study begins, African resistance had become more assertive, motivated in part by Christian beliefs that pushed in the direction of active resistance. The goal was more ambitious: one-man-one-vote in a unitary system. Passive resistance against unjust laws replaced *beggar* tactics, the *sinfulness* rather than the *goodness* of the white man in time came to be stressed, and armed struggle eventually was condoned as the *lesser of evils*. Christianity, then, was never a static dogma but was continually reinterpreted in the light of new exigencies. Thus, the Christianity espoused by Albert Lutuli was quite different from that articulated by Steve Biko—and led to different strategies.

This study looks at four individuals—Albert Lutuli,[13] Robert Sobukwe, Steve Biko, and Desmond Tutu—and explores how each leader's Christian beliefs shaped the political strategy he pursued within the ANC, PAC, BCM, and UDF, respectively. It focuses on their leadership in four major episodes of resistance: the Defiance Campaign of 1952, the Sharpeville Massacre of 1960, the Soweto Uprising of 1976, and the Opposition to the Tricameral Parliament of 1983.

The selection of these four particular individuals[14] is based on their significant roles in these major campaigns, or "moments of resistance," to use Motlhabi's phrase.[15] His term is more accurate than the more commonly used "watershed events" because these campaigns were largely unsuccessful.[16] To quote Le May, they were "'turning points' where nothing turned."[17] But it was the very *failure* of these campaigns that forced their leaders to face up to the ineffectiveness of the prevailing tactics and the need to devise new ones, always in the context of a religious explanation and justification. These four campaigns, then, provide an opportunity for a snapshot look at African resistance politics as it developed over thirty years.

Among these four individuals, politics tended to gravitate toward two poles, or two opposing views of nationalism. Lutuli and Tutu represent the inclusive multiracial approach, sometimes called the Charterist position for its affinity with the ideals espoused in the Freedom Charter. Sobukwe and Biko typify the exclusive blacks-only approach, referred to as the Africanist position. These were two distinct approaches around which much of twentieth-century African politics has tended to gravitate. This study examines how theology has been variously employed to justify both the moderate Charterist and the radical Africanist schools of thought.


## REINHOLD NIEBUHR AND RELIGION

One can readily understand why certain Christian doctrines might be stressed to the exclusion of others. Undoubtedly, the fact that the African tends to see God as liberator and the Afrikaner views Him as the maintainer of order reflects the different social, political, and economic positions, and, ultimately, interests of those theologizing.

According to Reinhold Niebuhr, by some accounts the most important American contributor to twentieth-century political thought, both schools of thought—"prophetic criticism" which stresses the evils of government in history and "priestly sanctification" which sees government as an ordinance of God—are armed with proof texts for their respective positions.[18] Theology, Niebuhr reminds us, is subject to the "ideological taint" of all human knowledge, which, although gained from a particular perspective, nevertheless pretends to be final and ultimate.[19] He argues that the Church is subject to the faulty insights and sinful ambitions of specific individuals, groups, and classes that comprise it. The religious man is tempted to claim divine sanction for the very human and frequently sinful actions which he takes. In short, he is tempted to equate his particular interests with eternal truths.[20]

Niebuhr's analysis takes us a long way in accounting for the theological differences one would expect between Afrikaners and Africans, conditioned as they were by their different circumstances. But Africans were never monolithic in their beliefs. To what extent can different interests among Africans explain the variety of ways they came to apply the Christian gospel to politics? The Charterists and the Africanists broadly shared a similar political goal, the dismantling of apartheid, yet they diverged widely in their methods for accomplishing it. In most respects, their leaders shared a comparable economic position and social status in South African society. Circumstances alone do not determine the dominance of one idea over another. A similar multiracial mission education made a different impression on Lutuli than on Sobukwe, the former valuing multiracial alliances and the latter shunning them. There is a sense, then, in which beliefs are more than a reflection of circumstances. The affiliation to the Charterist or the Africanist position cannot always be explained by objective conditions, since Africans from the same economic class with similar life experiences opted for opposing movements.

It was the task of the individual leader, therefore, to make his position appealing, and Christianity, which claimed the loyalty of most Africans, was employed in the service of legitimating various strategies and objectives to the African masses. Rationalization of means and ends, addressed to a society where Christianity was the earliest and most potent ideological frame of reference, was invariably couched in Christian language. Gerhart notes that the "ingrained morality" of the Charterist position vied with the "new moral perspective" of the Africanist approach in every young African's heart and mind.[21]

Lutuli and Tutu could advocate multiracial alliances on the grounds that God's universal fatherhood made all South Africans *brothers*. To claim that all whites were irredeemably evil was to deny the power of Christ to convert the sinful. If the goal was a future harmonious multiracial society, certainly the means had to be consistent with that end, involving all the people of South Africa. Tutu emphasized that "we cannot afford to use methods of which we will be ashamed when we look back."[22] Likewise, Lutuli was wary of any revolution fueled by hatred of whites being capable of establishing a political order in which whites would be accepted without rancor. But the primary reason he eschewed violence was that it could not be morally justified given the sacredness of the human person made in God's image.

Sobukwe and Biko, on the other hand, believed that the Charterist approach drew too heavily on the Christian tradition that stressed the goodness of man. They were skeptical about the possibility of white conversion, feeling that it was naive to believe that the white man would willingly give up his many advantages without being forced. They were especially cynical of the motives of those apparently sympathetic whites who claimed to share their objective of dismantling apartheid since they so clearly benefited from the system. Polarization was seen as necessary to draw attention to who the enemy was—the entire white population.

Sobukwe and Biko, like Lutuli and Tutu, were interested in maintaining an aura of moral respectability. The former rejected cooperation with whites because paternalistic whites undermined the black man's dignity. Excluding whites was morally superior to cooperating with them, because multiracial alliances tended to perpetuate a sense of black inferiority and degradation, encouraging blacks to doubt their own efforts, to wonder whether they were the children of God, or merely his *step-children*.

*Love of Africa* was the highest good; therefore, hating whites was ethically justified for it was tantamount to loving Africa. Later, after black rule, whites would again be loved as brothers because all who accepted black majority rule would be counted as *Africans*. The belief that God was on the side of the oppressed helped dissolve any moral ambiguities surrounding the use of violence. Just-war theories further removed any moral qualms about resorting to armed struggle. It came to be argued that Africans have a *divine right* to liberate themselves from the tyranny of the state because the government had lost any legitimacy as a God-ordained institution.

Invariably, political pronouncements for mass consumption were couched in Christian terms that all levels of a church-attending society—the educated and uneducated—could understand. The use of religious justifications by African political movements demonstrates, as Niebuhr has pointed out, that man is nearly incapable of claiming some desired object without seeking to prove that it is desirable in terms of some wider system of values.[23] The "value of the end," he writes, "is necessary to sanction the fact that it is desired."[24] Advancing the cause of black political rights became, thus, a *Christian duty*. The liberation of black South Africans was seen as having wider implications: the *liberation of mankind*. Likewise, the tactics employed—nonviolent or violent, multiracial or exclusivist—were presented within a moral framework, appealing to values beyond mere pragmatism. It was the task of these four leaders, vying for recruits to their political cause, to direct and to manipulate mass attitudes through the language of Christian protest.

The role of religion, however, is twofold. Religion is not only an *instrumentality* but an *absolute standard* by which to judge all finite structures. The two forces of religion contend with each other—the *utilitarian*, which seeks to harness the ultimate to one's immediate purpose, over against the *transcendent*, in which man truly desires to submit his will to the divine.[25] Niebuhr writes, "We seek in the same act and the same thought to conform our will to God's and to coerce God's will to our own."[26] The tendency to hide interest behind more inclusive ideals arises from the fact that man is a transcendent being able to contemplate a more general realm of value than his own interests. If man were not capable of transcending the temporal, he would have no concern for unconditioned truth and thus would not feel compelled to claim absolute validity for his partial perspectives and particular insights. He would not be tempted to confuse *his* truth with *the* truth.[27] But, Niebuhr asserts, the self never follows its own interest without pretending to be obedient to obligations beyond itself. "It transcends its own interests too much to be able to serve them without disguising them in loftier pretensions."[28] Political man justifies his immediate purposes by ultimate principles, "always trying to prove that what [he is] doing is in accord with God's will or with ultimate truth or with the supreme good. Thus, even a religion which is primarily the servant of human purposes points beyond itself."[29]

The capacity of man for self-transcendence permits a more absolute standard for judging his necessarily finite perspectives in the light of a more inclusive truth.[30] Man's transcendence forces him to ask how *his* truth is related to *eternal* truth.[31] Despite their corruption, universal norms not only exist in the rhetoric of political leaders, but also are reflected, albeit imperfectly, in reality. Although ideals are undoubtedly colored by temporal interests, man nevertheless sees "the possibility of a truth which is more than his truth and of a goodness which is more than his goodness."[32] The Kingdom of God, present in the world through the redeemed but not fully realizable in history, nevertheless exerts a pressure upon the conscience of man and represents an ideal by which to judge the present. Despite the impossibility of attaining the ideal of love in political communities, it is relevant all the same as a yardstick by which to judge society's tentative solutions at building justice, which for Niebuhr meant merely an "approximation of brotherhood under the conditions of sin."[33]

According to Niebuhr, religion provides a source of moral insight for individuals to oppose the false sanctities of governments, it offers a vantage point from which to discount the "pretensions of demonic Caesars,"[34] and it points to the fact that God is not the ally of ruling groups but, alas, their judge.[35] The value of religion lies in its ability to raise up "sensitive minorities" who can act as the conscience of the nation, subjecting its actions to criticism.[36] A prophetic faith enables the opposition to detect the spurious claims of impartiality and universality endemic in every community.[37]

Spanning a half century, Niebuhr's works sought to illuminate the contribution of religion to the realm of politics. He spoke particularly to the racial problem in editorials he penned for *Christianity and Society* and *Christianity and Crisis*; and on at least three separate occasions, he wrote directly on the South African situation.[38]

Today's readers will find many of his statements unenlightened if not altogether condescending. For instance, in a report issued by the Detroit Mayor's Race Committee which he chaired, Niebuhr urged black people to pay attention to the personal appearance and demeanor of themselves and their children. The same report also proposed teaching urban blacks in Detroit to maintain their homes and yards without pointing to the more serious problem of white slumlords' near total neglect of inner-city housing.[39]

Despite his sometimes trivial recommendations, Niebuhr nonetheless believed that issues of racial justice comprise that area of human relations demanding "the first charge of the Christian conscience."[40] In fact, the seriousness with which he addressed the issue of racial justice is borne out by Martin Luther King Jr., who stated that Niebuhr, "probably more than any other thinker in America" stressed the need for a transcendent faith with which to carry out the Gospel's demand for justice.[41]

Without doubt, Niebuhr is at his most insightful in those writings that deal theologically, rather than practically, with the problem of racism in America and abroad. Racism, he believed, is mankind's major collective sin, a virulent expression of group pride, the "sinful corruption of group consciousness."[42] For Niebuhr, racial bigotry is a form of pride and arrogance behind which man seeks to hide his general insecurity. Racial bigotry, he believed, is more than a problem of ignorance; it is ultimately a problem of idolatry, of man's "partly conscious and partly unconscious effort to make himself and his race and his culture God." In short, racism is a form of "original sin."[43]

Racism as an expression of group pride raises the question of the possibility of morality for collective man. In Niebuhr's first major work, *Moral Man and Immoral Society*, he elaborated the thesis that a sharp distinction had to be drawn between the moral and social behavior of individuals and of groups—whether national, racial, or economic. For Niebuhr, society transmutes individual altruism into collective egoism, with no group capable of acting from purely unselfish interests.[44] Given the egoism of collective man, the inability of groups to sacrifice their self-interest, and the impossibility of the love ethic to be applied to the political realm, is racism, in which a dominant racial group oppresses less powerful groups, inevitable?

For Niebuhr the answer would be no. Racial prejudice could be broken, not by enlightenment on the part of whites, as the naive optimists believed, but rather by repentance. Churches and, more specifically, the "prophetic minorities" within the churches, have a role in piercing the myths of racial superiority often sanctioned by orthodox religion, and in leading the country to repentance. In his writings on racism, Niebuhr did not deal directly with the issue of force, but his political philosophy as a whole justifies the use of violence to bring about the repentance of ruling groups. His social analysis led him to the conclusion that violence was an indispensable element in the dynamics of social change. Force was proper when its discriminate use provided greater opportunities for justice than did the denial of violence. In fact, precisely because groups cannot transcend their self-interest, politics is bound to be a contest of power.[45]

Niebuhr's thinking at various times mirrors the thinking of either the Charterists or the Africanists. Beginning his career as a self-styled liberal, optimistic about the capacity of man to change through education and enlightenment, convinced of the possibility of applying the love ethic to political problems, and supporting a strict pacifism which eschewed all forms of violence, Niebuhr resembles the early Lutuli and Tutu. Later in life he adopted a Christian Marxist position which rejected the "illusions" of the "idealists," the possibility that powerful groups would give up their privilege short of revolution. His writings from this period are reminiscent of the Africanists as well as perhaps the mature years of the Charterists. Finally, Niebuhr's thinking coalesced into a Christian realist stance which advocated not an absolute ethic of love but a proximate ethic of justice, based on mutual accommodation rather than self-sacrifice, and use of force to create a balance of power which alone makes justice possible.

We will see these various themes at play in South African resistance politics. A host of black leaders in South Africa carried on the Niebuhrian task of demonstrating the relevance of religion to the political struggle of dismantling apartheid. They owe Niebuhr a tremendous, if largely unrecognized, theological debt.

Concentrating on religion as I have in this study is justified not only because the topic has been neglected by scholars of South Africa, but also because nowhere has the interplay between religion as instrumentality and transcendent truth been more evident than in that country. Religion has been the touchstone both for political ideas and the vehicle for the dissemination of those ideas in South Africa. As a pervasive force—the "unbreakable thread"[46] in South African resistance politics—it deserves to be taken seriously as a catalyst for change.

## IDEOLOGICAL INFLUENCES

To focus on the importance of religion is not to ignore the significance of other ideological influences on African nationalism. Liberalism, Garveyism, Pan-Africanism, and communism are but a few of the most significant ideologies to have an impact on twentieth-century African resistance politics in South Africa. Christianity did not *compete* with these philosophical systems; African leaders borrowed from various secular ideologies what was compatible with their faith and personal predisposition and what made sense in the context of the prevailing conditions in South Africa.

Lutuli especially was influenced by liberalism. Gradualism, optimism, and faith in constitutional methods—all hallmarks of the liberal tradition—held sway over Lutuli's thinking and that of the early ANC. Kuper remarks that the ANC under Lutuli was proceeding "on the basis of a liberal humanitarian creed, which asserts the dignity of the human personality, the belief that all men are born equal, the conviction that the human being is educable, and the assumption that history is the story of the unfolding of freedom."[47] The first half of the twentieth century, writes Walshe, was devoted to attempts to "prise open the doors of discrimination so as to establish a gradual and evolutionary process of African participation in the structures set up by whites."[48]

Lutuli's mission education was no doubt responsible for his predisposition towards Western liberalism. Steeped in the liberal tradition, students from mission schools invariably accepted the belief in man's capacity for enlightenment and the inevitability of progress. Thus, writes Gerhart, they were predisposed towards wishful thinking, tending to substitute moralistic analyses for hard political calculations.[49]

In addition to the impact of Western education was the tradition of the Cape Province, which had been founded in 1820 by English settlers, who brought with them the ideals of liberal democracy. There a nonracial, if limited, franchise had existed since 1854, offering a working precedent of the liberal principle of nonracialism. There was hope among Africans in the ANC that in time political rights would be extended to all Africans. However, in 1936 all hope of extending the franchise to the other republics was shattered, as the Hertzog Bills disenfranchised the Africans living in the Cape Province.  The Charterists were also influenced by their ties to English liberals in Parliament, perceived as friends of Africans, who urged patience and moderation from them.  Sparks notes that the significance of the English, politically powerless themselves, was that they nevertheless "implanted political ideas that have given shape to the whole conflict."[50]

The example of the black American experience also had a role in shaping the evolution of a liberal ethos.  Blacks in America were struggling for the extension of civil liberties, and the emphasis there on cooperation across color lines made an indelible impression on black South Africans.[51]  The nonracialism of an earlier generation of African-Americans, including Frederick Douglass, Booker T. Washington, and W. E. B. Du Bois, made an impact in black South African intellectual circles.[52]

Another plank in the liberal platform in South Africa was Gandhi's legacy of nonviolent passive resistance.  His Indian Congress in South Africa, which was formed to protect Indian rights, provided a working model for the ANC.  The ANC's early commitment to nonviolence was formed in part by the liberal creed of nonviolence espoused by Gandhi.

While liberalism's emphasis on conciliation, compromise, and constitutional methods did not survive the second half of the twentieth century, liberalism's other tenets—multiracialism and rejection of violence—endured, the latter until 1961 and the former flourishing in the UDF of the 1990s.

The acceptance of liberal creeds was reinforced by Christian beliefs that stressed the equality of all men as brothers under the fatherhood of God.  The oneness made possible by Christ, who had broken down the walls of partition between Jew and Greek, male and female, was seen as having a practical implication: the unity of all people born in South Africa in one multiracial society. Furthermore, the Christian command to love one's neighbor required non-racialism and nonviolence, so thought Lutuli and his fellow liberals in the ANC.

By the time of the Defiance Campaign, however, Lutuli had become disillusioned with liberalism as a creed and with white liberals in particular. "Only a few," he lamented, "like Huddleston and Reeves and Blaxall . . . share our troubles with us."[53]  The truly committed few, unfortunately, were peripheral to the power structure and hence proved ineffectual at promoting reform.  Lutuli never gave up hope that white South Africans could change, but experience made him more realistic about the persistence of self-interest among white South Africans.  Realizing that moral suasion alone would not suffice, he was forced to face up to the implications of his faith, writes Robertson.[54]

A proper understanding of the doctrine of original sin would have gone far in preventing his initially overly optimistic view of human nature.  The Christian view of man emphasizes not only man's glory but also his misery.  A "mature" faith would have prevented the unfounded optimism of the early ANC regarding the white man's willingness to change.  It recognizes that there "is clearly something more stubborn and mysterious in human wrongdoing than some easily corrected sloth or malice."[55] Man's egotism and will-to-power are persistent and not readily overcome. Thus, preaching the Gospel will not overcome evil in history, and moral entreaties are insufficient in restraining one group from taking advantage of another.[56] The implication of the doctrine of original sin in time became clear to Lutuli: political pressure buttressed by power was necessary to back up moral claims.

Sobukwe and Biko appear to have commenced their political lives with a realistic appraisal of whites' unwillingness to change without having to evolve to that position. One explanation for why they so readily stressed the sinfulness of whites is that they came of age in an era of white intransigence to political reform. Lutuli had been born into a society in which apartheid had not yet been institutionalized. His world was one in which economic advancement for middle-class blacks was not altogether impossible. The South Africa that Sobukwe and Biko entered, on the other hand, was a harsher world in which every aspect of their lives was controlled by a myriad of apartheid laws and in which there were progressively fewer opportunities for success. Thus, they grew up with fewer illusions about the nature of white rule, according to Gerhart.[57]

Ever the realist, Sobukwe asserted, "History has taught us that a group in power has never voluntarily relinquished its position."[58] He had little faith in the inherent goodness of the white man. Experience had taught him the tenacious hold of interest on group behavior and the stubbornness of sin in all political communities.[59] His rejection of multiracialism as a strategy reflects a profound awareness of the limits of self-sacrifice in politics. It is not in the interest of other groups—white liberals and communists—to bring about black majority rule; hence, alliances with these groups would stifle black aspirations, he believed. Both Sobukwe and Biko rejected liberalism's penchant for gradualism, constitutionalism methods, multiracialism, and nonviolence.

The Africanists' political realism stems from a "more profound version"[60] of the Christian faith than the early Charterists that stressed the sinfulness of man and hence the need for action, not sermons. Their political program was based on the recognition that pure conscience seldom defeats an unjust system.[61] They recognized that inordinate power tempts its holders to abuse it, and that only power can challenge power. The inability of humans to transcend their own interests significantly to consider the rights of others in contrast with their own makes force inevitable,[62] they discovered. Armed with the truth about man's nature which Christian teaching supplies, Sobukwe and Biko accepted the need for force in politics. However, given the gross inequality in strength between blacks and whites, the Africanists were content to emphasize psychological emancipation. Forced to face the truth that only commensurate power could counter power to wrench changes, the PAC and BCM instigated status campaigns aimed at increasing black confidence and bargaining power in order to eventually confront whites on an equal footing.

Sobukwe and Biko appear to apply the doctrine of original sin exclusively to the white man and assume that the downtrodden Africans possessed a monopoly on virtue. Given their view of the nearly total depravity of the white man, it is not surprising that the Africanists found Garveyism, which stressed the evils of the white man and the moral superiority of the black man, congenial. Garvey's ideas were in circulation in South Africa beginning in the 1920s, but his racialist assertions and visions had little influence on the ANC, given its strong belief that God's fatherhood of all men pointed to the ideal of nonracialism. Garvey's impact on South Africa was a delayed one, writes Walshe, contributing to the ideas of the later Africanists.[63]

Garveyism had been brought to South Africa by James Thaele, a follower of Garvey's Universal Negro Improvement Association, who had picked up its tenets from study in the United States. When Thaele returned to South Africa, he joined the Western Cape Congress of the ANC, pushing it in a Garveyist direction. The Cape ANC's organ was named *The African World* to identify it with Garvey's *Negro World*, and it published Garvey's treatise on "African fundamentalism" into Sotho with a message that "this letter is a guideline of the principles of government that shall be ours."[64] In addition, the Johannesburg ANC newspaper *Abantu Batho* defended Garvey's ideas in its columns.[65] However, by the end of the decade, the Garveyist influence had receded and the ANC returned to its nonracial, moderate style.[66]

Garvey's racialism was compatible with that of the Africanists in the PAC and BCM, who embraced his slogan "Africa for Africans." And although the PAC dissociated itself from the corollary slogan "to hurl the white man into the sea," one PAC member admitted "[People] liked it privately! But we didn't want to go down on paper . . . it would damage us with our friends overseas."[67] It also found its way into the separatist churches that Sobukwe was courting through their connection with black-exclusivist sects in America who were its champions. Mangena Mokone had established the Ethiopian Church in Pretoria under Garvey's slogan: "Africa for Africans."

Closely related to the racialist overtones of Garveyism was the equally racialist ideology of Pan-Africanism. Pan-Africanism, which stressed predominant African power, had a negligible effect on the ANC, which had sought throughout its history the extension of rights to Africans. (Even when in the mid-1940s the ANC demanded an open franchise—which given the size of its population would have placed dominant political power in African hands—it stressed in its writings and speeches that it wanted to *share* power rather than *usurp* power, in order to placate white fears of black domination.[68] Never did the ANC speak of *seizing* power.) The concept of predominant political power was subsequently developed within the Youth League and later by the Africanists of the PAC and BCM. In developing an ideology of African nationalism, the Africanists began to direct their attention to the African continent as a whole,[69] envisioning a Pan-African unity stretching "from Cape to Cairo, Madagascar to Morocco."[70]

Another link between racialist theories from abroad and the Africanist movement was forged in the 1960s. The Black Power movement in the United States was having an impact on South Africa through the writings of Eldridge Cleaver, Stokely Carmichael, and Charles Hamilton. Malcolm X in particular was a favorite among young South Africans. A former South African Students' Association (SASO) member recalls that the group had twelve recordings of Malcolm X's speeches: "Compared to Martin Luther King, we felt that Malcolm's preachings were much more gutsy, much more in tandem with what we were thinking and feeling."[71] Debates on the similarities and differences between blacks in the United States and South Africa were popular among black-consciousness groups. The widespread use of the term *black* as a positive expression is a legacy of the Black Power movement in the United States, and the raised fist to connote black power was adopted enthusiastically from that movement.[72]

The religious wing of the Black Power movement, represented by black theology, was having an equally strong impact. A taped address by American black theologian James Cone on black theology was heard at the first conference on black theology in South Africa. While the South African black theology movement was largely coterminous with rather than dependent upon the American movement, there is no doubt that American black theology was the single most important external influence on South African politics in the 1960s and 1970s.

By the 1970s, Gerhart writes, never had such a thorough-going effort been made to selectively adapt foreign ideas to the South African situation. This she attributes to the general explosion in worldwide telecommunications and the widespread availability of overseas literature on race relations.[73] But the political conditions in South Africa better explain why foreign exclusivist ideologies took root in the hearts and minds of young Africans. Racialist ideas from abroad predictably found a warm reception on the now blacks-only campuses throughout South Africa. This should not be surprising; Lutuli had attributed his education in an integrated environment with forestalling hatred against whites. Likewise, Tutu looked back at his time in England, where normal relations between the races was possible, as significant in instilling in him a commitment to the multiracial ideal. These experiences were not available to the generation of Africans coming of age in the 1960s. The generation of leaders schooled in Christian liberal aspirations of being accepted as participants with whites in running the state was replaced by a generation for whom control, not assimilation, was sought and openly articulated. Africanism was especially strong in the Boer republics, where race relations had always been strained. Gerhart notes that living in the Orange Free State or the Transvaal may have bred an ingrained mistrust of whites not found among the blacks from the Cape and Natal provinces, where the core of the ANC leadership has originated.[74]

Garveyism, Pan-Africanism, and black power—secular ideologies which stress black exclusivism—are all compatible with Christian doctrines that stress God's preferential option for the poor, which in the hands of black theology has come to mean God's siding with the oppressed black nation. Scriptures that stress God's special relationship with the elect support the Africanists' claim for a special destiny based on the color of their skin, the cause of their oppression. The Exodus story—a favorite with the Afrikaners who saw a parallel between God's deliverance of the Israelites from the Egyptian oppressors and their own Great Trek away from the English imperialists—has been appropriated by black theologians to describe God's special concern for the oppressed black nation under white domination. Tutu and other moderate black theologians have been quick to warn their more racialist brothers that God sides with them, not because they are better or more deserving than their oppressors, but simply because they are oppressed.[75] Neither did Tutu see the whites as *irredeemable devils* as do some black theology proponents.

Communism was another salient ideology at play in South African society. The Communist Party of South Africa (CPSA) opened its membership to Africans in the mid-1920s, and there were always some Africans with simultaneous memberships in the Communist Party and ANC. The National Party victory in 1948, based in part on the promise to discriminate against Indians and Coloureds as well as Africans, made joint action seem possible, and some of the young Africanists in the Youth League, including Nelson Mandela and Oliver Tambo, moderated their earlier rejection of communist alliances. The banning of the Communist Party in 1950 led to even greater unity between the ANC and communists since the ban was seen as a threat to all extraparliamentary opposition.[76]

The fact that the communists have been the most radical voice in South African politics in terms of urging the complete dismantling of apartheid helps to explain the historically warm relations between ANC members and Communist Party members. In addition, communist countries have welcomed visiting Africans, who on their return helped spread knowledge of communist theory. The Soviet Union's forceful denunciation of apartheid in the United Nations, compared to the West's mild protest in that body, also explains the camaraderie between the communists and ANC members. Furthermore, the Soviet Union welcomed Africans to its consulate in Pretoria (before it was closed in 1956), while the United States banned Africans from all social functions at its embassy in South Africa until 1963. This contrast could not fail to make a lasting impression on Africans, who also benefited from the night schools conducted by communists in South Africa. A more mundane explanation for the closeness between the ANC and communists is the fact that the ANC did not have its own national newspaper and relied on the communist organ the *New Age* to put forth the ANC position in a positive light, which it did not fail to do.[77]

The small number of communists who were ever members of the ANC is disproportionate to the large impact of communism on that organization. By emphasizing class analysis—the importance of working-class solidarity among black and white workers—communists encouraged the Charterists to think in terms other than exclusively racial ones.[78] Communism's long-term impact on the Charterists, then, was to reaffirm the ideal of multiracialism. Lutuli and Tutu, consistent with their belief in multiracial efforts, have welcomed assistance from all quarters. They have been receptive to working with individual communists but less receptive to communist ideas, which they considered to be based on a false religion, the deification of a particular class and worship of the state.

Yet during the Treason Trial, Lutuli conceded that they had "picked up the language" of communist theory.[79] This is evident in the economic platforms of the Freedom Charter: "The People Shall Share in the Country's Wealth" and "The Land Shall be Shared Among Those Who Work It." The Freedom Charter's economic policies advanced the earlier Program of Action's aim of winning political rights. Obviously, the new emphasis on the redistribution of wealth and land reflected the views of the communists in the Congress of Democrats (COD) as well as the general realization by the ANC that it was necessary to champion the ideas of the rank and file to build the ANC into a true mass movement. However, the fact that there was no detailed economic program indicates the less-than-perfect correlation between the ANC's priority, political democracy, and the communists' ultimate aim for a socialist revolution following the democratic one. The Communist Party's commitment to eradicate capitalism was not synonymous with the ANC's deepest concerns, according to one view. In fact, Lutuli favored retaining some ownership of private property and hoped that blacks would join whites as capitalists.[80]

Sobukwe and Biko, more so than the Charterists, were deeply hostile to communism. They rejected communist theory as irrelevant in a country where race, not class, was the decisive division. They were convinced that communists' interests could not coincide with black aspirations, because (white) communists would lose out in a black majority government.

Benson writes that their opposition to communism sprang from their religious training. They had been taught, she explains, that communists were the anti-Christ.[81] Perhaps their rejection of communism sprang also from a Christian awareness that all mankind is fallen. Christianity reveals the myth of a perfect class which is inherently benevolent. The Christian doctrine of man's fallen state is inconsistent with a view that sees a perfect harmony of wills after the dictatorship of the proletariat ushers in a utopia. The Africanists could not bring themselves to view all sin as residing in property, and their religious background predisposed them to reject a materialist view of man as simply an "economic animal."[82]

However, the Africanists borrowed from communist theory in devising policies that aimed at the redistribution of wealth. There was a recognition that without deep economic changes, political equality would be inconsequential. But their commitment to the socialization of property was conditioned as much by their belief that Christianity required economic justice as by a conversion to scientific socialism. God's concern for the whole man translates into interest in his physical as well as spiritual well-being, the Africanists argued. Later, Tutu was to insist that Christianity did not preach an other-worldly pie-in-the-sky-when-you-die theology but recognized that "people want their pie here and now, and not in some future tomorrow."[83] Socialism, he theorized, was superior in providing economic justice than was capitalism, which he believed was based on man's baser instincts.[84]

Although the BCM borrowed more extensively from Marxism-Leninism than the earlier resistance movements, Biko claimed that his economic views were based on an *indigenous* African socialism rather than a *foreign* import. He endorsed *African Socialism*, which was based on ideals such as mutuality, cooperation, and neighborliness which presumably existed in precolonial Africa. Like Lutuli and Sobukwe before him, Biko was clearly more interested in the nonmaterial aspects of liberation, as Tutu would be later. As Christians, they based their assault on apartheid more on its devaluation of the dignity of God-created beings than on its economic exploitation of them.

## RACIST LEGISLATION

As important as any abstract ideas in fueling opposition movements was the reality of living under the harsh conditions of apartheid. The choice of strategies pursued was shaped in large measure by the actual circumstances of repression in South Africa. In other words, a black political culture of protest evolved under the impact of external ideological influences and against the backdrop of racist legislation.

It was the color-bar clauses of the South Africa Act (1909) prohibiting Africans from doing skilled work in the mines; the Natives Land Act (1913) outlawing Africans from buying land outside the reserves or living outside the reserves unless employed by whites; the pass laws restricting the movement of Africans; and the Masters and Servants laws making breach of contract by unskilled workers a criminal offense that was behind the formation of the ANC. The history of the fledgling ANC in this early period was marked by fruitless attempts and endless appeals to persuade whites on the basis of a shared Christian morality to remove the discriminatory legislation. In 1936, the Hertzog Bills were passed, including the Representation of Natives Bill, which whittled away the limited black franchise in the Cape Province, and set up the Natives' Representative Council as an advisory board for black participation outside the mainstream of political life.

Following the election in May 26, 1948, which the National Party won on the promise to enforce apartheid (*apartness*), race became the overriding consideration in organizing society. Building on earlier laws and practices, segregation became more fully entrenched. After 1948, the color bar, previously limited to mining, was extended throughout industry. A host of new laws was passed that further attenuated black rights. One of the first bills passed by the new government was the Prohibition of Mixed Marriages Act (1949) forbidding interracial marriage, followed by Immorality Acts (1950, 1957) restricting interracial sex. The Population Registration Act of 1950, the cornerstone of apartheid, assigned each person to one of three racial groups: white, Coloured, or African. The Bantu Authorities Act (1951) strengthened the power of tribal authorities in the reserves and paved the way for the Promotion of Bantu Self-Government Act (1959), which recognized the reserves as the *homelands* for the various tribes, and the only arena in which Africans would exercise their political rights.

It was the comprehensive apartheid legislation instituted by the Nationalists under D. F. Malan—and the growing realization that appeals for change had been unsuccessful—that was the impetus for the ANC's decision to adopt more militant action and to openly defy unjust laws in the Defiance Campaign of 1952. Following the campaign, instead of dismantling apartheid, the government instituted more draconian legislation in 1953: the Public Safety Act, which permitted the government to declare a state of emergency and then issue emergency regulations; the Criminal Law Amendment Act, which mandated severe penalties to protesters of any law; and the Bantu Education Act, which took control of education away from the churches and required that black children be taught in blacks-only schools. By the end of the 1950s, the homelands policy of self-government for Africans in the bantustans continued apace under the Verwoerd government. This decade also saw the Extension of University Education Act, which, far from *extending* educational opportunities, prohibited blacks from attending the major English universities of Witwatersrand, Cape Town, and Natal.

From this environment of harsh legislation, the recognition that opportunities for African political and economic advancement were being systematically cut off, and disillusionment with the ANC's unsuccessful efforts of protest, the PAC was formed, committed to new methods of struggle: the rejection of cooperation across racial lines with white sympathizers and the acceptance of violence as an option. When the 1960 Pass Campaign was brutally put down by police at Sharpeville, and the ANC and PAC were subsequently banned, resistance politics became more assertive as violence came to be embraced by the military wings of the exiled groups, as well as entertained as an option by the BCM.

After Sharpeville, tough new laws aimed at curbing dissent were passed. The Sabotage Act of 1962 was built upon the earlier Internal Security Act of 1950. The Terrorism Act became law in 1967, which expanded on the earlier two acts to include actions which "embarrass the administration of the affairs of the State."[85] These acts authorized detentions and bannings of those suspected to be a danger to state security. In 1968 the Prohibition of Political Interference Act was passed, which outlawed multiracial political parties. Thus, blacks were excluded from joining the Liberal and Progressive Parties and from influencing the policies of those groups that many blacks felt were acting on their behalf. The Group Areas Act was revised in 1966 to create separate group areas in towns and cities for the three racial groups.

By the 1970s ten homelands had been officially designated by the government and under the Bantu Homelands Constitution Act (1971) were on the way to acquire *independent nations* status. In addition, legislation had established by 1967 the Urban Bantu Councils, which limited black political participation to minor local matters. In 1976, the government passed a new law that required the use of Afrikaans as the medium of instruction in the secondary schools. Outraged by this new law, and dissatisfied with Bantu education, which was marked by poor instruction, overcrowded schools, and limited postgraduation employment prospects, students took to the streets in protest only to be assaulted by police fire in what came to be known as the Soweto Uprising. The protest reflected a deep resentment among young people with the myriad of apartheid laws regulating their lives and putting limits on their future opportunities. The crushing of opposition, the banning of black-consciousness organizations, and the exodus of thousands of young people to join the ANC in exile set the scene for the continued militancy of the 1980s.

The context for black resistance politics in the following decade was the government's attempts to modify apartheid in order to gain allies. To this end, new township councils with broader powers than the earlier urban councils were established to distinguish a privileged class of urban blacks from the migrant workers whose only political rights were confined to the tribal homelands. Furthermore, a new constitution was passed with three chambers—extending some political rights to Indians and Coloureds to dissuade them from forming a united front opposition with Africans. Despite some relaxation of *petty apartheid* legislation—dismantling segregation in some public places—the pillars of apartheid were kept in place: the Population Registration Act, the Natives Land Act, and the Group Areas Act. The UDF's *One Million Signatures* campaign urging Coloureds and Indians to boycott the 1984 election was successful if judged by the number of people who stayed away from the polls, but it did not cause the government to repeal the new constitution. The campaign did usher in the longest sustained era of protest in South African history, witnessed the release of Nelson Mandela from Robben Island, the unbanning of the ANC, the dismantling of most apartheid legislation including the Group Areas and Population Registration Acts, and the beginning of talks to usher in a new political settlement.

As important as the actual conditions of life under apartheid or the impact of ideologies on shaping a political culture of protest was the effect of world events. Rights that were being won elsewhere were being compared with the diminution of rights for blacks in South Africa. The right of small nations for self-determination articulated by Woodrow Wilson after World War I made an impression on black South Africans, who could not fail to see that these same rights being enunciated in the Fourteen Points—which they had hoped would apply equally to them—were being denied them in South Africa. World War II made an even greater impact on black thinking. After all, it had been a war fought against racism, or so thought black South Africans, who believed their loyalty and support for the war effort would be rewarded following the Allied victory. The Atlantic Charter's endorsement of national self-determination and the United Nations Universal Declaration of Human Rights encouraged black South Africans to expect that these liberties would apply to them as well.

All this lit a flame of expectation, writes Sparks, "and when decolonization began the flame burned brighter still."[86] The example of Indian independence from Great Britain in 1948 and the swift decolonizations that followed in Indonesia, Indochina, India, Pakistan, Ceylon, Philippines, Jordan, Syria, Libya, Morocco, Tunisia, and Egypt did not escape the attention of blacks in South Africa. By the 1960s almost all of Africa had been decolonized, and when Portugal, the oldest colonial power in Africa, was vanquished in the mid-1970s, followed by the transfer of power to the black majority in Rhodesia in 1980, the effect was a renewal of militancy, the belief in the total unacceptableness of minority rule, and an affirmation of faith in eventual victory.

It is within this setting of a steady torrent of apartheid legislation, the introduction of ideological currents from abroad, combined with the growing awareness of successful liberation struggles worldwide that the opposition to apartheid must be viewed. Intolerable laws were defied, resistance met with defeat, disillusionment set in, new ideological forces were adopted, and different strategies were tried. According to Anthony Marx, "Opposition movements . . . refined abstract ideas against the harsh realities of experience, and failure has been a powerful teacher."[87] Disillusionment with past strategies that had failed encouraged leaders to adopt new strategies based on different ideological assumptions that might better serve them.

For instance, if violence in time became an acceptable option, it had as much to do with the intransigence of white South Africans to change as with Garveyist and other exclusivist ideas being studied on campuses. The failure of whites to dismantle apartheid meant the repudiation of those tactics that had been tried and found wanting. Disillusionment invariably ushered in new militancy; the multiracial moderation of the ANC under Lutuli came to be replaced by the radical exclusivist approach of the BCM under Biko. The brutal crushing of the student revolt at Soweto, followed so closely by the mysterious death of Biko in police custody, and the banning of the black-consciousness groups, strengthened arguments for a just revolution that have been articulated in the 1980s.

Christianity was a vital factor in the evolution of a black political culture of resistance. It was never the single ideological influence, but it combined with other forces to produce a people bent on defiance of unjust laws and of minority rule. Christianity is, however, the one and only *unbreakable thread* that ties these opposition movements together.  What these four leaders shared—despite their attraction to sometimes opposing secular ideologies—was a belief in a transcendent God to whom one owed total allegiance.  Rather than a force that pushes in the direction of apolitical escapism, Christianity, they believed, requires resolute action in the world, for there is no area of life "in which God's writ does not run."[88]  The greatest sin, they agreed, "was to allow oneself to be oppressed."[89] Niebuhr writes, "The promises of another world may prompt the weak man to resign, but they will encourage the strong man to deeds of superhuman heroism."[90]  Certainly, this applies to Lutuli, Sobukwe, Biko, and Tutu, as they strove to approximate the Kingdom of God within history.  Despite the moral ambiguities inherent in politics, they felt called to enter the fray, taking their faith with them, as Lutuli had said, "and praying that it may be used to influence for good the character of the resistance."[91]  Lutuli, Sobukwe, Biko, and Tutu were courageous men of action persuaded that religious faith had implications for politics, even if they saw those implications somewhat differently.

## NOTES

1. Study Commission on U.S. Policy Toward Southern Africa, *South Africa: Time Running Out* (Berkeley: University of California Press, 1981).

2. David Bosch, cited in James Young, "South African Churches: Agents of Change," *Christian Century* (November 24, 1982), p. 1201.

3. Eighty percent of South Africa's population are members of Christian churches.

4. John W. de Gruchy, cited in Simon Maimela, *Proclaim Freedom to My People* (Johannesburg: Skotaville, 1987), p. 12.

5. There are actually three main white Dutch Reformed Churches: Nederduitse Gereformeerde Kerk, Nederduitsch Hervormde Kerk, and Gereformeerde Kerk.

6. See T. Dunbar Moodie, *The Rise of Afrikanerdom: Power, Apartheid and the Afrikaner Civil Religion* (Berkeley: University of California Press, 1975); William A. de Klerk, *The Puritans in Africa: The History of Afrikanerdom* (London: Rex Collings, 1975); and J. Alton Templin, *Ideology on a Frontier: The Theological Foundation of Afrikaner Nationalism, 1652-1910* (Westport, Conn.: Greenwood Press, 1984).

7. Thomas Karis, "South African Liberation: The Communist Factor," *Foreign Affairs* (Winter 1986-1987), p. 287.

8. Peter Walshe, *The Rise of African Nationalism in South Africa: The African National Congress 1912-1952* (Berkeley: University of California Press, 1971).

9. Gail Gerhart, *Black Power in South Africa: The Evolution of an Ideology* (Berkeley: University of California Press, 1978).

10. Mokgethi Motlhabi, *Challenge to Apartheid: Toward a Moral National Resistance* (Grand Rapids, Mich.: William B. Eerdmans, 1988); and Mokgethi Motlhabi, *The Theory and Practice of Black Resistance to Apartheid* (Johannesburg: Ravan, 1984).

11. Cited in Ernie Regehr, *Perceptions of Apartheid: The Churches and Political Change in South Africa* (Scottsdale, Ariz.: Herald Press, 1979), p. 212.

12. Charles Villa-Vicencio, "To Be Servant of the People: The Church and Change in

South Africa," *Sojourners* (December 1992), p. 28.

13. Lutuli preferred this spelling of his name. See Thomas Karis and Gwendolen Carter, *From Protest to Challenge: A Documentary History of African Politics in South Africa, 1882-1964*, vol. 3 (Stanford: Hoover Institution Press, 1972-1977), p. xviii.

14. Some prominent leaders whose political perceptions were shaped by their Christian convictions include John Dube, Z. K. Matthews, Nelson Mandela, Oliver Tambo, Anton Lembede, and Allan Boesak. The majority of African political leaders were Christians whose faith had political implications and who articulated the struggle within a theological framework.

15. Motlhabi, *Challenge to Apartheid*, p. 37.

16. It might be argued that the opposition to the Tricameral Parliament was a success in that record numbers of Coloureds and Indians boycotted it. It certainly ushered in the longest period of political agitation in South African history, culminating in the release of Nelson Mandela and other political prisoners, the dismantling of much apartheid legislation, and the unbanning of the ANC. Nonetheless, it was over a decade before black South Africans were granted the most elemental of political rights, the vote.

17. G. H. L. Le May, cited in John Daniel, "Radical Resistance to Minority Rule in South Africa: 1906-1965" (Ph.D. dissertation, Buffalo: State University of New York, 1975), p. 284.

18. Reinhold Niebuhr, *The Nature and Destiny of Man*, vol. 2: *Human Destiny* (New York: Charles Scribner's Sons, 1964), p. 270.

19. Reinhold Niebuhr, *The Nature and Destiny of Man*, vol. 1: *Human Nature* (New York: Charles Scribner's Sons, 1955), p. 194.

20. Reinhold Niebuhr, *Beyond Tragedy: Essays on the Christian Interpretation of History* (New York: Charles Scribner's Sons, 1937), pp. 121-122.

21. Gerhart, p. 75.

22. Desmond Tutu, *The Words of Desmond Tutu*, ed. Naomi Tutu (New York: Newmarket Press, 1989), p. 48.

23. Reinhold Niebuhr, *Christian Realism and Political Problems* (Fairfield, N.J.: Augustus M. Kelley Publishers, 1977), p. 77.

24. Niebuhr, *Christian Realism and Political Problems*, p. 88.

25. Niebuhr, *Beyond Tragedy*, p. 78.

26. Niebuhr, *Beyond Tragedy*, p. 81.

27. Niebuhr, *The Nature and Destiny of Man*, vol. 1, p. 197.

28. Niebuhr, *The Nature and Destiny of Man*, vol. 2, p. 109.

29. Niebuhr, *Beyond Tragedy*, pp. 79-80.

30. Niebuhr, *The Nature and Destiny of Man*, vol. 2, p. 214.

31. Niebuhr, *The Nature and Destiny of Man*, vol. 2, p. 240.

32. Niebuhr, *Beyond Tragedy*, p. 61.

33. Niebuhr, *The Nature and Destiny of Man*, vol. 2, p. 254.

34. Reinhold Niebuhr, *The Children of Light and the Children of Darkness: A Vindication of Democracy and a Critique of Its Traditional Defense* (New York: Charles Scribner's Sons, 1944), p. 82.

35. Niebuhr, *Beyond Tragedy*, p. 56.

36. Niebuhr, *The Children of Light and the Children of Darkness*, p. 183.

37. Niebuhr, *Beyond Tragedy*, p. 56.

38. For his writings on racism, see Reinhold Niebuhr, "The Negro Ministry and Its Fate in a Self-righteous Nation," *Social Action/Social Progress* 35 no. 59 (October 1968), pp. 53–64; "Christian Faith and the Race Problem," *Christianity and Society* (Spring 1945); Editorial Notes, *Christianity and Crisis* 12, no. 23 (January 5, 1953); "The Christian Faith and the Race Problem," *Christianity and Society* (Spring 1945); "The Race Problem," *Christianity and Society* (1942); "Bad Days at Little Rock," *Christianity and Crisis* 17, no. 22 (December 26, 1955); "The Negro Issue in America," *Christianity and Society* (Summer 1944). For his writings that deal particularly with racism in South Africa, see Reinhold Niebuhr, "The South African Tragedy," *Christianity and Society* 20, no. 2 (Spring 1955); "The Supreme Court on Segregation in the Schools," *Christianity and Crisis* 16, no. 4 (March 19, 1956); "The Church and the South African Tragedy," *Christianity and Crisis* 20, no. 7 (May 2, 1960), pp. 53–54.

39. Report of the Mayor's Committee on Race Relations (Detroit, 1926), cited in Ronald Stone, *Reinhold Niebuhr: Prophet to Politicians* (Nashville, N.Y.: Abingdon Press, 1972), pp 32–33.

40. Niebuhr, Editorial Notes, *Christianity and Crisis,* p. 178, cited in Gordon Harland, *The Thought of Reinhold Niebuhr* (New York: Oxford University Press, 1960), p. 256.

41. Kenneth Smith and Ira Zepp. *Search for the Beloved Community: The Thinking of Martin Luther King, Jr.* (Valley Forge, Penn.: Judson Press, 1974), p. 31, cited in Ernest F. Dibble, *Young Prophet Niebuhr: Reinhold Niebuhr's Early Search for Social Justice* (Washington, D.C.: University Press of America, 1979), p. 296.

42. Niebuhr, "The Race Problem," *Christianity and Society*, cited in Harland, p., 259.

43. Niebuhr, "The Christian Faith and the Race Problem," *Christianity and Society*, cited in Harland, p. 259.

44. Reinhold Niebuhr, *Moral Man and Immoral Society* (New York: Charles Scribner's Sons, 1932), p. xi.

45. Reinhold Niebuhr, "Human Nature and Social Change," *Christian Century*, vol. 1 (1963), p. 363.

46. Julie Frederikse coined the phrase in reference to nonracialism, which she sees as the continuous link in African resistance politics. See Julie Frederikse, *The Unbreakable Thread: Non-racialism in South Africa* (Johannesburg: Ravan, 1990).

47. Leo Kuper, *Passive Resistance in South Africa* (New Haven: Yale University Press, 1957), p. 109.

48. Peter Walshe, *Black Nationalism in South Africa* (Johannesburg: Ravan, 1973), p. 33.

49. Gerhart, *Black Power in South Africa*, pp. 34–35.

50. Allister Sparks, *The Mind of South Africa* (New York: Ballantine Books, 1990), p. 51.

51. Walshe, *The Rise of African Nationalism in South Africa*, pp. 416–417.

52. Walshe, *The Rise of African Nationalism in South Africa*, pp. 12–15.

53. Anthony Sampson, *The Treason Cage: The Opposition on Trial in South Africa* (London: Heinemann, 1958), p. 195.

54. Janet Robertson, *Liberalism in South Africa* (Oxford: Clarendon Press, 1971), p.

104.

55. See Niebuhr, *Beyond Tragedy*, p. 141.

56. See Niebuhr, *The Nature and Destiny of Man*, vol. 2, p. 49.

57. Gerhart, p. 46.

58. Mangaliso Robert Sobukwe, *Speeches of Mangaliso Sobukwe, 1949–1959* (no publishing information available), p. 11.

59. For a discussion on the differences between individual and group morality, see Niebuhr, *Moral Man and Immoral Society*.

60. Niebuhr, *The Nature and Destiny of Man*, vol. 2, p. 87.

61. See Niebuhr, *Beyond Tragedy*, p. 285.

62. See Niebuhr, *Moral Man and Immoral Society*, p. 6.

63. Walshe, *The Rise of African Nationalism in South Africa*, p. 165.

64. Sparks, p. 254.

65. Walshe, *The Rise of African Nationalism in South Africa*, p. 168.

66. Sparks, p. 254.

67. Cited in Gerhart, p. 216.

68. Karis and Carter, *From Protest to Challenge*, vol. 3, p. 317.

69. Walshe, *The Rise of African Nationalism in South Africa*, p. 335.

70. "Manifesto of the Africanist Movement," cited in Gerhart, p. 207.

71. Lindy Wilson, "Bantu Steve Biko: A Life," in N. Barney Pityana, Mamphela Ramphele, Malusi Mpumlwana, and Lindy Wilson, *Bounds of Possibility* (Cape Town: David Philip, 1991), p. 29.

72. Gerhart, p. 295.

73. Gerhart, p. 273.

74. Gerhart, p. 142.

75. Shirley du Boulay, *Tutu: Voice of the Voiceless* (Grand Rapids, Mich.: William B. Eerdmans, 1988), p. 237.

76. From its founding in 1921 until its banning in 1950, the Communist Party was known as the Communist Party of South Africa (CPSA). In 1953, it reestablished itself as the South African Communist Party (SACP).

77. Thomas Karis, "South African Liberation: The Communist Factor," *Foreign Affairs* (Winter 1986–1987), p. 276.

78. Walshe, *The Rise of African Nationalism*, p. 369.

79. Robertson, p. 171.

80. Albert Luthuli, "Statement taken from Chief Albert Luthuli," Treason Trial lawyer's brief (Carter-Karis Collection), cited in Gerhart, pp. 119–120.

81. Mary Benson, *Nelson Mandela* (London: Panaf, 1980), p. 33.

82. James Leatt, Theo Kneifel, and Klaus Nurnberger, eds., *Contending Ideologies in South Africa* (Grand Rapids, Mich.: William B. Eerdmans, 1986), p. 94.

83. Desmond Tutu, *Crying in the Wilderness: The Struggle for Justice in South Africa* (Grand Rapids, Mich.: William B. Eerdmans, 1982), p. 28.

84. Tutu, *Crying in the Wilderness*, pp. 100, 112.

85. Study Commission on U.S. Policy Toward Southern Africa, *South Africa: Time Running Out*, p. 69.

86. Sparks, p. 237.

87. Anthony Marx, *Lessons of Struggle: South African Internal Opposition, 1960–1990* (New York: Oxford University Press, 1992), p. 27.

88. Desmond Tutu, *Hope and Suffering* (Grand Rapids, Mich.: William B. Eerdmans, 1984), p. 170.

89. Steve Biko, *I Write What I Like*, ed. Aelred Stubbs (San Francisco: Harper & Row, 1978), p. 31.

90. Niebuhr, *Moral Man and Immoral Society*, p. 65.

91. Albert Luthuli, *Let My People Go* (London: Collins, 1962), p. 155.

# 1

# Albert Lutuli and the African National Congress

Albert Lutuli was born in 1898 in Bulawayo, Rhodesia into a devout Christian home. His grandfather had been the first Christian convert of the Umvoti Mission Reserve in Groutville, a mission established by American Congregationalists in Natal in 1836.[1] His father at the time of Lutuli's birth was employed as an evangelist-interpreter at the Congregationalist mission near Bulawayo. At this mission, Harcourt writes, "Christian living was a reality, there were no distinctions in color or station; on the contrary, the black man was taught to recognize his own worth and to walk straight with the tallness of his ancestors."[2]

## STUDENT AND TEACHER

After his father's death, the family returned to Groutville where he attended the local mission school, Groutville Primary. He continued his education at Ohlange Institute at Inanda;[3] Edendale, a Methodist school in Pietermaritzburg; and Adams College, an American Missionary Board institute in Amanzimtoti.

At this time in South Africa, any schooling available to Africans was provided by the churches.[4] Gerhart notes that missionary schools were responsible for creating an African middle class with knowledge of the wider world.[5] Consequently, writes Zulu, it was from this class that the efforts to develop the black man politically first arose.[6] The educated were the first to argue that liberty, equality, and fraternity about which they were taught should apply equally to Africans. Reflecting on the impact of his early education on his political ideas, Lutuli says, "It was at Edendale, I think, that I began to wake up and look about me."[7]

Equally significant to these future African leaders as the academic training was the integrated environment. According to Hinchliff, mission education promoted a deliberate mixing of the races.[8] Lutuli found this multiracial setting, in which two cultures met and were enriched, advantageous.[9] Certainly, the intellectual and spiritual experiences during this period laid the foundation for his later political leadership.

His first job was as a school principal in Blaauwbosch[10] where he was challenged by two African Christians to think through the Christian beliefs he had taken for granted. Until then, he admits, he was a Christian "by accident of upbringing rather than by conscious choice."[11] Shortly thereafter, since there was no local Congregational Church, he was confirmed in the Methodist Church and became a lay preacher. Forever after, Benson writes, his faith would be a vital influence on his development;[12] and, according to Carter and Gerhart, "The language of the Bible and Christian principles profoundly affected his political style and beliefs for the rest of his life."[13]

Within a few years he was awarded a scholarship to pursue teacher training at Adams College where he stayed on as the first African teacher of Zulu Culture and Music. He attributes the Christian ethos he developed to the varied contacts made over a number of years at Adams.[14] He benefited greatly from the spirited discussions with overseas visitors connected with the American Mission Board. Thus, while somewhat isolated from political realities within South Africa, Lutuli absorbed global ideas far advanced to most South Africans, black or white.

In particular, he points to the influence of a fellow teacher at Adams, a liberal Afrikaner who associated freely with blacks. Lutuli comments, "More than any one person, this man helped me to forestall intolerance of whites in general and of Afrikaners in particular."[15] This colleague[16] gave him a sense of Afrikaners as victims of their own past. "It did enlarge my understanding of the forces which go to the making of men, and it gave me some insight into the dilemma of whites, particularly Afrikaners, which has possibly served in later years as a real protection against hatred and bitterness."[17]

He credits Adams with instilling in him the belief that Christianity was not a private affair without relevance to society but a belief which had to be applied to the conditions of one's time. "Adams taught me what Edendale did not, that I had to *do* something about being a Christian, and that this something must identify me with my neighbour, not dissociate me from him."[18]


## CHIEF OF GROUTVILLE

Reluctantly, Lutuli left Adams in 1936 to take over the duties of chief of the Umvoti Mission Reserve in Groutville. While his experiences as an academic had provided him with an understanding of Christianity as a belief which equipped one to meet the challenges of society, his role as chief opened up his eyes to exactly what those challenges were. He writes, "At Adams College I had had no particular cause to look far beyond the walls of the institution. I was, of course, aware of the South African scene, but Adams was in some ways a protected world, and the South Africa outside did not reach in in those days. . . . All that came to an end when I became Chief of Groutville. Now I saw, almost as though for the first time, the naked poverty of my people, the daily hurt to human beings."[19]

For seventeen years, Lutuli immersed himself in the affairs of his people and gained first hand experience of African political problems. He became aware of the land hunger of his people, confined as they were to 14 percent of the land, and thereby forced to sell their labor to subsist. He was confronted by the need of African men to migrate to the mines and cities, causing families to be split apart.[20] He saw that this exploitable proletariat was discriminated against in opportunities for employment, conditions for work, and recognition as workers. And in time he came to see that his people were helpless without the vote.

As a Christian, what he found unforgivable about the government's policy was its utter indifference to the suffering of individual persons who lose their land, their homes, and their jobs in the government's pursuit of an unholy division of mankind.[21] Lutuli's concern, however, was not just that segregation impoverishes Africans but that it is "a most humiliating affront to their person and dignity."[22] Lutuli considered personal dignity more deserving of redress than economic bondage. He wrote, "This matter of dwarfing our personalities and trying to make us believe we are nobodies is the worst sin the whiteman [sic] has committed against Africans."[23] He held an essentially Christian[24] belief in the sacredness of the human person, and therefore viewed apartheid as an affront to the humanity of the oppressor as well as to the oppressed, since it appealed to his baser instincts: selfishness, greed, and personal aggrandizement.[25]

## OVERSEAS AMBASSADOR

During this time Lutuli made two overseas speaking trips on behalf of Christian missions. Woodson notes that these trips were critical to his philosophical development, providing a rare opportunity for a nonwhite South African to observe nonwhites in societies without segregation.[26] In 1938, having been elected to the executive committee of the South African Christian Council, he served as a delegate to the International Mission Conference in Madras to discuss the place of indigenous churches in missionary endeavors. Davey writes that Lutuli was impressed with the freedom enjoyed by Indians under the British Raj. The mixing of races in debate, worship, and fellowship at the conference also made a decisive impact upon Lutuli, for it exposed the segregation of South Africa in all its shame.[27]

It is in India that he experienced the political implications of Christianity. He was thrilled to witness a vigorous Christianity, actively grappling with issues and facing challenges. He contrasts this with the church in South Africa which tended to accommodate itself to society, not leading, but waiting for its African converts to push it into belated action.  From discussions on the interaction of the Christian faith and rising nationalist movements in the Third World, he discovered that in South Africa Christianity had a long way to go.  He came home, he writes, "an incisive critic of South African Christianity."[28]

Ten years later, a second invitation to travel overseas arose out of his church activities.  Under the aegis of the American Mission Board and the North American Missionary Conference, he was invited to the United States to speak on Christian missions.  During that trip, he warned Americans that Christianity was facing its severest test in South Africa because of the evil of racial discrimination.  Having witnessed the power of the growing civil rights movement, he was reluctant to return to South Africa, for it was refreshing, he admits, to enjoy normal relations with white people.[29]

He credits travel abroad with helping him see South African issues more sharply, and in a different and larger perspective.  But he denies he was "spoilt" by travel abroad.  He writes, "I was spoilt by being made in the image of God."[30]  His deeply held religious belief that men are equal in the sight of God is the fundamental source of his political ideas, and his opposition to apartheid is based on its splintering of the family of man.  Trips abroad only opened his eyes to how other societies had dealt more positively with race relations.


## POLITICAL LEADER

Lutuli was being challenged not only by experiences abroad but by political events within South Africa.  In 1936, the Hertzog Bills were passed, which presaged the full-scale implementation of apartheid in 1948.[31]  These bills included the Representation of Natives Bill which removed Africans from the Cape roll of voters to a separate roll,[32] and the Land Act, which while expanding the boundaries of the reserves—those areas designated by the government as homelands for the various ethnic groups—laid out in the 1913 Land Act, still prohibited any African from owning land elsewhere or from living outside the reserves unless employed by whites.  Benson writes, "As [Lutuli's] deeply held religious beliefs were applied to these facts, almost for the first time he felt the poverty and daily hurt to human beings inflicted by the system of rule by a privileged white minority."[33]

As part of the Representation of Natives Bill, the Natives' Representative Council (NRC) was established with Africans as members to advise the government on African concerns.[34]  Lutuli was elected to it in 1946,[35] and although Lutuli says that the African leaders "were never warm about the Representation of Natives Act of 1936," they nevertheless accepted it in the spirit of "Let us put the white man on trial."[36]  At his first Council meeting, realizing the impotence of this body to bring about meaningful change, he succeeded in having the members vote to adjourn indefinitely.[37] Lutuli explains, "The feeling was growing apace that there was work to be done. The days of fruitless talking were sliding into the past. . . . Men with a desire to air grievances gave way to men with a purpose."[38]

The previous year, Lutuli had joined the African National Congress (ANC) Natal chapter and increasingly felt that the ANC was the better vehicle through which to press African demands to the government. He explains that his introduction to Congress had been almost accidental. He had been impressed for a long time by the stands made by the ANC against the 1913 and 1936 Land Acts and against passes, and was for years a part of Congress in all but the technical sense.[39]

But it was more than just a whim of accident that brought Lutuli into the ANC at this time. World War II had brought an industrial revolution to South Africa with the accompanying population movement from rural to urban areas.[40] Many of Lutuli's subjects were becoming directly and harshly affected by the administration of discriminatory legislation as they migrated for jobs in the city. When John Dube, president of the Natal chapter, died suddenly in 1946, Lutuli found himself on the executive committee under the new president, A. W. G. Champion. As membership in Natal grew under Champion's leadership, Lutuli writes, "at last we began to turn away from thinking in terms of an amelioration here and a concession there, and to get down to fundamentals. We began, in other words, to demand our rightful place in the South African sun, where before we had been petitioning to be treated a little less harshly in the place assigned to us by whites."[41]

With the adoption of the Program of Action in 1949, following on the heels of the Nationalist victory the previous year, new goals were clarified: "We were no longer interested in ameliorations and petty adjustments. There was no longer any doubt in our mind that without the vote we are helpless."[42] Likewise, new methods were stressed: illegal but nonviolent countrywide demonstrations, strike actions, and civil disobedience were to replace words. The new strategy reflected concern that the Nationalists under D. F. Malan were bent on expanding customary segregation into systematic apartheid. New, more militant tactics were thought to be necessary.

Lutuli views his political activity in the ANC as the expression of his Christian faith: "For myself I am in Congress precisely *because* I am a Christian. . . . My own urge, *because* I am a Christian, is to get into the thick of the struggle . . . taking my Christianity with me and praying that it may be used to influence for good the character of the resistance."[43] He began to feel that the Church too often evaded its responsibility for the whole of man's life. Lutuli warned against a misapplication of Christian trust, the idea that "God will give us freedom when He is ready." Such belief encouraged the abandonment of personal responsibility, resulting in a "resigned fatalism, a daydream about what God may do in the future, while the present slips by." For Lutuli, a passive view of Christianity could not be reconciled with the "Christian principle of work *and* pray."[44]

## DEFIANCE CAMPAIGN

Opportunity to put his faith into action arose when, as the newly-elected Natal provincial president of the ANC,[45] he found himself embroiled in the Defiance Campaign, the first major episode of passive resistance led by the ANC. Champion, unsure of the advisability of the campaign, had not informed the Natal chapter of the plans. Lutuli was astonished to learn of the campaign for the first time at the end of 1951 at the ANC's national conference. He decided to argue for it in principle but plead for postponement so that he could prepare the Natal ANC membership. He feared that an ill-prepared action would be worse than none, because of the possibility of its leading to violence. Lutuli's objections were heard, but the ANC voted to go ahead with the June 26 date, with the stipulation that Natal could enter when it felt ready.

Congress decided to apply its new method—nonviolent civil disobedience—to "all those particular discriminatory laws . . . which were not informed by morality."[46] However, the fact that the Indian Congress—presumably experienced in passive resistance, since Gandhi had developed this technique during his sojourn in South Africa—and the African Congress participated jointly in the campaign limited the scope of what could be done since apartheid laws oppressed these groups differently.[47]   What they did share, writes Lutuli, was the humiliation of discrimination in public places.[48] Thus, the *main* focus of the campaign was against the *Europeans only* prohibition. Defiers were urged to disregard *separate but equal* facilities. The idea was for the two congresses to openly disobey these laws and to accept arrest and imprisonment peacefully. "The method was to send in groups of carefully trained 'volunteers' to disobey publicly," explained Lutuli.[49] Forman notes that they made certain that they would be caught red-handed, even making appointments with the police for their arrests.[50] The aim was to fill the prisons, thus paralyzing the system of justice and forcing the government into concessions.[51]

In fact, some 8500 volunteers—mainly Africans, but some Asians and a few Europeans—trained in the methods of nonviolent resistance, used segregated public amenities, patronized the European section of post offices and train coaches, and sat on white park benches. Led by 250 leaders of the ANC, the campaign was to consist of three phases: (1) defiance by small groups in cities, (2) extension throughout the countryside, and (3) mass defiance involving industrial centers.

Lutuli's role in the campaign was that of a staff officer. He writes, "I did not myself defy any law. My job was to remain in the background, to keep up the pressure and to organise."[52] In particular, Lutuli's job was to tour the rural areas, recruiting volunteers. But the campaign never fully reached into the countryside as planned. In fact, 70 percent of those arrested came from the small towns and cities of the eastern Cape.[53] Lewin's explanation for this pattern of concentration is that they were better educated and more Christianized after longer contact with Western civilization. Emphasizing the religious roots of the ANC's campaign, he notes that resistance in this area was marked by notable religious fervor and was supported by African clergy.[54]

In October 1952, Lutuli was summoned to Pretoria by W. W. M. Eiselen, secretary of Native Affairs, to discuss his Congress activities. He explained that he was in Congress precisely because of the things to which chieftaincy had opened his eyes. When he refused to resign either posts, seeing no conflict with serving God in two realms, he was deposed as chief. In response, Lutuli issued a statement: "I have embraced the Non-Violent Passive Resistance techniques in fighting for freedom because I am convinced it is the only non-revolutionary, legitimate and humane way that could be used by people denied, as we are, effective Constitutional means to further aspirations."[55]

At the annual ANC conference in December 1952, Lutuli was elected president general by an overwhelming majority, succeeding J. S. Moroka who at his trial during the Defiance Campaign had disgraced himself by dissociating himself from the other defendants. Lutuli later had this to say about his election at so crucial a time: "I felt it was an overwhelming call of the people—and the voice of the people is sometimes the voice of God."[56] In the wake of harsh, new legislation,[57] he quickly brought the campaign to an end six months after it began. In a press statement, he explains the reason for his involvement in the campaign: "Laws and conditions that tend to debase human personality—a God-given force—be they brought about by the State or other individuals, must be relentlessly opposed in the spirit of defiance shown by St. Peter when he said to the rulers of his day: 'Shall we obey God or man?'"[58]

He believed the new tactics were consistent with Christian teaching: "I sin if I submit to the indignities that are hurled at me. I am a guardian of the divine dignity within me, and it is my duty to defend it."[59] Later, he wrote, "We are performing a divine duty when we struggle for freedom."[60] In his Nobel Peace Prize acceptance speech, he eloquently summarizes the Christian convictions that led to his involvement in the Defiance Campaign:

I . . . as a Christian and patriot could not look on while systematic attempts were made almost in every department of life, to debase the God-factor in man or to set a limit beyond which the human being in his Black form might not strive to serve his Creator to the best of his ability. To remain neutral in a situation where the laws of the land virtually criticized God for having created men of colour was the sort of thing I could not, as a Christian, tolerate.[61]

Until the Defiance Campaign, the Christian conviction of the ANC leadership was manifested not in active political self-assertion but in verbal appeals on moral grounds for justice. The ANC had traditionally relied on petitions and deputations, hoping that South Africans could be enjoined to live up to the standards of Christianity. Despite disillusionment over the years with efforts to pursue justice, "a Christian vision of nonracial justice persisted," writes Walshe, and the "most common form of protest consequently remained a moral assertion of human dignity with its roots in the Christian ethic."[62] The leaders of the ANC continued into the 1950s to rely "on the assumption that nonracial justice in political and economic matters was grounded in the Christian message of God's fatherhood, the brotherhood of man, and the command to love one's neighbor as oneself."[63]

Lutuli says this about the early strategy of Congress:

In its early days Congress gave voice to the many day-to-day grievances of the people. It appealed (fruitlessly) to the whites, it made representations, and it busied itself with the spadework of creating unity. It did not at that time attack the fundamental issue—participation in ownership and government. Realistically—for it was dealing with people who were still politically unawakened—it addressed itself to such sources of hardship as the 1913 Land Act and the Pass System. In these early stages it was asking for alleviation rather than demanding votes.[64]

The legacy of Christianity up to this point in South African history was to support an unrealistic optimism in white South Africans' willingness to change. This view, with its unquestioning faith in the white man's basic instinct for fair play, "ill-prepared [black South Africans] to come to grips with the realities of power politics and the selfish drive of organized white interests."[65] However, with the realization that appeals to these fellow white Christians would not bring political reform, the ANC gradually accepted the need for mass organization and assertion of black political power, culminating in the Defiance Campaign.

Lutuli's explanation for rejecting the early strategy was simply that it had not worked: "Who will deny that thirty years of my life have been spent knocking in vain, patiently, moderately and modestly at a closed and barred door? What have been the fruits of . . . moderation?"[66] In fact, the Africans' situation had worsened dramatically over the years:

The past thirty years have seen the greatest number of laws restricting our rights and progress until today we have reached a stage where we have almost no rights at all: no adequate land for our occupation; our only asset, cattle, dwindling; no security of homes; no decent and remunerative employment; more restriction to freedom of movement through passes, curfew regulations, influx control measures; in short, we have witnessed in these years an intensification of our subjection to insure and protect white supremacy.[67]

Therefore, the new strategy was justified: "It is with this background and with a full sense of responsibility that, under the auspices of the ANC, I have joined my people in the new spirit that moves them today, the spirit that revolts openly and boldly against injustice and expresses itself in a determined and non-violent manner."[68]

## THE CHURCH

An inclination to moralize on the basis of Christian ethics survived the transition from reliance on the moral regeneration of society to the acceptance of the need for mass demonstrations.[69] Despite the change in tactics, the Church was still relevant. Lutuli writes:

Obviously, we do not expect to see the Church organizing political movements. But it must be *with* the people, *in* their lives. I have no admiration for the political predikant. But I know something of the thirst of my people for spiritual guidance in the situation which confronts us now and will continue to be our lot for some time yet. The Church must be in among us all. If it stands on the outskirts, we cannot expect our religion to survive and be respected—we are untrue to our mission and that is suicide. Too often the flock has been left to its own devices in pressing matters of the moment.[70]

While seeing an important role for the Church, Lutuli nevertheless criticized it for not living up to its responsibility. In a speech given during the Treason Trial, in which he along with 155 other leaders of all races was tried on charges of high treason,[71] he laments:

White paternalist Christianity—as though the whites had invented the Christian Faith—estranges my people from Christ. Hypocrisy, double standards, and the identification of white skins with Christianity, do the same. For myself, for very many of us, nothing short of apostasy would budge us. We know Christianity for what it is, we know it is not a white preserve, we know that many whites—and Africans for that matter—are inferior exponents of what they profess. The Faith of Christ persists in spite of them.[72]

The Church he accuses of supporting government policy: "The churches above all were to have brought us not apartheid but fellowship one with another. Have they? Some measure of human failure is inevitable. Even so, have not many of the churches simply submitted to a secular state which opposes expressions of fellowship and our membership one of another? Have not some even gone so far as to *support* the outlook of the secular state?"[73]

The churches burned during the Defiance Campaign had become to Africans symbols of oppression:

They stand for an ethic which the whites have brought, preached, and refused to practise. . . . "You close your eyes obediently to pray," goes the saying, "and when you open them the whites have taken your land and interfered with your women." These churches represent something alien from the spirit of Christ, a sort of patronising social service . . . Do not many Christian ministers talk down to us instead of coming down . . . among us, as Christ did and does?[74]

In conclusion, he urges that it is not too late for white Christians to look at the gospels and redefine their allegiance: "But, if I may presume to do so, I warn those who care for Christianity, who care to 'go into *all* the world and preach the Gospel.' In South Africa the opportunity is three hundred years old. It will not last forever. The time is running out."[75]

For the most part, the churches watched passively from the sidelines during the Defiance Campaign. Lutuli, nevertheless, was encouraged by what little support was offered. When the Christian Council initially refused to issue a statement during the Defiance Campaign, feeling it would be an inappropriate action for a coordinating body of member churches, Lutuli, serving on its executive committee, persuaded it to draft one. The Council resolved that the individual Christian had to bring his conscience to bear; obedience to a Higher law than man's justified disobedience to man's laws. Lutuli found it a "sound and useful statement" which saved the Christian Council from charges of evasion.[76] In a flight of hyperbole, Lutuli writes, "At long last there were clear signs that the churches were becoming involved in the South Africa struggle *as churches*. Here and there individuals have acted and spoken out all along. Now African Christians, involved in making moral decisions about passive resistance, wanted the guidance of their churches speaking officially with voices not African or European but Christian."[77] Twelve years later he was still urging the Church to be much more courageous and forthright in speaking out against oppression.[78]

## COMMUNISTS

Lutuli had one major criticism of the churches. Christians were criticizing the communists "from a deep armchair" when Communists were among those deeply involved in the opposition.[79] Communists had been some of the ANC's earliest allies. The Communist Party of South Africa (CPSA) dated back to 1921 with some ANC members carrying dual memberships in the ANC and CPSA. After the CPSA was banned in 1950 under the Suppression of Communism Act, the Party dissolved itself but re-emerged in 1953 as an underground organization calling itself the South African Communist Party (SACP). It too welcomed ANC members into its ranks.[80]

Lutuli writes, "For myself I am not a Communist. Communism seems to me to be a mixture of a false theory of society linked on to a false 'religion.' In religion I am a Christian and the gods of state worship (as in Russia) are not my Gods." But, according to Lutuli, the principle concern is liberation, and "we are not going to be side-tracked by ideological clashes and witch hunts. When I co-operate with Communists in Congress affairs I am not co-operating with Communism. We leave our differing political theories on one side until the day of liberation, and in the meantime we are co-operating in a defined area, in the cause of liberation." After the dismantling of apartheid, "we will sort ourselves out into conventional political parties."[81]

Given his Christian background, it is not surprising that Lutuli expressed his willingness to cooperate with communists in terms of the principle of the dignity of man before God and the command to love one's neighbor. He writes:

The Communist philosophy I reject. But Communists are people, they are among the number of my neighbours, and I will not regard them as less. . . . The strength to combat and rectify their false doctrines, as with the false doctrines of white supremacists, does not lie in my depersonalising them and going apart into an anti-somebody camp. It lies rather in the things I believe in, it lies within me. I am confident . . . that I can serve my neighbour best by remaining in his company.[82]

Jordan Ngubane, a one-time Youth Leaguer, publicly debated Lutuli on this issue. He warned Lutuli that he was in danger of being used as a "cat's paw" of Moscow.[83] Yet Lutuli continued to affirm his position and to work alongside communists such as Walter Sisulu, a member of the Youth League, and communists in the Congress of Democrats (COD). Of the latter he says, "All we know is that these men came to help us. I don't deny that some might have ulterior motives, but all I am concerned about is that they came to assist me fight racial oppression, and they have no trace of racialism or being patronizing, just no trace of it at all." To make his point, he reminds his critics of the biblical story of the blind man healed by Christ. When people asked him, "Who healed you? Was he not a sinner?" the blind man said, "I don't care who he was. All I know is that he healed me."[84]

## MULTIRACIALISM

Because Lutuli believed in the brotherhood of all men, the equality of the races before God, he believed that the tactics employed should be multiracial and, likewise, any final political solution should be multiracial, involving all the peoples of South Africa—white, Indian, and Coloured, as well as black. Briggs and Wing write, "As a Congregationalist he stood for those values which are an integral part of the Congregational witness . . . the liberty and the unity of all men within the family of God." He believed, according to Briggs and Wing, "that the unity between the races which had been achieved in Congregationalism, where our oneness in Christ transcends our racial differences, was a practical policy for South Africa."[85]

At Bloemfontein, the ANC had endorsed the decision to undertake the Defiance Campaign in conjunction with the Indian Congress and with any others who would join in. In speech after speech, Lutuli affirms his willingness to accept whites in the struggle. Lutuli praised the emergence of cooperation between races during the Defiance Campaign "not merely because it increases the impact of resistance, but because it is the beginning of a non-racial South Africa."[86] As the following passage makes clear, his advocacy of multiracialism was clearly a moral decision over a merely tactical one:

I believe that a racially exclusive resistance is the wrong reply to a racially exclusive
oppression.  It is *morally* the wrong reply, and it is also a demonstration of the wrong
method if we think of the ideal it sets before our children.  Tactically, the drawing in of
our horns and the concentration of our forces may have some advantages, but in the long
run it will obstruct the way to a South Africa that embraces all her citizens.[87]

Never once did Lutuli advocate a narrow black nationalism; he stood for a
form of political partnership in which each group would make its own contribution to the growing fullness and enrichment of all.  He made it clear that he was
not opposed to whites per se but to their system: "Africa as a whole is sick of
. . . whites as perpetual 'senior partner.'  This is not the same as being sick of
whites."[88]  The Defiance Campaign, he made clear, was undertaken to resist
unjust laws, not whites.  In fact, because of his moderate multiracialism, many
whites correctly saw Lutuli as a devoted Christian, concerned about their well-
being.  According to Choonoo, Lutuli became a "Moses figure," whom his
followers saw not exclusively as a black nationalist but as a black man concerned
about the destiny of all men.[89]

Lutuli, reelected president general in 1955, brought together at Kliptown,[90] on
the symbolic date of June 26, the Congress of the People,[91] members of the Indian
and Coloured Congresses as well as the Congress of Democrats.[92]  The Congress
of the People was to be a demonstration of what South Africa's first national
convention in 1903 should have been, namely representative of all racial groups.
The Congress's agenda was the ratification of the Freedom Charter, which Lutuli
had helped write.[93]  The Freedom Charter[94] summarized the posture of the ANC
as well as Lutuli's own philosophy on the principle of a multiracial South Africa:
"South Africa belongs to all who live in it, black and white, and . . . no
government can justly claim authority unless it is based on the will of all the
people."[95]  Lutuli explained that the Freedom Charter was based on the fact that
all races that had made South Africa their home were entitled to ownership:
"What is important for our situation is that we are all here . . . and no one desires
to change it or should desire to change it.  And since we are all here, we must
seek a way whereby we can realize democracy, so that we can live in peace and
harmony in this land of ours."[96]

Kuper points out that the Freedom Charter did not demand a transfer of power
to Africans but urged a sharing of power.[97]  Motlhabi explains that the moderate
language, a forty-year habit with the ANC, was retained to allay white fears and
prevent an all-white backlash.[98]  Of course, the *implication* of the Charter's
preamble was black majority rule, but the *tone* of the document was color blind
with no *Africanist* invocation.

According to Gerhart, the legacy of Christianity in the ANC was the
acceptance of a multiracial ideal of nationalism.  The ANC under Lutuli's
leadership stood for African rights within the framework of a pluralistic demo-

cracy, "the [nation] being ultimately defined not as the community of black Africans only, but as a multi-racial community of all people born in South Africa."[99] Lutuli was clear on this point: "[W]e would as strongly be opposed to Black domination, or any other kind of domination from whatever source, as we are uncompromisingly opposed to white domination."[100] For "we do not desire to dominate but to share as between brethren."[101]

## VIOLENCE

According to Gerhart, the other legacy of Christianity on the ANC was a rejection of violence.[102] For Lutuli, cooperation with some whites necessarily excludes violence against other whites. Lutuli sums up his beliefs: "Had Congress ever been an organisation which placed reliance on bloodshed and violence, things would have been simpler. What we have aimed to do in South Africa is to bring the white man to his senses, not slaughter him. Our desire has been that he should co-operate with us, and we with him."[103] For Lutuli, the claim of human dignity precludes force. "With those who recognize it we are at one. We cannot discard it in our dealings with those who deny it."[104]

Lutuli believes that a nonviolent approach had practical implications as well. It would make reconstruction and reconciliation in a new South Africa easier, because there would not be the bitterness bound to follow a violent struggle. But the main reason for choosing the nonviolent approach was moral, because "our better natures and our conscience demand this of us."[105]

Lutuli urges nonviolence because as a Christian he felt no other methods were moral, or for that matter, necessary. The belief in the rightness of their cause was a tremendous source of encouragement to Lutuli and his followers. He writes, "I trust that the consciousness of the justice of our cause and a belief in the divine approval of our struggle will give us strength and courage to bear it until victory is won."[106] Lutuli saw the struggle as one of right against wrong, good against evil, and saw the conclusion as foregone. Having a "divine origin," the yearning for freedom can never be permanently gagged, he assured his followers.[107] Apartheid will perish, he believed, as must any system founded on "contempt for human beings."[108] He urges, "The road to freedom may be long and thorny but because our Cause is just, the glorious end—Freedom—is ours."[109]

His faith in the inherent goodness of man translated into the conviction that whites could be persuaded to change their ways. By the time of the Defiance Campaign, there was an awareness that whites had not had a change of heart. Still, Lutuli did not advocate wrenching power from whites. Rather, the nonviolent passive resistance was to demonstrate to white South Africa the lengths that Africans were prepared to go to demonstrate their unhappiness with apartheid. White South Africans would be so moved as to modify their opinions, it was hoped. "We will shake to repentance the hearts of white South Africans,"

Lutuli writes.[110] Daniel notes that the ANC never expected that these campaigns would be immediately successful; they were, instead, undertaken to rejuvenate the faith of the protesters in the rightness of their cause.[111] Lutuli did not harbor an apocalyptic view of God's intervening on their behalf, but he did see the struggle in terms of spiritual warfare. "We do not struggle with guns and violence, and the supremacist's array of weapons is powerless against the spirit," he wrote.[112]

Callan is convinced that Lutuli never wavered from his commitment to nonviolence even as late as 1960 on the eve of Sharpeville: "Our situation in the Union may be grim, but it is not hopeless. There is still enough good will and charitableness among South Africans, Black and White—if only leaders, both Black and White, and the government would get together to talk things over."[113] The Legums note that nine years after the Defiance Campaign, on the occasion of receiving the Nobel Peace Prize, there was still no oscillating in Lutuli's belief:

I firmly believe in non-violence. It is the only correct form which our work and our struggle can take in South Africa. Both from the moral and the practical point of view the situation in our country demands it. Violence disrupts human life and is destructive to perpetrator and victim alike. . . . To refrain from violence is the sign of the civilized man. . . . Yet I do not regard peace as a passive thing. The non-violence policy I am advocating is a positive one. . . . It demands moral courage and taxes our physical courage.[114]

Perhaps Lutuli's position is more complex. In his Nobel acceptance speech, he reaffirms his belief in nonviolence, while at the same time recognizing the legitimacy of armed struggle elsewhere in Africa. Furthermore, he asserts that violence is not an appropriate method for the ANC, but he admits it is not an impossibility given white intransigence. Lutuli wrote:

It has naturally crossed our minds to wonder whether anything but indiscriminate bloodshed and violence will make any impression, so impervious do they seem. It will do neither them nor us any good, and if they get it, it would not be from Congress. It will be simply the result of unendurable provocation, of trading for too long on a patience which has its limits. If the whites continue as at present, nobody will give the signal for mass violence. Nobody will need to.[115]

Gerhart writes that Christian morality was the touchstone of all the ANC's political policies. Therefore, "an aggressively anti-white stance could perhaps be ruled out on grounds of practicality alone, but more important to the genuine Christian—and there were many in the ANC—no African organization could ever be regarded as *morally* justified if its appeal for support was based on the policy of an eye for an eye."[116]

But emerging at this time within the ranks of the ANC was a nationalist-minded coalition, calling themselves Africanists, at odds with both the moderation and multiracialism of Lutuli. Walshe writes that there was much "heart-searching and frustration" as this new strand of thought established itself.[117]

## NOTES

1. The founder, Alvin Grout, is also known as the man who loaned a copy of the U.S. Constitution to the Voertrekkers, who founded a Republic in Natal.

2. Melville Harcourt, "Albert Lutuli," in *Portraits of Destiny* (New York: Sheed and Worrel, 1966), p. 103.

3. Ohlange was founded by the Reverend John Dube, the first president general of the ANC. Educated in the United States, he was influenced by Booker T. Washington's program for educational self-help.

4. The Bantu Education Act of 1953, implemented in 1954, took control of education away from the churches. The act arose out of concern that mission schools were inculcating in black students a desire for equality with whites. Bantu education, on the other hand, would prepare blacks for an economically useful role while denying them higher achievements. See Shaun Johnson, "Youth in the Politics of Resistance," in Shaun Johnson, ed., *South Africa: No Turning Back* (Bloomington: Indiana University Press, 1989), p. 98.

5. Gail Gerhart, *Black Power in South Africa: The Evolution of an Ideology* (Berkeley: University of California Press, 1978), p. 33.

6. Lawrence Zulu, "Nineteenth Century Missionaries: Their Significance for Black South Africa," in Mokgethi Motlhabi, *Essays on Black Theology* (Johannesburg: University Christian Movement, 1972), p. 88.

7. Albert Luthuli, *Let My People Go* (London: Collins, 1962), p. 28.

8. Peter Hinchliff, *The Church in South Africa* (London: SPCK, 1968), p. 88.

9. Luthuli, *Let My People Go*, p. 31.

10. Luthuli was the entire staff.

11. Luthuli, *Let My People Go*, p. 32.

12. Mary Benson, *Chief Albert Lutuli of South Africa* (London: Oxford University Press, 1963), p. 7.

13. Thomas Karis and Gwendolen Carter, *From Protest to Challenge: A Documentary History of African Politics in South Africa, 1882-1964*, vol. 4 (Stanford: Hoover Institution Press, 1972-1977), p. 61.

14. Luthuli, *Let My People Go*, p. 42.

15. Luthuli, *Let My People Go*, p. 40.

16. The colleague was de Villiers, who, ironically, later became head of the government department responsible for applying the Bantu Education Act.

17. Luthuli, *Let My People Go*, p. 40.

18. Luthuli, *Let My People Go*, p. 42.

19. Luthuli, *Let My People Go*, p. 57.

20. Group areas legislation kept families from living with the male head of household in the "white" areas.

21. Albert Luthuli, "Africa and Freedom," *Vital Speeches* 28 (February 1962), p. 269.

22. Albert Luthuli, "The Effect of Minority Rule on Nonwhites," in Hildegarde Spottiswoode, *South Africa, The Road Ahead* (London: Bailey Bros. and Swinfen, Ltd., 1960), p. 112.

23. "Presidential Address by Chief A. J. Lutuli," ANC Annual Conference of December 16–19, 1954, in Karis and Carter, vol. 3, p. 140 (Document 7a).

24. Edward Callan, *Albert John Luthuli and the South African Race Conflict* (Kalamazoo: Western Michigan University Press, 1962), p. 51. He notes that the idea of sacredness of the person is an African as well as Christian concept. For the similarities between African traditional religions and Christianity, see also John de Gruchy, *The Church Struggle in South Africa* (Grand Rapids, Mich.: William B. Eerdmans, 1986), p. 157.

25. "African Nationalism," Message to the Annual Conference of the ANC in Bloemfontein, December 16–19, 1955, in Albert Lutuli, *The Road to Freedom is via the Cross* (London: ANC, n.d.), p. 32.

26. Dorothy Woodson, "Albert Luthuli and the African National Congress: A Bio-Bibliography," *History in Africa* 13 (1966) p. 347.

27. Cyril Davey, *Fifty Lives for God* (London: Oliphants, 1973), p. 109.

28. Luthuli, *Let My People Go*, p. 80.

29. Luthuli, *Let My People Go*, p. 84.

30. Luthuli, *Let My People Go*, p. 85.

31. Hertzog's was the first Afrikaner National Party victory. Lutuli did not take part in the All-African Convention in the late 1930s to oppose the Hertzog Bills. Natal was still politically isolated. This convention, however, included other respected church dignitaries. See Karis and Carter, vol. 2, p. 6.

32. This removed Cape blacks to a separate roll for the purpose of electing three white native representatives to the lower house, and, by indirect means, electing four white senators to the upper chamber. Before the removal, it had been hoped that the franchise for property-owning Africans effective in the Cape Province since 1854 would be extended to the other three provinces. This did not happen, and the Coloureds in the Cape lost their franchise as well in 1955.

33. Benson, p. 12.

34. This was merely a consultative body that advised the government. The NRC had twenty-three members—seven whites and sixteen Africans. Twelve of the latter were selected by indirect elections.

35. Lutuli defeated Selby Msimang in a by-election for a successor to John Dube, who had died.

36. Callan, p. 22.

37. The NRC was abolished by the government in 1951 under the Bantu Authorities Act which transferred the administration of Africans to the minister of Native Affairs, then Dr. Hendrik Verwoerd.

38. Luthuli, *Let My People Go*, pp. 97–98.

39. Luthuli, *Let My People Go*, p. 99.

40. For the effect of post-World War II industrialization on African nationalism, see Peter Walshe, *The Rise of African Nationalism in South Africa: The ANC 1912-1952* (Berkeley: University of California Press, 1971), pp. 328–332. For a discussion of postwar economic development as an impetus for uniting blacks, Coloureds, and Indians in a common milieu, see Karis and Carter, vol. 2, p. 70.

41. Luthuli, *Let My People Go*, p. 100.

42. Luthuli, *Let My People Go*, p. 109. "African Claims" in 1943 had stated "our

undisputed claims to full citizenship." Earlier that year, the ANC's revised constitution did not mention the franchise explicitly, but the 1947 constitution was clear about insisting on the principle of one-man-one-vote.

43. Luthuli, *Let My People Go*, pp. 154–155.

44. Luthuli, *Let My People Go*, p. 190.

45. With the support of the Youth League, he was able to defeat narrowly George Champion.

46. Luthuli, *Let My People Go*, p. 109.

47. Just three years earlier, Africans had rioted against Indians in Durban, which made this joint effort all the more remarkable.

48. The six categories of laws they were protesting were: pass laws, stock limitation, Group Areas Act, Separate Representation of Voters Act, Suppression of Communism Act, and Bantu Authorities Act. See Edward Feit, *South Africa: The Dynamics of the ANC* (London: Oxford University Press, 1962), p. 27.

49. Luthuli, *Let My People Go*, p. 117.

50. Lionel Forman and E. S. Sachs, *The South African Treason Trial* (London: John Calder, 1957), p. 139.

51. John Daniel, "Radical Resistance to Minority Rule in South Africa: 1906–1965" (Ph.D. dissertation, Buffalo: State University of New York, 1975), p. 149.

52. Luthuli, *Let My People Go*, p. 119.

53. For a description of the Defiance Campaign and its aftermath, see Muriel Horrell, *A Survey of Race Relations in South Africa, 1952-1953* (Johannesburg: SAIRR, 1953), pp. 27-30.

54. Julius Lewin, *Politics and Law in South Africa: Essays on Race Relations* (London: Merlin Press, 1963), p. 47.

55. "The Road to Freedom is via the Cross," November 1952, in Lutuli, *The Road to Freedom is via the Cross*, p. 10.

56. Benson, pp. 24–25.

57. New legislation had been enacted in 1953: The Public Safety Act enabled the government to declare a state of emergency and then issue emergency regulations. The Criminal Law Amendment Act mandated severe penalties—fines up to 500 pounds or five years imprisonment—to protesters of any law.

58. "The Road to Freedom is via the Cross," November 1952, in Lutuli, *The Road to Freedom is via the Cross*, pp. 9–10.

59. Colin Legum and Margaret Legum, *The Bitter Choice: Eight South Africans' Resistance to Tyranny* (New York: World Publishing Co., 1968), p. 62.

60. Albert Luthuli, "Let Us Speak Together of Freedom," *Fighting Talk* (October 1956), p. 5.

61. Lutuli, "Africa and Freedom," text of the Nobel lecture delivered by Lutuli in Oslo on December 11, 1961, in Lutuli, *The Road to Freedom is via the Cross*, pp. 56–57.

62. Walshe, pp. 158–159.

63. Walshe, p. 341.

64. Luthuli *Let My People Go*, p. 91.

65. Gerhart, p. 36.

66. "The Road to Freedom is via the Cross," November 1952, in Lutuli, *The Road to Freedom is via the Cross*, pp. 7-8.

67. "The Road to Freedom is via the Cross," November 1952, in Lutuli, *The Road to Freedom is via the Cross*, p. 8.

68. Lutuli, "The Road to Freedom is via the Cross," November 1952, in Lutuli, *The Road to Freedom is via the Cross*, p. 8.

69. Walshe, p. 345.

70. Luthuli, *Let My People Go*, p. 138.

71. The Treason Trial lasted from 1956-1961. The treason charges against Lutuli were dropped at the end of 1957, but he was involved as a defense witness for the next three years. The prosecutor cited October 1952, the peak of the Defiance Campaign, as the starting point of the treasonable acts. It has also been said that the Freedom Charter itself was on trial. (Eventually, all 156 defendants were acquitted. The prosecutor was unable to prove either that the Freedom Charter was a communist document or that the accused had conspired to overthrow the state.)

72. Luthuli, *Let My People Go*, pp. 131-132.

73. Luthuli, *Let My People Go*, p. 132.

74. Luthuli, *Let My People Go*, p. 131.

75. Luthuli, *Let My People Go*, p. 132.

76. Luthuli, *Let My People Go*, p. 137.

77. Luthuli, *Let My People Go*, p. 136.

78. Peter Walshe, *Church versus State in South Africa: The Case of the Christian Institute* (Maryknoll, N.Y.: Orbis, 1983), p. 35.

79. Luthuli, *Let My People Go*, p. 138.

80. The Communist Party was opened up to Africans in the mid-1920s. The ANC's relationship to the party was mainly with individual members, not the party itself.

81. Luthuli, *Let My People Go*, pp. 153-154.

82. Luthuli, *Let My People Go*, p. 155.

83. Anthony Sampson, *The Treason Cage: The Opposition on Trial in South Africa* (London: Heinemann, 1958), p. 194.

84. Benson, p. 31.

85. D. Roy Briggs and Joseph Wing, *The Harvest and the Hope: The Story of Congregationalism in Southern Africa* (Johannesburg: United Congregationalist Church of Southern Africa, 1970), p. 291.

86. Luthuli, *Let My People Go*, p. 186.

87. Luthuli, *Let My People Go*, p. 186.

88. Luthuli, *Let My People Go*, p. 188.

89. R. Neville Choonoo, "Parallel Lives: Black Autobiography in South Africa and the United States" (Ph.D. dissertation, New York: Columbia University, 1982), p. 152.

90. Illness kept Lutuli from attending.

91. June 26, 1952 was the date of the Defiance Campaign. June 26, 1950 had been National Day of Protest and Mourning. Since then, June 26 has been observed as South African Freedom Day. At the Congress of the People, there were 2,844 delegates: 2,182 Africans, 320 Indians, 230 Coloureds, and 112 whites.

92. The Congress of Democrats was formed during the Defiance Campaign. It

included many communists, since the Communist Party had been banned in 1950.

93. The Freedom Charter was not penned by one person but based on thousands of ideas forwarded from all around the country. See Forman and Sachs, p. 142.

94. The Freedom Charter was divided into the following ten headings:
The people shall govern!
All national groups shall have equal rights!
The people shall share in the country's wealth!
The land shall be shared among those who work it!
All shall be equal before the law!
All shall enjoy human rights!
There shall be work and security!
The doors of learning and of culture shall be opened!
There shall be houses, security and comfort!
There shall be peace and friendship!

95. "Freedom Charter," adopted by the Congress of the People, June 26, 1955, in Karis and Carter, vol. 3, p. 205 (Document 11).

96. "Our Vision is a Democratic Society," speech to Congress of Democrats, 1958, in Johannesburg, in Lutuli, *The Road to Freedom is via the Cross*, p. 49.

97. Leo Kuper in Monica Wilson and Leonard Thompson, *The Oxford History of South Africa: 1870-1966*, vol. 2 (Oxford: Clarendon Press, 1971), pp. 463-464.

98. Mokgethi Motlhabi, *Challenge to Apartheid: Toward a Moral National Resistance* (Grand Rapids, Mich.: William B. Eerdmans, 1988), p. 44.

99. Gerhart, p. 12.

100. "Call for Dialogue," letter to Prime Minister Strijdom, May 28, 1957, in Lutuli, *The Road to Freedom is via the Cross*, p. 40.

101. Luthuli, *Let My People Go*, p. 209.

102. Gerhart, p. 42. Even for those ANC members whose political convictions had no religious foundation, the moral position of the ANC was important. See Gerhart, p. 100.

103. Luthuli, *Let My People Go*, p. 113.

104. Luthuli, *Let My People Go*, p. 116.

105. Benson, p. 64.

106. Albert Luthuli, "The Necessity of a 'Black' South African Church History," in Hans Jergen Becken, ed., *Relevant Theology for Africa* (Durban: Lutheran Publishing House, 1973), p. 113.

107. Lutuli, "Freedom in Our Lifetime!" Presidential Address to the 42d Annual Conference of the ANC, Queenstown, December 18-20, 1953, in Lutuli, *The Road to Freedom is via the Cross*, p. 11.

108. Albert Luthuli, "Foreword," in Leslie Rubin and Neville Rubin, *This is Apartheid* (London: Christian Action, 1966), p. 3.

109. "Message to the Annual Conference of the ANC in Bloemfontein," December 16-19, 1955, in Lutuli, *The Road to Freedom is via the Cross*, p. 32.

110. "Presidential Address to the 42d Annual Conference of the ANC, Queenstown, December 18-20, 1953, in Lutuli, *The Road to Freedom is via the Cross*, p. 26.

111. Daniel, p. 197.

112. Luthuli, *Let My People Go*, p. 229.

113. Luthuli, "The Effect of Minority Rule on Nonwhites," in Spottiswoode, p. 117. See Callan, p. 54.

114. Cited in Legum and Legum, p. 61.

115. Luthuli, *Let My People Go*, p. 113.

116. Gerhart, p. 99.

117. Walshe, *The Rise of African Nationalism in South Africa: The ANC 1912-1952*, p. 247.

# 2

# Robert Sobukwe and the Pan-Africanist Congress

That new thought established itself in a political organization founded in 1959, the Pan-Africanist Congress (PAC), with Robert Sobukwe as president. Born in 1925 in the Afrikaner town of Graaff-Reinet in the northern Cape, Sobukwe "grew up with Christianity as his earliest ideological frame of reference," Gerhart writes.[1] His father, a Methodist lay preacher, insisted on regular church attendance for his family, and it was not unusual for the children to be quizzed on the weekly text and sermon.[2] Sobukwe's other religious example was his brother, an Anglican priest who later became a suffragen bishop, only the third black bishop in the church at that time.

Sobukwe's schooling was provided through the sixth grade by the local Methodist mission school which accepted both black and Coloured students. At age fifteen, he was sent to Healdtown, a Methodist boarding school established by British missionaries.[3] The Christian influence at Healdtown was thorough: grace before meals, daily prayers, weekly church attendance and scripture class, and monthly communion. Pogrund comments that the young boarder was religious but not a zealot.[4] A Christian atmosphere pervaded also at Fort Hare, which Sobukwe entered in 1948.[5] As at Healdtown, this institution, founded by Glasgow missionaries, required daily prayers and weekly church services of its students.[6]

## YOUTH LEAGUE

It was during his first year at Fort Hare that Sobukwe joined the Youth League, the youth division of the African National Congress (ANC). It was the Youth League which had decided that the ANC's early goal, the improvement of the black man's lot, was inadequate and had by 1944 prodded the ANC into accepting its point of view that only the franchise could guarantee blacks' rights.[7] Sobukwe took an active role in pushing the movement towards adopting a restricted black nationalist approach which shunned help from concerned whites. He had been part of the group that wrote the Youth League's Manifesto, which was later incorporated in the ANC's 1949 Program of Action.

In 1949, he was elected both president of the Fort Hare Students Representative Council and national secretary of the Youth League. With two friends, he prepared a daily commentary on political issues called *Beware*, in which he endorsed the Africanists' view of noncollaboration, fiercely attacking the Natives' Representative Council and advisory boards.[8] According to A. P. Mda, a cofounder of the Youth League, Sobukwe went on to develop his and Anton Lembede's thinking to a higher level.[9] But, following graduation,[10] Sobukwe began a period of relative isolation from the mainstream of resistance politics. While these were turbulent times for South Africa, they were quiet years for the new teacher Sobukwe. In 1950, he began teaching at Jandrell Secondary School in Standerton but was temporarily suspended for publicly supporting the Defiance Campaign in 1952. According to Pogrund, Sobukwe's involvement in the Defiance Campaign was limited to asking the ANC to send a speaker to a political meeting prior to the campaign—Sobukwe was secretary of the Standerton branch of the ANC—and briefly addressing that meeting. Sobukwe himself was not a defier. His explanation in later years was that he had been told by the ANC leadership in Johannesburg to stand by and wait for a call to action, which never came. But, Nthato Motlana, the speaker sent by the ANC to Standerton, remembers that teachers generally were not called to defy since they would surely lose their jobs. Secondly, the ANC would not have asked people in Standerton, a small country town, to defy since the laws there were so vicious.[11] After the Jandrell School Committee, comprised mainly of local clergymen, appealed to the Transvaal director of native schools, Sobukwe was reinstated.

In 1954 he was appointed languages lecturer in the Department of Bantu Studies at the University of Witwatersrand in Johannesburg.[12] During this time he was chairman of the ANC branch at Mofolo, one of Johannesburg's newer townships, and gradually became the unofficial leader of the Orlando Africanists, editing the Orlando Youth League's journal *The Africanist*, and guiding the maturation of the Youth League's ideas.[13]

During the ANC conference in Durban in November 1958, the Africanist wing of the Youth League attempted to take over the leadership from Lutuli and his moderate supporters. On that occasion, Lutuli addressed the conference to criticize the Africanists' exclusivist position: "The African National Congress stands or falls by a free democracy. It is opposed to a racial majority masquerading as democracy, as it is opposed to a minority of any kind—racial or otherwise—dominating others because it seized full control of the state."[14]

Unable to take over the leadership of the ANC, and to change its direction, the Africanists under Sobukwe's leadership broke away in April 1959 and formed the

Pan-Africanist Congress.[15]   In a letter of secession, signed by Selby Ngendane but actually drafted by Sobukwe,[16] they explained their parting: "We are launching out openly, on our own, as the custodians of the ANC policy as it was formulated in 1912 and pursued up to the time of the Congress Alliances."[17] By this they meant a return to what they believed was the militancy and the all-African character of the earlier ANC.


## MULTIRACIALISM

The PAC disagreed sharply with the ANC on the value of multiracial efforts. Sobukwe rejected collaboration with sympathetic whites, believing that multiracial cooperation between slave owner and slave was an "ungodly alliance."[18] Unlike Lutuli, Sobukwe denied that there could be such a thing as a *good* white in South Africa.  The PAC consistently rejected appeals to alliances with whites based on any notion of white morality.

Silk explains that Sobukwe was convinced that all whites impede African aspirations.  Certainly, the *bad* whites, the Nationalist Boers, want to keep the African in his place.  But, the *good* whites, the missionary and liberal alike, also thwart African progress by destroying the African's confidence in his own strength and ability.  He writes, "Although their motives and techniques differed, Sobukwe realized that their effect on African spirit and initiative was similar."[19] In a speech given in Soweto, Sobukwe lambasted three *good* whites—the Reverend Ambrose Reeves, Anglican bishop of Johannesburg; Father Trevor Huddleston, an Anglican priest and later archbishop; and Patrick Duncan,[20] member of the Liberal Party and editor of the liberal newspaper *Contact*—as examples of well-meaning whites who actually undermined blacks' ability to free themselves.

In a graduation speech at Fore Hart in 1949, Sobukwe explained his stand: "We have been accused of bloodthirstiness because we preach 'non-collaboration.' I wish to state here tonight that that is the only course open to us.  History has taught us that a group in power has never voluntarily relinquished its position. It has always been forced to do so.  And we do not expect miracles to happen in Africa."[21]

Africans are the only people, Sobukwe believed, who can be truly interested in the complete overhaul of the present system.  Although there were some whites who are "intellectual converts" to the African's cause, they benefit materially from the present set-up, and so cannot completely identify themselves with that cause.[22]  If some whites seem sympathetic to African demands, he writes, it is only in so far as those demands do not threaten their privileges.  If they offer assistance, it is for the purpose of directing and controlling the struggle to ensure that it does not become too radical.[23]

Whereas Lutuli viewed whites as brothers, Sobukwe saw them as colonizers.[24]

Lutuli saw the foe as the present Nationalist government, but Sobukwe believed the enemy was the entire foreign minority.[25] Sobukwe accused the ANC of fighting just the present Nationalist government and its policies: "The fact that the Nats are a logical product of past South African history and that what they stand for is approved and supported by the overwhelming majority of whites in the country has apparently escaped the notice of the ANC."[26] Because of the ANC's narrow definition of the enemy, everyone but the nationalist government was regarded as an ally.    The PAC, on the other hand, aimed at complete overthrow of white domination; it wanted political control, not merely political participation in a new white government.  Thus, to say, as did the ANC, that there existed some *good* whites obfuscated the true nature of the struggle.

Sobukwe criticized the ANC for thinking of South Africa as an exceptional case in Africa—an independent state and not a colony.[27] Before the formation of the PAC, according to Khopung, South Africa had been excluded from the list of African countries to be liberated.  African leaders had convinced the masses that South Africa was not a colony but an independent state and, therefore, an exception from the rest of Africa.[28]  The Simons concur that whereas elsewhere in Africa national liberation meant overthrowing an external imperial government; in South Africa under the ANC liberation was construed as sharing power with a white minority.[29]

This view Sobukwe emphatically rejected.  He felt that the nationalist aspect had been underemphasized by the ANC because of its mistaken belief that South Africa was not a colony.  Sobukwe linked the nationalist struggle against *colonialism* in South Africa with the other revolutionary struggles throughout Africa.  He subscribed to the Pan-Africanist view that sought the creation of a "United States of Africa, stretching from Cape to Cairo, Morocco to Madagascar."[30]

The PAC drew on the long tradition of Pan-Africanism which existed in the United States, Europe, and Africa.  W. E. B. Du Bois, Kwame Nkrumah, and George Padmore—the fathers of Pan-Africanism—envisioned Africa as one united country, a vision readily adopted by the PAC.  Gerhart notes that George Padmore's book, *Communism or Pan-Africanism?*, published in 1956, was compulsory reading in Africanist circles by the time the PAC was founded.[31]

But this ideology was not simply imported; it was a return to the outlook of Anton Lembede, the founder of the Youth League, who had also preached a Pan-Africanist doctrine of African unity and had advocated the complete replacement of white minority rule.  But it was not until the All-African Peoples Conference in Accra in December 1958 which gathered together leaders from all parts of the continent in a show of unity that Pan-Africanism was fully embraced by the Africanists in South Africa.  The Africanists, "always pan-Africanists at heart" were so inspired by the All-African Peoples Conference that they incorporated not only *Pan-Africanism* into its organization's name but every tenet of Pan-Africanist doctrine into PAC ideology as an article of faith.[32]

Gerhart believes that political expediency as well as sincere conviction led the PAC to espouse Pan-Africanism. She points out that a perspective of Africa as a single nation made it easier to dismiss South Africa's few million whites as an insignificant minority within the larger population.[33] Denying the uniqueness of South Africa made it possible to deny the necessity for a unique political solution. Therefore, like the nationalist movements to the north, the PAC could justify the complete overthrow of white domination and the setting up of a black majority government. The PAC rationalized noncollaboration with sympathetic white liberals, comparing the tactic to the example of the nations to the north who had liberated themselves without help from *foreigners*. A Pan-African ideology of black unity linking South Africa's struggles to those elsewhere on the continent gave legitimacy to the Africanists' fledgling organization. Who could fail to be impressed by cables of congratulations sent to the PAC Inaugural Convention from nationalist heros like Sekou Toure of Guinea and Kwame Nkrumah of Ghana, who using the same methods the Africanists advocated, had proven their ability to vanquish the European imperialists?[34]

## OTHER OPPRESSED MINORITIES

Sobukwe's rejection of multiracial collaboration extended to Indians as well as to whites. He granted that the Indians were an oppressed group. Certainly, the "down-trodden, poor stinking coolies" of Natal could identify with the African majority in its struggle to overthrow the white minority. Unfortunately, the Indian leadership was the merchant class which identifies with the white oppressor.[35] The PAC's position on Coloureds was more ambiguous. Pogrund asserts that there had been a change of policy regarding them, thanks to Sobukwe. He argues that John Gomas, a Coloured activist in Cape Town, wrote Sobukwe after the PAC's founding conference pledging his support. Gomas had been a member of the Communist Party when it dissolved itself in 1950, but was excluded from membership when the party reorganized itself three years later. His rejection by the hated communists made Gomas more welcomed than a Coloured would otherwise have been to Sobukwe. Since Sobukwe did not want to exclude Gomas from membership in the PAC, he went about first persuading the executive committee and then the branches to change the policy disqualifying Coloureds. Having accomplished that, Sobukwe spoke as if it had always been the policy of the PAC to include Coloureds.[36]

Sobukwe's antipathy towards communists requires some explanation. According to Benson, the Africanists opposed communists because their religious upbringing had taught them that communists were the anti-Christ.[37] Partially for that reason, the presence of communists in the Congress Alliance had led to the Africanist breakaway.[38] Sobukwe also feared that a united front approach would mean communist control of the resistance. Furthermore, he rejected Marxism as a "foreign" ideology not relevant to the South African situation since Africans were oppressed not as a class but as a nation. Class analysis was, at best, a "distraction," he believed.[39] He called the "leftists" in South Africa "quacks" and concluded that communism in South Africa, like Christianity, "has been extremely unfortunate in its choice of representatives."[40] Despite his renunciation of communism, his thinking nevertheless relied on a Marxist-Leninist economic analysis. In a postapartheid South Africa, no differentiation of wages would be tolerated, Sobukwe maintained, and confiscation of property also would be in the hands of the people.[41]

## PSYCHOLOGICAL LIBERATION

Sobukwe believed it was necessary for Africans to build up their bargaining power before they could collaborate or negotiate with other groups. Only when the African could be sure that his dignity as a person would be respected could he meet with others as equals. To accomplish that end, Sobukwe announced on Hero's Day, the twelfth anniversary of the death of Lembede, a Status Campaign to exorcise the slave mentality and to encourage black self-respect. The campaign's stated purpose was to accustom Africans to the idea of acting collectively in order "to force the pace of progress toward freedom."[42] The immediate target was to have been shops and businesses that did not give courteous service to Africans. These businesses would have been boycotted until they eliminated the substandard treatment of Africans. The task was to arouse and consolidate the masses, to mobilize black spending power, so that they could be made conscious of their power. Having been "conscientized," they would realize they could rely on themselves, rather than on sympathetic whites negotiating on their behalf. Having built up their bargaining power, they would be worthy of respect and could negotiate as equals.

Until the time comes when Africans are treated as equals, he rejected the advice of so-called "responsible preachers" who suggest "cooperation as a solution."[43] Rather, Sobukwe urged, "Watch our movements keenly and if you see any signs of 'broad mindedness' or 'reasonableness' in us, or if you hear us talk of practical experience as a modifier of men's views, denounce us as traitors to Africa."[44]

One legacy of Sobukwe's upbringing is that he never failed to see the spiritual dimension to the struggle for freedom. The Status Campaign was to "free the mind of the African—and once the mind is free, the body will soon be free."[45] Both he and Lutuli viewed the evil of apartheid more in its affront to human dignity than in the economic deprivation it wrought. Sobukwe explained why his primary concern was with the intangible: "Certain quarters have accused us of being concerned more with our status, with being addressed as 'Sirs' and 'Maam' than with the economic plight of the African people. Our reply is that such accusations can come only from those who think of the African as an economic animal—a thing to be fed—and not as a human being."[46] He saw the movement towards self-reliance on the part of Africans as a spiritual transformation, a religious experience, in which "we shall become purer and purer, leaving all the dross of racialism and similar evils behind."[47]

The importance of this *spiritual* dimension should not be neglected, believes Daniel. He says that the real importance of the PAC, often overlooked in analyses that concentrate on its exclusivist orientation, was its awareness of the necessity for a mental revolution as a prerequisite to political revolution.[48] He notes that Sobukwe was stressing the same theme as Frantz Fanon in Algeria—that centuries of colonial oppression had produced a degraded self-image, which first had to be overcome.[49] Pogrund also stresses Sobukwe's debt to Marcus Garvey, who recognized that as long as one thinks like a slave, he will remain a slave.[50]

It is in this context that Sobukwe's rejection of multiracialism should be understood. Sobukwe believed that multiracialism perpetuated the inferiority complex of Africans. According to Daniel, he recognized that Africans had internalized a belief in the innate superiority of whites and an acceptance of their own inferior status which resulted in an unconscious sense of shame in their blackness and a habit of dependence upon whites.[51]

For Sobukwe, admitting whites into alliances inevitably led to white domination in those groups. Whereas an educated middle-class African might value the symbol of multiracial cooperation and might not feel the ANC was being dominated by whites and Indians, the average African would view it differently. Sobukwe felt that the existence of the alliance would reinforce his doubts about the ability of his own people.[52] Lutuli, on the other hand, advocated cooperation with those whites he distinguished as *progressive*. He differentiated between the redeemed whites and those yet to be redeemed whose hearts he believed in time could be "shaken to repentance."[53]

## MINORITY RIGHTS

Sobukwe's concept of a future South Africa likewise differed from Lutuli's vision. While the ANC had supported the need for an electoral system that would guarantee the rights of the white minority,[54] the PAC rejected the idea of a minority guarantee, believing it was contrary to the goal of a nonracial society. Sobukwe, whose Christian faith was the source of respect for individual rights,[55] considered the guarantee of individual rights the highest protection necessary. He saw no reason why a predominantly black electorate should not elect a white man to Parliament "for colour will count for nothing in a free South Africa."[56] Those whites and Indians prepared to regard themselves as Africans would have an equal say but no special privilege.

In addition, the Pan-Africanist view of a united Africa would make irrelevant the problem of minorities. Sobukwe maintained that "In a United States of Africa there will be no 'racial groups' and I am certain that with freedom of movement from Cape to Cairo, Morocco to Madagascar, the concentration of so-called minority groups will disappear."[57]

Sobukwe expressed the view to the PAC Inaugural Convention that multi-racialism is pandering to European bigotry and arrogance and a method of safeguarding white interests, implying proportional representation, irrespective of population figures. Multiracialism implies that basic differences between the various national groups exist and that the best course is to keep them permanently in a kind of democratic apartheid.[58] Multiracialism, according to Sobukwe, represented the aspirations of an elite stratum of Africans which has embraced the liberal idea of gradually being assimilated into the ruling class while the vast majority of Africans continue to be exploited and denied democratic rights on the grounds of their "unreadiness, backwardness and illiteracy."[59]

He criticized the ANC leadership which "claims to be fighting for freedom when in truth it is fighting to perpetuate the tutelage of the African people. It is tooth and nail against the Africans gaining the effective control of their own country. . . . It is fighting for the 'constitutional guarantees' or 'national rights' for our alien nationals."[60] He emphatically denied that multiracialism was a "virtue." Rather, the granting of "rights" on the basis of "ethnological origin" amounted to the "continued maintenance of contempt for human worth and disregard for human dignity."[61] There is *one* race, the *human* race, he preached, and he condemned all forms of racialism, including multiracialism.[62]

While Lutuli had made it clear that his organization was fighting apartheid, and not whites, Sobukwe reversed this. "We do not fight apartheid alone. We fight the whole of white supremacy."[63] But, he denied he was antiwhite:

In every struggle, whether national or class, the masses do not fight an abstraction. They do not hate oppression or capitalism. They concretise these and hate the oppressor, be he the Governor General or a colonial power, . . . or, in South Africa, the white man. But they hate these groups because they *associate them with their oppression*! Remove the association and you remove the hatred. In South Africa, then, once white domination has been overthrown, and the white man is no longer "white-man boss" but is an individual member of society, there will be no reason to hate him and he will not be hated even by the masses.

We are not anti-white, therefore. We do not hate the European because he is white! We hate him because he is an oppressor. And it is plain dishonesty to say I hate the sjambok [lash] and not the one who wields it.[64]

Indeed, he hated whites as *oppressors*, not as persons. More than that, he hated the ideology that buttressed white oppression. He wrote, "We are fighting against the Calvinist doctrine that a certain nation was specifically chosen by God to lead, guide and protect other nations."[65] It was against the ideology of racial superiority that he vented his hatred. Ambiguously, he warned against that destructive emotion: "[A] doctrine of hate can never take people anywhere. It is too exacting. It warps the mind. That is why we preach the doctrine of love, love for Africa."[66]

The ANC had accepted that South Africa belonged to all who lived in it. The PAC, on the other hand, asserted that Africans, as well as being the majority, are the indigenous "sons of the soil" from whom whites had stolen the country through conquest and, therefore, are the true owners.[67]

Sobukwe affirmed the Youth League's Manifesto of 1944, later adopted in the Program of Action of 1949, which asserted the Africans' "primary, inherent and inalienable right to Africa which is his continent and Motherland."[68] Thus, the Africans' right to effective control is unchallengeable. It accused the ANC of repudiating the "nation-building" strategy of the Program of Action by endorsing the Freedom Charter, which effectively auctioned the Africans' land "for sale to all."[69] The PAC's objectives coincided with the resolutions adopted at the All-African Peoples Conference in 1958, which embraced the slogan "Africa for Africans."[70] The PAC, however, dissociated itself from the extreme Garveyist aim "to hurl the white man into the sea."[71] Peter Molotsi, discussing the PAC's decision to avoid the slogan, admitted that people voiced the sentiment personally but decided against publicly endorsing it since it would damage the PAC with its friends overseas.[72]

Eventually whites can be counted as *Africans*, once the country is returned to its rightful owners, if their first allegiance is to Africa and the concept of majority rule: "Politically we stand for government of the Africans for the Africans by the Africans, with everybody who owes his loyalty only to Africa and who accepts the democratic rule of an African majority, being regarded as an African."[73] In this context, his doctrine of "love for Africa" makes sense alongside his hate of the white oppressor; love is possible towards those whites who are not opposed to black majority rule, for they are true Africans.

That same conference compelled Lutuli to reiterate the ANC's stand: "We of the ANC have no desire to dominate others by virtue of our numerical superiority. We are working for a corporate multi-racial society. We are opposed to the outlook that the colour of one's skin should determine one's politics. We are prepared to extend the hand of friendship to White South Africans who are our brothers and sisters."[74] Of course, both Lutuli and Sobukwe were advocating universal suffrage. The ANC had evolved by the 1950s to that demand; early on, it had merely sought the representation of Africans in Parliament, not questioning the present structure of government. There was no question, of course, that recognition of African voting rights would lead to a black majority government. The ANC had merely avoided speaking openly about a predominantly black government, lest any suggestion of African control provoke violent reactions from the white minority population. The PAC, on the other hand, deemed white opinion irrelevant and hence was explicit about who would rule Africa.

## CHURCHES

While Lutuli had believed intensely in multiracial efforts and appealed specifically to the multiracial, English-speaking churches,[75] Sobukwe's rejection of multiracialism prevented him from looking in that direction for support. Rather, it was to the African Independent Churches (AICs) that he turned.[76] The black independent churches had begun to split from the white churches by the late nineteenth century. It was predominantly from Methodism, Sobukwe's own denomination, that the schisms came. Meli explains that the Wesleyan Church had become associated with the imposition of colonialism; hence the large number of breakaways from that denomination.[77]

In 1884, Nehemiah Tile, a Tembu, seceded from the Wesleyan Methodist Church and founded his own sect, the Tembu National Church. Having grown impatient of European control, he wanted to establish a purely native church. Hewson believes that there can be no doubt as to the political significance of the movement. Tile's successor in the movement was another Wesleyan Methodist, Mangena Mokone, who in 1892 founded the original Ethiopian church in Pretoria, whose distinguishing feature was that it was composed of and controlled by Africans. According to Hewson, there was a decisively antiwhite aspect to it, its slogan being "Africa to the Africans."[78] Shortly afterwards, another African minister, James Mata Dwane, also left the Methodist Church to join the movement. According to Karis and Carter, he entertained visions of a national church that would play a leadership role in the Africans' fight for self-determination.[79] A fourth secession, described by Sundkler, was the Bantu Methodist Church, or the "Donkey Church," founded in 1932 on the Rand.[80]

Sundkler writes of an unmistakable nationalist spirit which inspired leaders and followers to breakaway from the mission churches.[81] The rapid development of independent churches after 1913 was a reaction against the Natives Land Act. He writes, "From 1913, the burning desire of the Africans for land and security provided the apocalyptic patterns of the Zionist or Messianic myths, whose warp and woof are provided by native land policy and Christian, or at least *Old Testament* material."[82] D. T. Jabavu also asserts that the religious breakaways symbolize "the general ambition of the Bantu for liberation, liberation from being underlings to the Europeans in various phases of life, namely: economic, political and religious."[83]

Kretzschmar adds her voice to those who see both religious and political reasons for the emergence of the African Independent Churches. She believes that not only were the new churches responding to Africans' desire to interpret the Bible in their own way, to engage in indigenous forms of worship, and to enjoy leadership opportunities; they were also reacting to a host of discriminatory laws that restricted Africans to the reserves, hampered opportunity to buy land, controlled employment advancement, imposed taxation, and denied representation in government.[84]

There is a feeling from some quarters, however, that the independent churches were not founded for political, economic, social, or racial reasons. Appiah-Kubi, for instance, warns against seeing these movements primarily as a reaction against white control. He argues that "spiritual hunger" was the main cause for their emergence. There was a need for "healing, divining, prophecying and visioning" that these churches fulfilled.[85] Hastings points out that many did not begin as conscious schisms but emerged because there was no mission church in the area. He likewise believes the most characteristic motivation was not a political rejection of colonialism or colonial churches "but the establishment of accessible rites of healing with a Christian reference and within a caring community by gifted and spiritual individuals claiming an initiative effectively denied them in the older churches."[86]

But his argument is belied by the fact that it was *political* events that were prone to trigger a popular movement. By his own admission, these included "the imposition of colonial regulations" and "the apparently irresistible loss of ancestral lands to incoming white settlers."[87] The evidence does in fact support the position that the independent churches were reacting to both political and ecclesiastical domination. De Gruchy correctly concludes, "There remains little doubt that the independent churches were concerned about more than just religious freedom. They wanted the liberty of their people from all unjust bondages. . . . But, at least for the time being, they had to be content with religious freedom."[88]

The fact that the government was suspicious of the new church bodies gives credence to the view that the independent churches were subversive, or at least potentially so. At the time of the Bambata Rebellion, especially, there was alarm over the political role played by the independent churches. Bamba, a Zulu chief, led an armed revolt against the British government in Natal in protest over the poll tax. The rebellion was marked by seditious preaching among the Ethiopian groups who urged African ascendancy over whites. Later, at Bulhoek in 1921, the potential for a religiously inspired resistance was again evident. The government ordered an Ethiopian church that was squatting on Crown Land to move. The church's leader, Mgijima, told his people to charge the troops, promising them that God would turn the army's bullets into water. According to Comaroff, the prophetic Zionist churches, whose members numbered among the most impoverished people in the land, were profoundly subversive. Their radical rejection of capitalism and the state perhaps more closely than any other church body replicated the PAC's own noncollaborationist stance.[89]

But, while the beginning of the independent church movement may have been coterminous with the rise of African nationalism, the AICs did become complacent in time. Regehr writes that separatist groups tended to stop short of a concept of African political assertion and went out of their way to establish their respectability.[90] This happened in part because of the churches' natural interest in public recognition by the government for such purposes as registration of marriages and purchasing of communion wine. By 1950, the second and third generations of independent church leaders were generally cautious about involvement in political protest, which came instead from the black elite within the missionary churches.[91] In some instances, preoccupation with the *Kingdom of God* distracted the independent churches—especially the Zionist groups—from political involvement. Rather than act, they tended to *withdraw* from the reality of racial discrimination, waiting for God himself to usher in the millennium.[92]

At the very least, though, the independent church leaders, more than their brothers in the multiracial churches, offered a stronger critique of the white Christian churches and its members. Walshe notes that many of the independent churches saw that white Christians had failed to be the light who Christ says his disciples are.[93] They did not harbor a naive trust in the inherent goodness of whites, nor did they make appeals for political freedom on the basis of a shared Christian morality.

It is to this section of Christendom that Sobukwe turned. The black independent churches were a natural source of converts to the PAC's cause, given the clear affinity between the PAC's *go it alone* spirit and the *antiwhite* mood of these churches. Ideologically, it was natural that the PAC sought to link the AICs' theology of separation to its political ends. Tactically, too, it made sense to turn to the AICs because through them the PAC had links to both rural peasants and urban workers. Had the PAC not been banned, Gerhart believes, it might eventually have redirected the energies of religious separation into political channels.[94] That it hoped to tap the latent political interests of the independent churches is evident from the PAC's invitation to Bishop Walter M. Dimba, a leading separatist and head of the Federation of Bantu Churches, to deliver the opening sermon at the PAC Inaugural Convention. According to a white observer, the ministers at the Inaugural Convention spoke wildly of "the hooligans of Europe who killed our God and have never been convicted."[95]

Use of such intemperate language—anathema to the cautious ANC—was the hallmark of the PAC. Using the Christian terminology dear to him, Sobukwe urged:

And we have it from the Bible that those who crucified Christ will appear before him on the judgment day. We are what we are because the God of Africa made us so. We dare not compromise, nor dare we use moderate language in the course of freedom. As Zik [Nigeria's Nnomdi Azikiwe] puts it, "Tell a man whose house is on fire to give a moderate alarm; . . . tell a mother to extricate gradually her babe from the fire into which it has fallen; but do not ask me to use moderation in a cause like the present.[96]

The PAC in exile years later boasted of politicizing the masses under the cloak of religion. The PAC's Revolutionary Command revealed, "The PAC Oath of Allegiance had taken the place of religious vows. This was not an isolated phenomenon. Throughout the country, the church and other 'innocent' forms of organisation had become the banner of the PAC underground activity."[97]

Surely, Sobukwe's mission-sponsored education had left a legacy on his political development quite different from Lutuli. By bringing Africans and whites together in new structures of relationship, dedicated to a universal ethic, Christian missions might be expected to counteract tendencies toward an exclusive nationalism.[98] However, the mission experience had a quite different impact on Sobukwe. The Legums explain that one consequence of mission education is student derision of missionaries as hypocrites. At least the Afrikaners are honest and consistent on where they stand on race. This hostility towards missionaries, they note, is often carried over to English-speaking Christians and to white liberals.[99]

Young Sobukwe reflected this attitude. When the principal of Healdtown made a speech at Fort Hare on the need for improved contact between the races, Sobukwe challenged him: "The moment I step out of your home, sir, after a show of the brotherhood of man, I will be picked up for a pass offense." When the principal protested that the pass law was not his responsibility, Sobukwe replied, "It will be sir. You're part and parcel of the set-up in this country." He then added an indictment on the church's accommodation to apartheid: "The Methodist Church itself is pursuing a segregationist policy; it has different stipends for Black and White ministers."[100]

Whereas Lutuli had been grateful to missionaries for their work among Africans, Sobukwe included them among the "friends" who "every time our people have shown signs of uniting against oppression" have come along and "broken the unity."[101] He explains that in the earliest days it was the missionary who broke the unity, between 1900 and 1946 it had been the liberal, and today it is again the missionary who fulfills this role: "After maintaining an unbroken and monastic silence for years while Smuts was starving the people out of the Reserves, the Missionaries suddenly discover, when the Africans unite, that the Africans have not had a fair deal."[102] Sobukwe asserts that Africans are no longer so gullible as to trust the Church's efforts on their behalf. "I am afraid these gentlemen are dealing with a new generation which cannot be bamboozled. 'What you are thunders so loudly that what you say cannot be heard.'"[103]

Lutuli had agreed that white Christians were not always good exemplars of their faith. But he continued to work with them and to affirm the efforts of the multiracial churches. Sobukwe refused to cooperate with the multiracial churches, instead looking for support in the African independent churches. It is significant that he did not reject religion in toto. Like Lutuli before him, Sobukwe saw the struggle in terms of the battle between good and evil, which he couched in Christian terminology. For instance, the following Methodist hymn contained the theme of his address to the 1949 graduating class at Fort Hare:

Once to every man and Nation
Comes the moment to decide,
In the strife of truth with falsehood
For the good or evil side. . . .
Then to side with truth is noble

When we share her wretched crust,
Ere her cause bring fame and profit
And 'tis prosperous to be just.
Then it is the brave man chooses
While the coward stands aside,
Til the multitude makes virtue
Of the faith they had denied.[104]

The "brave" men, according to Sobukwe, are those who espouse African nationalism; the "cowards" are its opponents.[105]

Sobukwe quoted regularly from scriptures in his political pronouncements, and spoke of fulfilling God's mission through politics. "You have a mission; we all have a mission. A nation to build we have, a God to glorify, a contribution clear to make towards the blessing of mankind," he urged his followers.[106] There was a recognition among the Africanists that politics had to be based on a Christian foundation. They stressed that the national liberation struggle had to be "strengthened by an unflinching faith in the Almighty God."[107] Anton Lembede,[108] Sobukwe's predecessor as the intellectual father of the PAC, had urged, "our ethical system today has to be based on Christian morals since there is nothing better anywhere in the world."[109] In fact, Africanists claimed a "divine destiny" to free Africa.[110]

Interestingly, both Lutuli and Sobukwe professed belief in the *inevitability* of success. "The final triumph of the liberation movement under the direction of the PAC," Sobukwe wrote, "is assured."[111] Sobukwe predicted that South Africa would be "independent" by 1963.[112] He no doubt believed this because of the example to the north; by 1957 Ghanian independence held forth the prospect that if Africans to the north could free themselves by their own efforts so too could the Africans in South Africa. By the time of Sharpeville, nine colonies had gained independence with four more due that year. For many politically aware Africans, including Sobukwe, independent Africa took on the quality of a "new Jerusalem," write Karis and Carter, and its leaders the appearance of "infallible prophets of freedom."[113] Also, Harold Macmillan's "winds of change" speech to the South African Parliament in February 1960 was seen by blacks as a warning that South Africa could no longer count on Great Britain's continual support, and inspired hope among them. In addition, Sobukwe's optimism was based on a genuine conviction that exclusive nationalism was the *true religion* to address South Africa's sin. The masses, he believed, were yearning for nationhood; all that had been lacking was the correct ideology, African nationalism. The PAC was ready to *preach a creed* that would show the way to self-realization that the masses desired. Surely the PAC could conclude that success could now be only a matter of time.[114]

Both Lutuli and Sobukwe believed in the rightness and justice of their cause. Sobukwe had said, "We are fighting for the noblest cause on earth, the liberation of mankind."[115] And Lutuli asserted, "Our cause is just and we have the Divine assurance that it must triumph over wrong."[116] Both men engaged their followers in prayer before the two campaigns in question. In addition, Lutuli believed that God would help the Africans by converting the whites to see the error of their ways. Nowhere in Sobukwe's writings, however, is there any indication that God was expected to intervene in any way. Certainly, Sobukwe felt it was unrealistic to believe that God would change the hearts of the white minority. But, if not God, then at least "history [is] on our side. *WE WILL WIN!*"[117]

Sobukwe's *go it alone* spirit seems applicable to the Almighty as well. Turner in a doctoral study on comparative ideologies posits the thesis that a belief in a personal, intervening God is associated with a leader's policy of nonviolence. A more *deist* concept of God, which Sobukwe held, corresponds to the acceptance of violence as an appropriate method of struggle.[118]

## VIOLENCE

Did Sobukwe, in fact, promote violence? The Orlando Youth League, the predecessor of the PAC, on remembering the Sophiatown removals, had been contemptuous of the ANC's nonviolent strategy: "What is the use of calling on the people of Sophiatown to 'resist' the removal 'non-violently?' How is this possible? Is it not a contradiction in terms? One either 'resists' violently or 'submits' unwillingly. . . . Since white domination is maintained by force of arms it is only by superior force of arms that it can be overthrown."[119]

The PAC shared the Youth League's view on this. But, on the eve of the antipass campaign, Sobukwe wrote to Major-General Rademeyer, the commissioner of police, emphasizing that the campaign would be nonviolent and imploring the commissioner to instruct his "trigger-happy, African-hating" policemen to refrain from violence in attempting to put down the demonstration.[120] He assured Rademeyer that his people would disperse if given clear orders and time to do so.

In a press conference on March 18, Sobukwe reiterated the nonviolent nature of the demonstration: "I have appealed to the African people," Sobukwe told the press, "to make sure that this campaign is conducted in a spirit of absolute non-violence, and I am quite certain they will heed my call."[121] In his final instructions to the PAC branches, Sobukwe warned, "Our people must be taught *now and continuously* that in this campaign we are going to observe *absolute nonviolence*. There are those in our ranks who will be speaking irresponsible [*sic*] of bloodshed and violence. They must be firmly told what our stand is."[122]

His call for a nonviolent pass demonstration was based on practical considerations, not on any philosophical commitment to passive resistance, as the ANC's had been.[123] Sporadic outbursts of violence during the Defiance Campaign eight years earlier had provided the government with an excuse to use force against the protesters. Sobukwe did not want to see that repeated. He explained that the only people who would benefit from violence were the police, who, after the dead are buried, would round up a few people "and the rest will go back to Passes, having forgotten what our goal had been."[124]

This is not to say that the ANC's decision to endorse nonviolence did not have a pragmatic component; certainly they were no more eager than the PAC to be blown away by the police. The point is that unlike the ANC, nowhere did the PAC link nonviolence with the morally correct behavior. Indeed, Daniel points to Sobukwe's frequent praise of violent protesters of the past as well as his statement—"We are ready to die for our freedom. We are *not yet* (emphasis added) ready to kill for it."—as proof he considered violence an acceptable, if future, option.[125] Pogrund writes that Sobukwe later told him that he had no alternative but to accept the inevitability of armed conflict between whites and blacks because whites would never freely relinquish their ruling position.[126] In a 1988 interview, PAC member Zeph Mothopeng described Sobukwe's view on violence: "[H]e was forced . . . to accept that the ruled could not avoid turning to violence. When you talk of non-violence, you presume that the other side has a conscience. . . . But the rulers in South Africa have not had a conscience."[127] If there is any doubt that the PAC did not rule out violence in principle, the PAC put this notion to rest when it admitted later to its earlier "pretence to non-violent struggle."[128] Peter Molotsi, one-time PAC executive member, admitted that the PAC accepted the inevitability of violence and in fact welcomed the possibility of open conflict.[129] Therefore, the constant references by the PAC to past heroes who fought in *self-defense* was to put violence within an acceptable moral framework and to appeal to those whose moral convictions might otherwise preclude violence.[130]

## SHARPEVILLE MASSACRE

At the first PAC conference, the decision had been taken to launch a Positive Action Campaign "to overthrow White domination and to attain freedom and independence."[131] The PAC had criticized the ANC's approach of reacting against individual apartheid laws. Such an approach, it was believed, led to a preoccupation with effects rather than the root cause, since "every year will bring forth, as every year has brought forth, new oppressive laws, on top of the ones we are opposing."[132] Thus, while fighting against Bantu education, passes for women would come along, and while they are preoccupied with that, new laws would emerge. Politically, the PAC's aim was to close the very source of South Africa's evil legislation. The task was to carry out the Program of Action item by item irrespective of what the government was doing.

One can see that the PAC's belief in noncooperation extended to the government as well as to Indians, communists, and sympathetic whites. The PAC's position was simply to have nothing to do with the government except to wrench power from it.  Sobukwe believed that the only way the white minority could maintain its domination was by enlisting the cooperation and goodwill of the oppressed.[133]  The PAC felt its approach was consistent with the Program of Action which advocated noncooperation with oppressive structures.

The ANC had interpreted this part of the Program of Action to mean rejection of Natives' Representative Councils and the like.  For the ANC, noncooperation meant civil disobedience if certain demands were not met, but it did not reject negotiations out of hand.  It normally began with negotiations, threatening noncollaboration if its demands went unmet.  Motlhabi sees in this process a refusal by the ANC to believe all its previous years of negotiations were futile, as well as an indication of faith in fellow human beings and their capacity for conversion.[134]  The PAC, seeing the ineffectiveness of this approach, put aside negotiation attempts altogether, except when it negotiated on a *technical* issue by cautioning the police commissioner not to use force during the Positive Action Campaign.

For all its criticism of the ANC for merely tinkering and fiddling—"here a boycott, there a demonstration, elsewhere a defiance campaign"[135]—and reacting to government policy, the PAC embarked on a demonstration not unlike the ANC's Defiance Campaign in 1952.  Earlier, Sobukwe had criticized the ANC for not turning the water off at the source, but instead bailing water out of a flooding house.  Lutuli responded, "[T]o get at the tap a good deal of wading through dirty water is necessary. . . . I suspect that when it emerges from theory, the PAC may well find itself committed, like us, not to a single master-stroke, but to a series of partial successes."[136]

There is some evidence that Sobukwe was opposed to the pass campaign, but went along with the decision of his executive committee, who wished to pre-empt the ANC's planned pass campaign scheduled later in the month.[137]  Nevertheless, there is a good reason why Sobukwe accepted the decision of the executive committee: to mobilize the masses.  No other feature of the apartheid system was as detested as the pass system.  It was considered the "linchpin" of apartheid, affecting employment, residence, and even marriage, for all classes of Africans.  Thus, Sobukwe felt that the pass campaign would generate support from all sectors of African society and be a vehicle for mass political education.  It was a step towards psychological liberation, which he believed was the key prerequisite for political liberation.  On a pragmatic note, the young militants within the PAC wanted action.  The PAC hoped to show that, unlike the ANC, they could produce results.  It was believed that the ANC's pass campaign would fizzle out and stir disillusionment among blacks in the country.

On March 18, Sobukwe called a press conference, announcing that two weeks earlier he had written Lutuli, inviting the ANC to join in the campaign under the banner "service, sacrifice, suffering."  The ANC wrote to reject Sobukwe's offer: "We must avoid sensational actions which might not succeed, because we realise that it is treacherous to the liberation movement to embark on a campaign which has not been properly prepared for and which has no reasonable prospect of success."[138] The day before the scheduled protest, Lutuli took the opportunity to publicly contrast the moderation of the ANC with the extremism of the PAC: "We do not want to kick you out of the country and we do not want to marry your sisters. All we want is a fair deal in our own country."[139]

On March 20, 1960, Sobukwe announced a national antipass campaign to be held on March 21, 1960,[140] in which his followers were to surrender themselves at police stations without passes under the slogan "no bail, no defence, no fines."[141] It was hoped that by insisting on arrest, the defiers would clog the jails, halt industry by their absence as workers, and thus force the government to accede to their demands. The leaders were to be in the forefront, inspiring the masses by their example of sacrifice. The PAC felt that the ANC's leaders had hung back at critical times, when the masses were prepared to forge ahead. The PAC also accused the ANC leadership of hiring lawyers, paying fines, and posting bail while the rank and file suffered imprisonment for acts of civil disobedience.[142] The night before the campaign, Sobukwe with his wife, Veronica, had prayed together for the welfare of the participants and for a successful operation.[143] In front of 200 followers who presented themselves for arrest at the Orlando Police Department, Sobukwe stated simply: "I am Sobukwe. We have no passes and we want the police to arrest us."[144]

Elsewhere the campaign had large turnouts, especially at Langa and Nyanga townships in Cape Town and in Vanderbijlpark and Sharpeville townships near Johannesburg.[145] At Sharpeville the crowd numbering some 5,000 to 20,000 protesters led by Myakale Tsolo was "noisy and excitable but not hostile, nor armed."[146] For all their singing and shouting, the protesters were more festive than belligerent, according to one account.[147] Upon reaching the police station, the leaders marched forward, asking the police to let them through so that they could surrender themselves for arrest for refusing to carry passes. Shortly after the PAC branch leaders had been let through into the police station, with no warning the police fired upon the assembled protesters, killing 69 people, most of them in the back, and wounding 186. At Langa, 1,000 miles away, in a similar situation, two were killed and forty-nine injured. Following the killings, the crowds went on a rampage, rioting and burning schools, public buildings, and others symbols of oppression.[148] In all, seventy-four people died throughout the country on this day of protest that Sobukwe had planned to be peaceful.

The Reverend Ambrose Reeves, one of the *do-gooder* white liberals earlier assailed by Sobukwe, made sure that the government could not whitewash the incident; he had lawyers immediately rushed to the hospitals to take statements from the victims.[149] The South African churches also responded quickly to the incident. A week after Sharpeville, twelve clergymen from the three Dutch Reformed Church bodies issued a statement rejecting apartheid as "unethical, unbiblical, and without any foundation in Scripture."[150] But nine leading members of the Nerderduitse Gereformeerde Kerk (NGK), while acknowledging mistakes made by the government in implementing apartheid, nevertheless approved of the policy of "independent, distinctive development, provided this was carried out in a just and honourable way, without impairing or offending human dignity."[151] The clergymen noted that it had always been accepted that apartheid in the early stages would create a certain amount of disruption.  In general, the English-speaking churches denounced the government's action in the Sharpeville Massacre, which was not surprising since these churches had been on record for years as opposing apartheid.

Significantly, Sobukwe was silent about the churches' pronouncements.  Unlike Lutuli, who was glad to see the churches taking a stand, Sobukwe had not been looking for allies from these quarters.  He no doubt viewed their pronouncements as the hypocritical response of liberals wishing to dissociate themselves from the government's policies, while at the same time benefiting from those very policies. Sobukwe had commented that Africanists were too sophisticated to be "bamboozled" anymore.  At any rate, he did not want help from the white churches.  "We are . . . on our own," he had urged his followers.[152]

Sobukwe's plan to be arrested was accomplished.  Police seized documents from his home and office and took him to Marshall Square, the central police station in Johannesburg.  There news reached him of the massacre at Sharpeville. "He was depressed and almost at the point of tears—the Sharpeville tragedy had hit him really hard," remembers journalist Stanley Motjuwadi.[153]  Lutuli immediately called for a day of mourning for the victims coupled with a stay-away from work on March 28.  He also urged blacks to burn their passes.

Sobukwe's reaction was immediate.  He called the ANC's day of mourning "rank opportunism."  He accused the ANC of "trying to bask in the sunshine of PAC's successes."  He criticized Lutuli for having the courage to burn his pass only after the government had suspended them.  (In the aftermath of Sharpeville, the government had temporarily suspended the pass laws but did not repeal them as the PAC wanted.)  "Supported and boosted by the white Press, he has been making one foolish statement after the other, pretending that he has a following in the country," Sobukwe complained.  He accused the ANC of trying to reap what the PAC had sowed.  "Our advice and warning to the ANC and its liberal friends is: Hands off our campaign.  We do not need your interference.  Go on with your coffin-carrying and other childish pastimes but leave the African people to fight the struggle without you.  Tell your bosses you cannot sell the African people because you do not control them."[154]  Pogrund suggests that Sobukwe misread the mood of the country; Lutuli's day of mourning protest was the biggest in the country's history.[155]

Consistent with his belief in noncollaboration, Sobukwe refused to defend himself on the charge of inciting people to violate the law.  After being sentenced along with eighteen other PAC members under the Criminal Law Amendment Act, which had been introduced in 1952 to break the Defiance Campaign, he made the following statement:

Your worship, it will be remembered that when this case began we refused to plead, because we felt no moral obligation whatsoever to obey laws which are made exclusively by a White Minority. . . . But I would like to quote what was said by somebody before, that an unjust law cannot be justly applied. We believe in one race only—the human race to which we all belong. The history of that race is a long history of struggle against all restrictions, physical, mental, and spiritual. We would have betrayed the human race if we had not done our share. We are glad to have made our contribution.[156]

After his three-year sentence was completed on Robben Island, Sobukwe was held for six additional years under a new measure, the General Laws Amendment Act of 1963, which allowed for continued detention "this side of eternity" of prisoners who had completed their sentences.[157]

By this time, both the PAC and ANC had been outlawed,[158] and efforts at peaceful change finally gave way to outright violence.[159] Having decided upon a course of violence,[160] the underground ANC established a military wing in 1961 called Umkhonto we Sizwe (*Spear of the Nation*) that committed sabotage.[161] The PAC simultaneously formed a military wing called Poqo (*Africans Alone*), that engaged in terrorism.

Carter and Karis argue that Lutuli himself came to adopt the belief that violence was at times a necessary evil in the struggle for justice. Just days after Lutuli received the Nobel Peace Prize, the ANC launched its first sabotage campaign, apparently with his tacit consent.[162] They offer no proof of his advance knowledge, other than the fact that he met with Mandela, the commander-in-chief of Umkhonto, in the days preceding the first bomb explosions on government installations. However, Callan notes that because of continued bannings in the late 1950s, it is doubtful that he was involved with the day-to-day operations of the ANC.[163] The executive committee of the ANC, responsible for major policy decisions, was drawn from members living within fifty miles of Johannesburg; Lutuli was thousands of miles away confined to the Groutville reserve. The better reading is that he did not lead the ANC into its new position and would not have had he been in a position to do so. But he understood how others were led to a course of violence because of closed legal means of protest. In a speech issued on June 12, 1964, after Nelson Mandela, Walter Sisulu and others were sentenced to life imprisonment in the famous Rivonia Trial for engaging in violence against the state, Lutuli stated:

The African National Congress never abandoned its method of a militant, nonviolent struggle, and creating in the process a spirit of militancy in the people. However, in the face of the uncompromising white refusal to abandon a policy which denies the African and other oppressed South Africans their rightful heritage—freedom—no one can blame brave just men for seeking justice by the use of violent methods . . . in order to establish peace and racial harmony.[164]

Meanwhile, what was Sobukwe's relationship with Poqo? He denied all links to it, pointing out that he was behind bars in Pretoria when the terrorist acts occurred. "I do not know what gave rise to it. I was not involved in it in any way at all," he insisted.[165] Also, by the time of Poqo, it is not clear that Sobukwe was still in control of the PAC. Hamilton Zolite Keke, jailed for ten years for membership in Poqo and later the PAC representative in London and Baghdad, doubts that Sobukwe knew anything about Poqo. It was too crude an organization and too lacking in political direction to have been a creation of Sobukwe, he maintains. "Had Sobukwe known of it," he believes, "he would have vetoed it. Sobukwe would not have sanctioned a situation where people with pangas and stones were given orders to attack well-trained Boers."[166] This assessment clearly deals with the practicality, not the morality, of using violence against a stronger enemy.

## CAPTIVITY AND FAITH

During his long captivity and subsequent home arrest in Kimberley, Sobukwe continued to uphold his religious convictions. While in prison in Pretoria, a Roman Catholic priest, Father Reg Webber, held weekly church services for the Methodist.[167] Father Webber maintained contact with Sobukwe when he was sent to Robben Island, writing him regularly. Sobukwe listened to religious broadcasts every morning—in English not Afrikaans—he liked to joke. As the leading political prisoner there, he frightened off the local chaplains who stayed clear of him. An Anglican minister ordered to visit him declined, saying the trip would make him seasick.[168] In 1965, the Methodist Church appointed the Reverend Theo Kotze, its minister in Sea Point, as part-time chaplain to Robben Island. Knowing that Sobukwe and Mandela were Methodists, he asked repeatedly to be allowed to visit them until finally the next year his request was granted. He saw Sobukwe three times before the Prisons Department cancelled his appointment as chaplain.

Unfortunately, his successor on Robben Island, the Reverend Francis MacCreath, nearly destroyed Sobukwe's beliefs. Pogrund explains that on MacCreath's first visit to Sobukwe, he lectured the prisoner on the wages of sin, saying that he deserved to be there. Sobukwe refused to see him again and asked that no ministers be permitted to visit him. Sobukwe described his break with the Church in these terms: "In the Christian religion I think that my difficulty is that Christ is hidden behind the pretensions, superstitions and arrogance of Western Europe."[169] This was a theme that was amplified later by the Black Consciousness Movement: white Christians were guilty of misusing the Gospel for their ulterior purposes. Sobukwe struggled with the relevance of Christianity for black South Africans, wondering if black South Africans were Christians simply because they were subjugated by Europeans who brought their religion. "If we had been subjugated by Turks, we would be fanatical Mohammedans as are eight million Africans on the continent. Similarly, if Indians had subjugated us we would be fanatical Hindus. There is nothing inevitable in our being Christians," he concluded.[170]

Despite his rejection of the Church and disappointment with white Christians, it is inaccurate to say that he lost his faith in prison. In a letter to Pogrund, he confessed, "My faith in God remains unshaken, Benjie. At the moment I don't care to know what He is like and where He resides. It is enough to know that He is and that His will will triumph."[171]

During his banishment to Kimberley, following nine years in jail, Sobukwe continued to display both an optimism about himself and South Africa, and a deep trust in God. "I am quite certain things will work out well. God has been too good to me, Benjie, to leave his promises unfulfilled," he confided to his close friend.[172] Although on Robben Island he had broken formally with organized religion, after he was released to Kimberley he began attending a Methodist Church. A skilled linguist, he was used as an interpreter during the Sunday service, translating the sermon into one language, then another. When the Security Police warned the local minister that he could be prosecuted as an accomplice to Sobukwe's breaking his banning orders by speaking at a gathering, he stopped using Sobukwe as an interpreter.[173]

Jim and Diana Thomson, two American visitors from Harvard University, were struck by Sobukwe's strong faith: "[H]e was deeply religious and deeply spiritual," remembered Diana Thomson. "He was a profound Christian. But he was not the kind of religious person who hits you over the head with God all the time. It was so deep in him that it pervaded everything he said without being blatant."[174] "And there was an unshakeable faith that God's good purposes would ultimately prevail in South Africa," added her husband, Jim.[175] Around the same time as the Thomsons' visit, Bernard Nossiter wrote a piece for the *Washington Post* in which he confirmed Sobukwe's "almost religious certainty" in the rightness of his cause and eventual triumph.[176]

The religious justification for the opposition to apartheid begun by Lutuli and continued by Sobukwe would be more fully articulated by the new generation of Africanists who came of age following a decade-long lull in resistance politics.[177] Led by Steve Biko, these young Africanists ushered in the Black Consciousness Movement.

## NOTES

1. Gail Gerhart, *Black Power in South Africa: The Evolution of an Ideology* (Berkeley: University of California Press, 1978), p. 183.

2. Benjamin Pogrund, *How Can Man Die Better: Sobukwe and Apartheid* (London: Peter Halban, 1990), p. 7.

3. The pupils at Healdtown were black but the staff was interracial.

4. Pogrund, p. 12.

5. Fort Hare was the offspring of Lovedale, a school founded by the Glasgow

Missionary Society as a showpiece of the church's multiracial efforts in education. When Sobukwe entered Fort Hare, there were 260 blacks, 29 Asians, and 35 Coloureds but no whites.

6. Pogrund, p. 20.

7. By 1944 explicit provision was made by the ANC for universal franchise.

8. Pogrund, p. 28.

9. Pogrund, p. 30.

10. Sobukwe graduated with a teaching degree from Fort Hare.

11. Pogrund, p. 54.

12. Sobukwe was one of less than half a dozen black academics on staff at this white university. While a teacher there, he simultaneously pursued an honours degree earning the distinction of being the last black student allowed to do an honours degree in the Department of Bantu Studies.

13. Thomas Karis and Gwendolen Carter, *From Protest to Challenge: A Documentary History of African Politics in South Africa, 1882-1964*, vol. 3 (Stanford: Hoover Institution Press, 1972-1977), p. 19.

14. *African Digest* 4 (February 1958), cited in Edward Callan, *Albert John Luthuli and the South African Race Conflict* (Kalamazoo, Western Michigan University Press, 1962), p. 39.

15. The PAC was formally constituted at a conference on April 6, 1959, five months after the breakaway from the ANC, on the 300th anniversary of the Cape landing of Van Riebeeck. Sobukwe was elected president by unanimous vote.

16. Pogrund, p. 87.

17. "Letter 'giving notice' of Africanist disassociation from the ANC (Transvaal)," November 2, 1958, in Karis and Carter, vol. 3, p. 506 (Document 37).

18. "Three African Freedom Movements," *Freedomways* 2, no. 1 (Winter 1962), p. 84.

19. Andrew Silk, "Understanding the Master: Robert Sobukwe's Legacy," *The Nation* 226, no. 12 (1978), p. 368.

20. Sobukwe's relationship with Patrick Duncan was complex. Early on assailed, Duncan later was appreciated. Forced to escape the country, Duncan became the PAC's first white member. When told in prison about the role of the Liberal Party in Sharpeville, Sobukwe said his men had been so impressed with what the liberals had done that they would have been willing to accept the amalgamation of PAC and the Liberal Party had the situation arisen. See Pogrund, p. 204.

21. Mangaliso Robert Sobukwe, *Speeches of Mangaliso Sobukwe 1949-1959*, no publishing information, p. 11.

22. Sobukwe, p. 23.

23. "Future of the Africanist Movement," Questions and Answers by R. M. Sobukwe, *The Africanist* (January 1959), in Karis and Carter, vol. 3, p. 508 (Document 38).

24. PAC, *Time for Azania* (Toronto: Norman Bethune Institute, 1976), p. 18.

25. "Opening Address," by R. M. Sobukwe, Inaugural Conference of the PAC, April 4-6, 1959, in Karis and Carter, vol. 3, p. 514 (Document 39a).

26. "Future of the Africanist Movement," Questions and Answers by R. M. Sobukwe, *The Africanist* (January 1959), in Karis and Carter, vol. 3, p. 507 (Document 38).

27. The ANC's leaders saw South Africa as an exception because of the large number

of non-Africans there.

28. Ethel Khopung, *Apartheid: The Struggle of a Dispossessed People* (Dar Es Salaam: Sharpeville Day Association Mbizana, 1972), p. 63.

29. Jack Simons and Ray Simons, *Class and Colour in South Africa 1850–1950* (London: International Defence Aid Fund for South Africa, 1983), p. 621.

30. Sobukwe, p. 16.

31. Gerhart, p. 207.

32. Karis and Carter, vol. 3, p. 322.

33. Gerhart, p. 208.

34. For a discussion of the influence of Pan-Africanism on the PAC, see Gerhart, pp. 204–211. See also Mary Benson, *The African Patriots* (London: Faber and Faber, 1963), pp. 49, 56–57, 117; and Peter Walshe, *The Rise of African Nationalism in South Africa: The ANC 1912–1952* (Berkeley: University of California Press, 1971), p. 566 ff.; and Karis and Carter, vol. 3, pp. 320–323.

35. Sobukwe, p. 19.

36. Pogrund, pp. 106–107. He then conveniently redefined Coloureds as "blacks."

37. Mary Benson, *Nelson Mandela* (London: Panaf, 1980), p. 33.

38. There were also whites and Indians in the Congress Alliance.

39. Walshe, p. 356.

40. "Future of the Africanist Movement," Questions and Answers by R. M. Sobukwe, *The Africanist* (January 1959), in Karis and Carter, vol. 3, p. 509 (Document 38).

41. Pogrund, p. 93.

42. Jordan Ngubane, *An African Explains Apartheid* (London: Pall Mall, 1963), p. 103.

43. Sobukwe, p. 8.

44. Sobukwe, p. 9.

45. Sobukwe, p. 34.

46. Sobukwe, p. 35.

47. Sobukwe, p. 36.

48. John Daniel, "Radical Resistance to Minority Rule in South Africa: 1906–1965" (Ph.D. dissertation, Buffalo: State University of New York, 1975), p. 218.

49. Daniel, p. 219.

50. Pogrund, p. 36.

51. Daniel, p. 219.

52. Karis and Carter, vol. 3, p. 319.

53. "South African Treason Trial Record," p. 32, cited in Ruth Turner, "Violence and Non-violence in Confrontation: A Comparative Study of Ideologies. Six Historical Cases: Paine, Lenin, Hitler, Gandhi, Luthuli, and King" (Ph.D. dissertation, Amherst: University of Massachusetts, 1979), p. 298.

54. The ANC Youth League also had a provision for protecting minority rights.

55. Walshe, p. 342.

56. Sobukwe, p. 25.

57. Sobukwe, "One Central Government in Africa," March 1960, in Karis and Carter, vol. 3, p. 563 (Document 46).

58. "Opening Address," Inaugural Convention of the PAC, April 4–6, 1959, in Karis

and Carter, vol. 3, p. 516 (Document 39a).

59. Robert Sobukwe, "PAC on Guard in Defence of PAC Policy and Programme," *The Africanist* (December 1959), p. 13, cited in Gerhart, p. 190.

60. Sobukwe, p. 42.

61. PAC, *Time for Azania*, p. 19.

62. Sobukwe, p. 43.

63. "Three African Freedom Movements," *Freedomways*, p. 84.

64. "Future of the Africanist Movement," Questions and Answers by R. M. Sobukwe, *The Africanist* (January 1959), in Karis and Carter, vol. 3, p. 508 (Document 38).

65. Colin Legum and Margaret Legum, *The Bitter Choice: Eight South Africans' Resistance to Tyranny*, New York: World Publishing Co., 1968, p. 114.

66. Sobukwe, p. 9.

67. Gerhart, p. 146.

68. "Basic Policy of Congress Youth League," Manifesto issued by the National Executive Committee of the ANC Youth League, 1948, in Karis and Carter, vol. 2, p. 324 (Document 57).

69. "Letter 'giving notice' of Africanist disassociation from the ANC (Transvaal)," November 2, 1958, in Karis and Carter, vol. 3, p. 505 (Document 37).

70. See Karis and Carter, vol. 3, p. 323. See "One Central Government in Africa," R. M. Sobukwe, (March 1960), in Karis and Carter, vol. 3, pp. 562–563 (Document 46). Also see Karis and Carter, vol. 2, p. 105.

71. Gerhart, p. 216.

72. Gerhart, p. 216.

73. Sobukwe, p. 25.

74. Callan, p. 40.

75. "English-speaking" refers to the churches of English origin who came to South Africa during the time of British Imperialism. The majority of their members are blacks. It includes the Anglican, Methodist, Presbyterian, and Congregational Churches but not the Lutheran and Catholic Churches.

76. AICs are usually divided into two groups—Ethiopianism and Zionism. Sundkler differentiates Ethiopianism from Zionism as follows: Ethiopianism broke away from the white churches but retained the outer forms, structure, and much of the teaching of the parent body. Zionism usually sprang up independently and blended together Christian faith with African traditions. See Bengt G. M. Sundkler, *Bantu Prophets in South Africa* (New York: Oxford University Press, 1961), pp. 53–60.

77. Francis Meli, *South Africa Belongs to Us: A History of the ANC* (Bloomington: Indiana University Press, 1989), p. 9. Thomas comments that while those in the multiracial churches cried "out," those in the apartheid (Dutch Reformed) cried "in," clamoring for closer unity. See David Thomas, *Councils in the Ecumenical Movement in South Africa* (Johannesburg; SACC, 1979), p. 35.

78. Leslie Hewson, *An Introduction to South African Methodists* (Cape Town: Methodist Publishing House, 1951), p. 94.

79. Karis and Carter, vol. 1, p. 7.

80. See Sundkler, pp. 40, 172.

81. Sundkler, p. 47.

82. Sundkler, p. 330.

83. D. D. T. Jabavu, "Foreword" to Lea, p. 11, cited in Hewson, p. 94.

84. Louise Kretzschmar, *The Voice of Black Theology in South Africa* (Johannesburg: Ravan, 1986), p. 47.

85. Kofi Appiah-Kubi and Sergio Torres, eds., *African Theology En Route* (Maryknoll, N.Y.: Orbis, 1979), pp. 117–118.

86. Adrian Hastings, *A History of African Christianity 1950–1975* (London: Cambridge University Press, 1979), pp. 69, 72.

87. Hastings, p. 73.

88. John W. de Gruchy, *The Church Struggle in South Africa* (Grand Rapids, Mich.: William B. Eerdmans, 1986), p. 45.

89. Jean Comaroff, *Body of Power, Spirit of Resistance: The Culture and History of a South African People* (Chicago: University of Chicago Press, 1985), pp. 255–263.

90. Ernie Regehr, *Perceptions of Apartheid: The Churches and Political Change in South Africa* (Scottsdale, Ariz.: Herald Press, 1979), p. 179.

91. Hastings, p. 74.

92. See Walshe, p. 10.

93. Peter Walshe, *Church versus State in South Africa: The Case of the Christian Institute* (Maryknoll, N.Y.: Orbis, 1983), p. 65.

94. Gerhart, p. 202.

95. Gerhart, p. 203.

96. Sobukwe, p. 12.

97. PAC, *PAC in Perspective*, p. 20.

98. Leo Kuper in Monica Wilson and Leonard Thompson, eds., *A History of South Africa to 1870* (Cape Town: David Philip, 1982), p. 434.

99. Colin Legum and Margaret Legum, p. 109.

100. Colin Legum and Margaret Legum, pp. 109–110. When the principal returned to Healdtown, he told the Caleys, Sobukwe's benefactors, that under no condition could Sobukwe return to teach at Healdtown as planned. See Pogrund, p. 41.

101. Sobukwe, p. 11.

102. Sobukwe, p. 11.

103. Sobukwe, p. 12.

104. Sobukwe, p. 10.

105. Sobukwe, p. 11.

106. Sobukwe, p. 9.

107. *Bantu World* (September 27, 1947), cited in Walshe, *The Rise of African Nationalism in South Africa*, p. 343.

108. Lembede, a devout Catholic, had been the first president of the Youth League.

109. Mary Benson, *South Africa: The Struggle for a Birthright* (New York: Funk and Wagnalls, 1969), p. 85.

110. "Basic Policy of Congress Youth League," Manifesto issued by the National Executive Committee of the ANC Youth League, 1948, in Karis and Carter, vol. 2, p. 324 (Document 57).

111. Sobukwe, p. 47.

112. Colin Legum and Margaret Legum, p. 14.

113. Karis and Carter, vol. 3, p. 321.

114. Karis and Carter, vol. 3, p. 326.

115. Sobukwe, p. 38.

116. Albert Luthuli, "South Africa Shall Have Its Freedom," *Africa Today* 3, no. 5 (September–October 1956), p. 3.

117. Sobukwe, p. 38.

118. See Turner, p. 30.

119. Article by "Nzana," *The Africanist* 1, no. 3 (May 1955), p. 6, cited in Karis and Carter, vol. 3, p. 27.

120. "Letter announcing the launching of the anti-pass campaign," R. M. Sobukwe to Major-General Rademayer, Commissioner of Police, March 16, 1960, in Karis and Carter, vol. 3, p. 566 (Document 48).

121. "Press Release: Call for Positive Action," announcing the launching of the anti-pass campaign [n.d.], in Karis and Carter, vol. 3, p. 566 (Document 49).

122. Sobukwe, p. 37.

123. Pogrund, p. 96.

124. Sobukwe, p. 37.

125. "Molotsi Reveals PAC Policy," *Contact* (June 18, 1960), p. 3, cited in Daniel, p. 224. Indeed, a PAC flyer issued at the same time declared that pass laws had to be "blown to oblivion this year, now and forever." See "The Pan Africanist Congress Has a Message for the Down Trodden Black Masses of Afrika," Flyer issued by the PAC [n.d.], in Karis and Carter, vol. 3, pp. 560–561 (Document 45).

126. Pogrund, p. 66.

127. Pogrund, p. 332.

128. PAC, *PAC in Perspective*, p. 16.

129. Daniel, pp. 224–225.

130. See Gerhart, pp. 100, 149, 200–201.

131. Colin Legum and Margaret Legum, p. 113.

132. "The Nature of the Struggle Today," Potlako K. Leballo, *The Africanist* (December 1957), in Karis and Carter, vol. 3, p. 503 (Document 36).

133. Sobukwe, p. 22.

134. Mokgethi Motlhabi, *The Theory and Practice of Black Resistance to Apartheid* (Johannesburg: Ravan, 1984), p. 83.

135. Albert Luthuli, *Let My People Go* (London: Collins, 1962), p. 187.

136. Luthuli, p. 188.

137. Ngubane explains that Sobukwe preferred the Status Campaign, but he was persuaded that dramatic results were necessary to increase the PAC's membership. See Jordan Ngubane, *An African Explains Apartheid* (London: Pall Mall, 1963), pp. 104–15.

138. Pogrund, p. 122.

139. Callan, p. 41.

140. The March 21 date was not Sobukwe's choice. He had chosen March 7, but the leaflets were not ready. The leaflets were still not ready close to the date, so Sobukwe spent the prior weekend duplicating some leaflets. There were still not enough for mass distribution.

141. R. M. Sobukwe, "Calling the Nation! No Bail! No Defence! No Fines!!!" Flyer announcing the launching of the anti-pass campaign, in Karis and Carter, vol. 3, p. 564

(Document 47).

142. See Gerhart, p. 230. During the Defiance Campaign, James Moroka had cut his own deal with the courts, dissociating himself from his fellow defendants.

143. Pogrund, p. 129.

144. Pogrund, p. 131.

145. Muriel Horrell, ed., *A Survey of Race Relations in South Africa, 1960* (Johannesburg: SAIRR, 1961), pp. 56–58.

146. Motlhabi, *Theory and Practice*, p. 94.

147. PAC, *Time for Azania*, p. 58.

148. Horrell, p. 73. For a detailed discussion of events at Sharpeville, see Ambrose Reeves, *Shooting at Sharpeville: The Agony of South Africa* (Boston: Houghton Mifflin, 1969); and Richard Gibson, *African Liberation Movements: Contemporary Struggles Against White Minority Rule* (London: Oxford University Press, 1972), pp. 55–57.

149. Pogrund, p. 136.

150. de Gruchy, p. 188.

151. de Gruchy, p. 189.

152. "Letter 'giving notice' of Africanist disassociation from the ANC (Transvaal)," November 2, 1958, in Karis and Carter, vol. 3, p. 506 (Document 37).

153. Pogrund, p. 137.

154. Pogrund, p. 141.

155. Pogrund, p. 142.

156. Colin Legum and Margaret Legum, p. 104.

157. This legislation, sometimes called the Sobukwe Clause, was designed especially for him and was never used against other prisoners.

158. In outlawing them, the government used the same reasoning it had against those charged during the Treason Trial. It charged that their fundamental aim was the violent overthrow of the government. No churches spoke out against the bannings.

159. Oliver Tambo says that the decision to resort to violence was the occasion of protests in 1961 against the formation of a republic. The army, not just the police, was mobilized against the protesters. He says it was a new situation that encouraged the ANC to embrace violence as a method of struggle. See Francis Meli, *South Africa Belongs to Us: A History of the ANC* (Bloomington: Indiana University Press, 1989), p. 148.

160. The official ANC, not its military wing, retained its position on nonviolence but refused to condemn Umkhonto. See Benson, *Nelson Mandela*, p. 239.

161. On the day that whites celebrate the defeat of Zulus in 1828, Umkhonto exploded its first bomb at government targets. Mandela explained that sabotage was the least undesirable and most morally justifiable type of violence, but that the struggle would escalate to guerilla warfare, then terrorism, and finally revolution if the earlier tactics were unsuccessful.

162. Karis and Carter, vol. 3, pp. 649–651. See also "The Role of Chief Luthuli" *African Communist* 70 (Fall 1977), p. 18 where it is suggested that Umkhonto had Luthuli's full support.

163. Callan, p. 30.

164. "On the Rivonia Trial," in Albert Lutuli, *The Road to Freedom is via the Cross* (London: ANC, n.d.), p. 92.

165. Pogrund, p. 204.

166. Pogrund, p. 183.

167. Pogrund, p. 177.

168. Pogrund, p. 270.

169. Pogrund, p. 292.

170. Pogrund, p. 272.

171. Pogrund, p. 291.

172. Pogrund, p. 309.

173. Pogrund, pp. 318–319.

174. Pogrund, p. 324.

175. Pogrund, p. 324.

176. Pogrund, p. 339.

177. The 1960s were a decade of quiescence since Lutuli was banned and Sobukwe, Mandela, Sisulu, and Mbeki were imprisoned. The ANC's underground leaders had been rounded up and arrested, and the PAC was in total disarray.

# 3

# Steve Biko and the Black Consciousness Movement

Born in 1946 in King Williams Town in the Cape Province, Steve Biko would become a major figure in the Black Consciousness Movement (BCM) of the late 1960s and early 1970s. He was raised in an Anglican family and educated at mission-founded institutions—Lovedale,[1] the Presbyterian academy in Alice; and St. Francis College, a Catholic boarding school in Marianhill. He later attended Natal University Medical School, but quit in 1972 to devote himself full-time to politics.[2]

A committed Christian, Biko nevertheless rejected the approach to politics associated with the Christian leadership of the African National Congress (ANC) under Lutuli, who accepted collaboration with whites concerned with justice. Gerhart writes, "Christian principles impressed him, as did the ideals of an eventual common, integrated society; but he was not satisfied to have any whites try to influence his thinking about the precise detail of either ends or means when it came to the future of Africans."[3]

## SOUTH AFRICAN STUDENTS' ASSOCIATION

It is no wonder, then, that in 1969 he founded the South African Students' Association (SASO), a splinter group from the mostly white National Union of South African Students (NUSAS), as an *all-black* student organization. The split arose out of a NUSAS conference at Rhodes University in 1967 at which black conferees were required to board at separate accommodations away from the conference site. Although this was in accordance with South African law, the fact that whites accepted it without question angered the black student.[4]

The next year Biko attended a student conference at Stuttenheim sponsored by the recently formed University Christian Movement (UCM).[5] There were two reasons for its attractiveness to blacks: its Christian orientation, which appealed to a population whose earliest and most potent ideological frame of reference was Christianity, and its black majority. More than half of the ninety delegates at the UCM conference were Africans, explained partly by the fact that unlike NUSAS it was allowed to exist on black campuses, having not yet developed a bad reputation with officials.[6] Still, its viewpoint and leadership were disproportionately white.

During subsequent debates among black students on the value of remaining in multiracial organizations, Biko in time came to see that black concerns did not coincide with white ones. But he admits that it was difficult to abandon faith in multiracial efforts: "I think I realized that for a long time I had been holding on to this whole dogma of nonracialism almost like a religion, and feeling that it is sacrilegious [sic] to question it."[7]

The following year at Turfloof, one of the government's *tribal* universities, the break was made. SASO provided this statement at its founding conference to explain its decision to go it alone: "The complexity of the South Africa scene makes it impossible to have a pluralistic organization that satisfies the aspirations of all member groups. Social and political stratifications in the country coupled with preferential treatment of certain groups result in differing aspirations prevailing in the different segments of the community."[8]

SASO explained that African students had unique interests and aspirations. Educated at ethnic universities apart from white students, Africans had entirely different problems than their white counterparts. Black students in student organizations tended to have concerns that transcended mere student issues. SASO's Manifesto explained, "We black students are an integral part of the black oppressed community before we are students."[9]

At first, the government welcomed the organization, as it fit in with its notion of separate development. Initially, it saw in black consciousness a manifestation of tribal consciousness which it was trying to foster through group areas, bantustans, and Bantu education. It did not at that time understand that BCM's goal was ultimately to counter white domination with black solidarity.


## THE WHITE QUESTION

Biko favored black solidarity over multiracial collaboration because of the dangers associated with alliances with white sympathizers. Biko wrote, "We must realise that our situation is not a mistake on the part of whites, but a deliberate act and that no amount of moral lectures will persuade the white man to 'correct' the situation."[10] Biko rejected the notion of the ANC under Lutuli that whites could be enjoined to live up to the Christian standards they professed. He denied that "beggar tactics" whereby "you choose to come to a round table to beg for your deliverance" accomplished anything but, rather, ensured the contempt of those in power.[11]

Biko believed that cooperation with whites for black deliverance was a self-defeating strategy. It led to an incongruous situation in which the white man was not only kicking the black man; he was instructing the black man how to react to the kick! "For a long time the black has been listening with patience to the advice he has been receiving. . . . With painful slowness he is now beginning to show signs that it is his right and duty to kick *in the way he sees fit.*"[12] Biko argued that the white liberal who claims to have a "black soul wrapped up in white skin"[13] still benefits from the apartheid regime:

Being white, he possesses the natural passport to the exclusive pool of white privileges from which he does not hesitate to extract whatever suits him. Yet, since he identifies with blacks, he moves around his white circles—white only beaches, restaurants and cinemas—with a lighter load, feeling that he is not like the rest. Yet at the back of his mind is the constant reminder that he is quite comfortable as things stand and therefore should not bother about change.[14]

In one respect, liberals did worse damage than those doing the "kicking." Seeking to control blacks' response to the "kick," they inevitably advocated moderation and gradualism. Thus, collaboration with white liberals, according to Biko, had been responsible for the lack of any real progress.[15]

Liberals were wrong in pinpointing the enemy. To the liberals, the enemy is strictly the National Party. Their assumption, according to Biko, is that all is well with the system "apart from some degree of mismanagement by irrational conservatives at the top."[16] Thus, the objective of white liberals was limited to replacing one white political party with another slightly less reactionary one and relaxing certain oppressive laws.

As suspect to Biko as the liberals were the more radical members of the left wing, the communists, who "tell us that the struggle is a class struggle rather than a race one."[17] But the true foe for Biko was neither the National Party nor the capitalist class, but rather white racism which needed to be faced by black unity. Biko believed that blacks needed to close their ranks to coalesce into a solid group to oppose the racism meted out by white society.[18]

Biko denied that his followers were themselves black racists: "Some will charge that we are racist but let us not take heed. . . . We do not have the power to subjugate anyone. We are merely responding to provocation in the most realistic way. Racism not only implies exclusion of one race by another—it always presupposes that the exclusion is for the purposes of subjugation."[19] However, he was aware of the ambiguity of the exclusive approach: "History has charged us with the cruel responsibility of going to the very gate of racism in order to destroy racism—to the gate not further."[20]

Biko advocated an exclusive black front, but, unlike Sobukwe, he accepted Coloureds and Indians in that front from the very beginning, including members from the Coloured and Indian campuses in SASO's executive committee from the start.  (Sobukwe, it will be remembered, in time came to accept Coloureds in the Pan-Africanist Congress and acted as if it had always been PAC policy to incorporate them.)  The BCM defined "black" as "those who are by law or tradition politically, economically, and socially discriminated against as a group in the South African society and identifying themselves as a unit in the struggle toward the realization of their aspirations."[21]  Certainly, the "stinking Coolies" Sobukwe had spurned were among the oppressed and deserved to be called "blacks."

Conversely, not all blacks were worthy of that appellation.  Biko wrote, "I must state categorically that there is no such thing as a Black policeman.  Any Black man who props the System up actively has lost the right to be considered part of the Black world."  Using a biblical allusion, he explains that he has sold his soul for thirty pieces of silver and has become an extension of the enemy into our ranks.[22]

Likewise, Biko rejected as "black" the homeland leaders, whom he described as "honorary whites" because they chose to accept the government's bantustans arrangement for "separate development."[23]  In his view, they were denying their God-given right to the whole country for some remote corner.  He criticized both Kaiser Mantazimo of the Transkei and Mangosuthu Gatsha Buthelezi of KwaZulu for aspiring for privileges for themselves within the established order.

Biko held the same view of any person who entered the Coloured Representative or Indian Councils, the Urban Bantu Councils (the advisory bodies in the townships) or any government boards or councils in the townships or reserves.  His opprobrium of these "dummy platforms" and "phoney telephones"[24] is reminiscent of Lutuli's disavowal of the Natives' Representative Councils as "toy telephones."

Their collaboration and compromise conflicted with the radical aims of the Black Consciousness Movement.  A SASO newsletter editorialized, "It is the elitist class, created by the very oppressed, that has joined hands with the oppressor in suppressing the legitimate aspirations of the masses of the people and they collect crumbs from the master's table for this dirty work."[25]  Trying to emulate whites, they are "insulting the intelligence of whoever created them black."[26]

Just as there were "a few bad blacks," Biko admitted that there were "a few good whites."[27]  But, for Biko, the exception merely proved the rule.  Even the "good" whites benefit from the system, so their sincerity in wishing to destroy that system is dubious.  And if they are sincere, that is "true liberals," then they are oppressed themselves and should fight for their own freedom and not for that of blacks with whom they can hardly identify.[28]  The role of whites is therefore limited; no group, however benevolent, can ever hand power to the vanquished on a plate, Biko stated.[29]  What the more aware whites can do is to work within their own community in a parallel *white consciousness* movement to educate their brothers for the future.  He wrote that the liberal must serve as a lubrication so that as the black majority shifts gears in moving South Africa in a new direction, there would be no grinding metal but an easy flowing movement characteristic of a well-tuned vehicle.[30]

## ASSIMILATION

Biko denied that blacks should seek assimilation into white society. He wrote, "This is white man's integration—an integration based on exploitative values in a society in which the whites have already cut out their position somewhere at the top of the pyramid. It is an integration in which black will compete with black, using each other as rungs up a step ladder leading them to white values."[31] It is an integration in which the black man first will have to prove himself in terms of the white man's values before meriting acceptance and assimilation.

Biko maintained that South Africa was different from the French former colonies where the chance of assimilation made it possible for blacks to aspire to "be white." In South Africa, on the other hand, whiteness has always been associated with political brutality and intimidation, early morning pass raids, and general harassment.[32] Biko concluded, therefore, that no black in South Africa really aspires to be white. Whereas Lutuli had admired Western culture, for Biko, in the South African context, it was evil. Equally important, it was not the *majority* culture. Biko explained:

If by integration you understand a breakthrough into white society by blacks, as assimilation and acceptance of blacks into an already established set of norms and code of behavior set up and maintained by whites, then YES I am against it. . . . I am against the fact that a settler minority should impose an entire system of values on an indigenous people. . . . For one cannot escape the fact that the culture shared by the majority group in any given society must ultimately determine the broad direction taken by . . . that society. . . . A country . . . in which the majority of the people are African must inevitably exhibit African values and be truly African in style.[33]

Thus, SASO's 1971 Policy Manifesto called for the necessity for blacks to develop their own value system. It stated: "The Black man must reject all value systems that seek to make him a foreigner in the country of his birth and reduce his basic human dignity. The Black man must build his own value systems, and see himself as self-defined and not defined by others."[34] A first step in self-definition was the refusal to refer to oneself as "nonwhite," opting for "black" instead. Biko wrote, "Merely by describing yourself as black you have started on a road towards emancipation, you have committed yourself to fight against all forces that seek to use your blackness as a stamp that marks you out as a subservient being."[35]

## BLACK CONSCIOUSNESS

SASO upheld the concept of black consciousness as the key to liberation. Biko explained, "[W]e cannot be conscious of ourselves and yet remain in bondage. We want to attain the envisioned self which is a free self."[36]   SASO wrote that black consciousness is an inward-looking process that seeks to reawaken blacks to their value as human beings and dignity as God's children.[37]   Its aim was to "pump back life into [the black man's] empty shell . . . infuse him with pride and dignity . . . remind him of his complicity in the crime of allowing himself to be misused and therefore letting evil reign supreme in the country of his birth."[38]

Like Sobukwe, Biko believed in the priority of psychological liberation. SASO's Policy Manifesto stated that the black man must be liberated *first* from psychological oppression springing from an  inferiority complex and, *second*, from physical oppression arising out of living in a white racist society.[39]   The emphasis on psychological liberation in the writings of the BCM sometimes overshadow the ultimate objective.   But it is clear that Biko believed that psychological liberation would create black solidarity and bargaining strength for the pursuance of its ultimate goal, which was, in short, a completely nonracial franchise: one-man-one-vote, with no reference to color.[40]

It is not clear how Biko envisaged getting from psychological to political liberation.   Clearly more concerned with the present than with the future, he wrote, "The future will always be shaped by the sequence of present-day events."[41]   Nevertheless, like Lutuli and Sobukwe before him, he had faith in ultimate success because, he asserted, "no lie can live forever."[42]   In addition, the successful revolutions in Angola and Mozambique were a source of encouragement, presenting the *possibility* of change in his lifetime.   However, unlike Sobukwe, he was prepared for a lengthy struggle: "We have set out on a quest for true humanity, and somewhere on the distant horizon we can see the glittering prize."[43]

Like his two predecessors, Biko believed, "Truth must triumph over evil."[44] He stated in court that "the white man . . . is going to eventually accept the inevitable."[45]   Davis notes that Biko provided his followers with a living hope in the future that could sustain them in the midst of oppression.  An eschatological vision enabled his people to live in the midst of their present oppression as though they were already liberated.  Biko "spoke as if the vanquished were already victorious.  He functioned prophetically, as if new Azania had already been born," Davis explains.[46]  If, as Moore argues, conquering the sense of inevitable subjugation is essential for political change, then Biko was responsible in reviving within the African people a sense of outrage against an intolerable situation that ought not be endured.[47]

Christianity for Lutuli, Sobukwe, and Biko provided the ethical critique of apartheid and with it the source of moral anger and hope that is vital to energize an oppressed people to take their salvation into their own hands.  For instance,

Biko wrote, "We have in us the will to live through these trying times; over the years we have attained moral superiority over the white man; we shall watch as time destroys his paper castles."[48]

Community development projects and leadership training seminars formed the bulk of SASO's work. SASO and the Black People's Convention (BPC), an adult organization Biko established in 1972, engaged in literacy campaigns, health projects, and community centers. Biko explained that they were undertaken in order to instill a sense of dignity and pride within the black man. Blacks benefited from seeing other blacks carrying out these projects. Previously, it had always been whites who offered charity; now it was blacks helping themselves. Biko wrote, "Our role was a simple one: to assist in the upliftment of the Black community and to help Black people . . . to diagnose their problems and to participate in the solutions of those problems."[49] He explained that self-help projects removed the defeatist attitude that good comes only from whites, and, thus, help in the building-up process. "This," he asserted, "is 'conscientization.'"[50] Community projects in addition to fostering self-reliance were to build a sense of oneness between leaders and masses without which any future resistance would be impossible.

## MAJORITY CULTURE

Like Sobukwe, Biko made no guarantees for minority rights: "We see a completely non-racial society. We don't believe, for instance, in the so-called guarantees for minority rights, because guaranteeing minority rights implies the recognition of portions of the community on a race basis. We believe that in our country there shall be no minority, there shall be no majority, just the people. And those people will have the same status before the law and . . . the same political rights."[51] *Individual* rights, however, would be respected in the observance of the United Nations Universal Declaration of Human Rights.

Biko, like Sobukwe, claimed that South Africa belonged to the Africans alone. Once it was independent, then whites could be accepted as equals, then whites would be invited to sit at the *Africans'* table: "We are aware that the white man is sitting at our table. We know he has no right to be there; we want to remove him . . . strip the table of all trappings put on by him, decorate it in true African style, settle down and then ask him to join us on our own terms if he wishes."[52]

He diagnosed the difference between black power in the United States and black consciousness in South Africa as the difference between a minority and majority philosophy. Black power, he explained, seeks participation by a minority in an already established society through pressure-group tactics. Black consciousness, on the other hand, aims at complete transformation of the system to make of it what the majority wishes.[53] South African blacks were no longer interested in becoming part of the system but in changing it, to make it more in keeping with traditional African values of communalism, compassion, and sharing. White society's elevation of individualism, greed, and materialism in which "the poor will grow poorer and the rich richer"[54] would be a thing of the past. The goal was a just, egalitarian society based on equal sharing of the country's wealth.

Although the ANC in its Freedom Charter had also linked political emancipation to economic transformation with an agenda that included some nationalization of industry and banks, rather than usher in a socialist state, the ANC sought the transfer of wealth to an African bourgeoisie class.[55] Lutuli had declared during the Treason Trial, "It is certainly not Congress policy to do away with private ownership of the means of production. The African business community has a full place in Congress and I personally regard African business enterprise as something to be encouraged."[56]

The PAC was more explicit than the ANC in its rejection of capitalism and imperialism. In Sobukwe's commencement speech at Fort Hare in 1949, he stated that the destruction of capitalism was central.[57] But, Hirson points out, Sobukwe never spoke in these terms again.[58] He was a cosignatory of the Youth League's proposed Program of Action whose economic demands were limited to the establishment of peoples cooperatives and incorporation of African trade unions into the ANC. The final Program of Action accepted by the ANC called merely for establishing commercial, industrial, transport, and other enterprises in both urban and rural areas and consolidating trade unions to improve the workers' standard of living.[59]

Fatton apparently believes that the Black Consciousness Movement advances beyond these conceptions. Certainly, Biko believed that South African blacks were *colonized* in terms of economic exploitation: "Their cheap labour has helped to make South Africa what it is today."[60] He saw economic greed as the reason for apartheid. Biko wrote, "The leaders of the white community had to create some kind of barrier between blacks and whites such that the whites could enjoy privilege at the expense of blacks and still feel free to give a moral explanation for the obvious exploitation that pricked even the hardest of white consciences."[61] And he was aware that substantial economic sacrifices, including freezing white salaries, would be required of whites in order for blacks to attain equity.[62]

But, Biko was far from seeing the struggle for independence in terms of class struggle. He explained, "There is for instance no workers in the classical sense among whites in South Africa, for even the most down-trodden white worker still has a lot to lose if the system is changed." The white worker is protected through job-reservation laws from competition with the majority, and because it is considered almost a sin to be black, poor whites demand the distinction between themselves and blacks. Hence, the most virulent antiblack feeling is found among the very poor whites whom Marxist class theory argues would align themselves with black workers in the struggle for emancipation.[63]

In short, if Biko rejected capitalism, he rejected communism as well as a "white ideology." He saw a third way, based on the African past, as the basis of the new society under African leadership. That third way was based on indigenous forms of communalism and was being articulated throughout the continent as *African Humanism, Negritude,* and *African Socialism.*[64] At its 1976 convention, the Black People's Convention adopted "black communalism" as its economic policy, which it defined as "an economic system which is based on the principle of sharing, lays emphasis on community ownership of land and its wealth and riches, and which strikes a healthy balance between what may legitimately be owned by individuals and what ought to be owned by the community as a whole."[65] Aspects of African culture, such as mutuality, cooperation, and neighborliness which had made poverty nonexistent in precolonial times, would be revived.[66]

Criticizing capitalism, Biko did not, however, make replacing it the central aspect of liberation. Like Lutuli, his attack on apartheid was based more on its assault on the dignity of man than on its economic exploitation of him. SASO held that liberation is primarily a "search for humanity and for existence as a God-created being."[67] Therefore, Biko was interested in the *nonmaterial* aspects of black liberation. Because of that, Fatton argues, he "failed to analyze in any systematic way the issues of class and economics."[68] That task, he writes, was left to later black consciousness-leaders who ascended after his banning and subsequent death.[69]

For Biko, the central problem was racism, not capitalism. The cause of our suffering is the color of our skin, he insisted.[70] Racial superiority, an ideology originally conceived for capitalism's demands for cheap labor, in time came to be believed, so that the race problem "has now become a genuine problem on its own."[71]


## THE CHURCH

Biko's preoccupation with the church stemmed from his study of its role in giving religious justification for apartheid. He could not fail to see how the Dutch Reformed Church's Calvinist theology had degenerated into ideology, rationalizing white privilege with the doctrine of the elect interpreted to mean God's special favor on the Afrikaners, and the story of the Tower of Babel employed to mean God's blessing on separate development. Even the multiracial churches, ostensibly progressive, were quietly sitting on the sidelines. Biko was especially contemptuous of these churches which he saw as hypocritical, issuing pious condemnations of apartheid yet taking no concrete actions either to stop the segregation within their own faith communities or to confront the state. Biko correctly saw the degree to which the white churches were themselves captive to the culture of apartheid rather than a true prophetic voice.[72] They publicly denounced apartheid as a sin and its theological justification a heresy, yet equivocated when it came to bold action.  As Villa-Vicencio puts it, these churches were "trapped within a theology of moderation and submission to the existing order."[73]

It was these moderate English-speaking churches which had traditionally urged reconciliation as a solution to the race problem.  African clergymen within the ANC, Biko believed, had been duped into accepting the importance of reconciliation, bridge building, and interracial cooperation, which the multiracial churches preached.  Under Biko's leadership, SASO lashed out at these churches in South Africa with their overemphasis on interracial fraternization as a solution to the problems of South Africa.  According to Biko, the real problem is land distribution, economic deprivation, and the disinheritance of the black people which no amount of Christian hand-holding between the races would change.[74]

Although criticizing the churches' self-serving use of the Gospel, Biko did not reject the role of Christianity in the struggle.  From a practical viewpoint, he knew that anyone trying to influence the black population politically who deemphasized religion would not succeed.[75]  Perhaps equally important, he believed passionately in God.  In a rare six-page document to his priest and friend, David Russell, in which he discussed his religious views at length, Biko wrote, "Does God exist?  I have never had problems with this question.  I am sufficiently convinced of the inadequacy of man and the rest of creation to believe that a greater force than mortals is responsible for creation, maintenance and continuation of life."[76]

He did, however, insist that the message of Christianity had to be made relevant.  In the following passage, Biko denounces the practice of Christianity in South Africa:

What is the white man's religion—Christianity?  It seems the people involved in importing Christianity to the black people steadfastly refuse to get rid of the rotten foundation which many of the missionaries created when they came.  To this date black people find no message for them in the Bible simply because our ministers are still too busy with moral trivialities.  They blow these up as the most important things that Jesus had to say to people.  They constantly urge the people to find fault in themselves and by so doing detract from the essence of the struggle in which the people are involved.  Deprived of spiritual content, the black people read the bible with a gullibility that is shocking.  While they sing in a chorus of "mea culpa" they are joined by white groups who sing a different version—"tua culpa."  The anachronism of a well-meaning God who allows people to suffer continually under an obviously immoral system is not lost to young blacks who continue to drop out of Church by the hundreds.[77]

However, he goes on to offer possibilities for change: "Too many people are involved in religion for the blacks to ignore.  Obviously the only path open for us now is to redefine the message in the bible and to make it relevant to the struggling masses. . . .  The bible must continually be shown to have something to say to the black man to keep him going in his long journey toward realisation of the self."[78]

Biko argued that Christianity elsewhere had been through various cultural adaptations from ancient Judea through Rome, through London, through Brussels and Lisbon, but "somehow when it landed in the Cape, it was made to look fairly rigid."[79]  He asserted that it was the task of black consciousness to unwrap the Western package from Christianity to let it speak to the black man's situation in Africa.

The first step was to incorporate insights from traditional African religion. It was important to put to death the notion that nothing good predated the advent of the white missionaries and colonizers. Rehabilitating traditional culture was seen as vital for African self-respect, since it was the disintegration of African traditions that had removed the anchor of African self-confidence.[80]  It was the goal of black consciousness, then, to rebuild self-confidence through a reassertion of pride in African culture and religion.[81]

Two aspects of traditional society were emphasized: a belief in God's immanence and the communalism of precolonial Africa.  In African religion, Mosala argues, God is not "simply a concept, or reality removed from the reality called the world.  He is more than the world but terrifyingly present in the human struggle for survival."[82]  God's deep involvement in the world is a truth that was emphasized in the BCM, and especially by the theologians in the movement, who came to stress God's concern in the here-and-now for the whole man—body, soul, and spirit—in his situation of oppression.  The this-worldly orientation of African religion was a necessary corrective to the other-worldly emphasis—the concern with personal piety and salvation—that was the focus, or so it seemed to Biko, of the white churches.

The second aspect of traditional religion incorporated in the movement was the corporate dimension.  In African religions, the whole community or group partakes of its ceremonies and festivals. According to the African kinship system, an individual cannot exist alone; he owes his existence to other people including past generations and his contemporaries.[83]  Traditional African society placed great store on individuals finding meaning through the community.  In precolonial Africa, children were brought up by the whole community and old people were cared for by all.[84]  The Xhosa proverb, "People are people through other people" highlights the concept that community welfare takes precedence over individual self-interest.[85]

Black consciousness sought to reawaken the corporate ideal, the oneness of the people, that had existed in African traditional life.  The individual's responsibility toward the whole community was stressed as it was argued that one's highest loyalty had to be to the black community.  Black consciousness sought to reawaken this past spirit of sharing, self-help, oneness of community, and unity of humanity and God that was at the heart of traditional society.  A sense of solidarity, it was believed, would create a united front of all blacks—rich and poor, educated and uneducated—which would be necessary in the political struggles ahead.[86]

Despite the interest in traditional religion within the Black Consciousness Movement, there was no wholesale rejection of Christianity, but, rather an attempt to incorporate insights from African traditional religion into a new awareness of Christian responsibility for community well-being.[87]

To be sure, there was an outright rejection of orthodox Christianity's inward orientation and concern with the *soul* to the exclusion of the outward life under conditions of oppression:

In a country teeming with injustice and fanatically committed to the practice of oppression, intolerance and blatant cruelty because of racial bigotry; in a country where all black people are made to feel the unwanted stepchildren of God whose presence they cannot feel; in a country where father and son, mother and daughter alike develop daily into neurotics through sheer inability to relate the present to the future because of a completely engulfing sense of destitution, the Church further adds to their insecurity by its inward-directed definition of the concept of sin and its encouragement of the "mea culpa" attitude.[88]

For Biko, the Church all too often stressed petty sins to the virtual exclusion of condemning the greater institutional sin inherent in the apartheid state. For instance, black ministers on Sunday preach against robbing, stabbing, murdering, and adultery without ever attempting to relate these vices to the poverty, unemployment, overcrowding, lack of schooling, and migratory labor brought about through apartheid.[89] Related to the Church's often irrelevant theology is its unwieldy bureaucracy which removes the Church from important priorities in order to concentrate on secondary issues like structures and finance, making the Church an "ivory tower."[90] Another feature which made the Church irrelevant to blacks is white control of that bureaucracy. While the membership of most non-Afrikaner churches is 90 percent black, 90 percent of the controlling power is in white hands. By accepting this situation, black Christians are allowing a minority which is not interested in making Christianity relevant to blacks remain in control of the workings of the churches.[91]

## BLACK THEOLOGY

Despite his criticism of the Church, Biko never rejected the validity of Christianity, for he recognized that "essentially the Black community is a very religious community."[92] Rather, he proposed that black theology be used to analyze the South African situation. He wrote, "Christianity can never hope to remain abstract and removed from the people's environmental problems. To be applicable to people, it must have meaning for them in their given situation. If they are oppressed people, it must have something to say about their oppression."[93]

He applauds black theology for relating the Christian faith to the black man's suffering. It shifts the emphasis from petty sins—stealing food when hungry, working without a pass, lying to the police—to the major sin—allowing an evil system to exist. Black Theology teaches the people not to suffer peacefully, but to fight against the greatest sin, which is allowing oneself to be oppressed.[94]

The role of the black theologian is to redirect the black man's understanding of God. Religion is significant for the black struggle against apartheid because for Biko "no nation can win a battle without faith." But it must be a proper faith for "if our faith in our God is spoilt by our having to see Him through the eyes of the same people we're fighting against then there obviously begins to be something wrong in that relationship."[95]

Biko's evident interest in black theology was sparked by his contact with it during his student days in the University Christian Movement. Basil Moore, a Methodist minister, was instrumental in bringing the works of black theologians in the United States to the attention of South African students. Biko was exposed to other radical theologies as well: political theology from Europe (Moltmann and Metz) and liberation theology from Latin America (Camara and Gutierrez) through his association with the Christian Institute, where studies of these writings were taking place under the direction of Catholic lay sister Anne Hope. However, it was the writings of James Cone and other African-Americans[96] on black theology that had the greatest impact on Biko and the Black Consciousness Movement. One African theologian, commenting on the contribution of Cone, said, "We feel . . . what Cone says in our bones."[97]

South African blacks were receptive to the ideas of Cone, such as God's identification with the oppressed, but the more militant aspects of American black theology were somewhat moderated in South Africa. Cone had written, "There is no use for a God who loves whites the same as blacks. . . . Black theology will accept only a love of God which participates in the destruction of the white enemy."[98]

SASO, on the other hand, argued, "There is a mile of difference between preaching Black Consciousness and preaching hatred of whites. Telling people to hate whites is an outward and reactionary type of preaching which, though understandable, is undesirable and self-destructive. It makes one think in negative terms and preoccupies one with peripheral issues." In fact, SASO saw hatred of whites as the expression of an inferiority complex "where the sufferer has lost hope of 'making it' because of conditions imposed upon him. His actual aspirations are to be like the white man and the hatred arises out of frustration." For SASO, black consciousness "takes cognisance of one's dignity and leads to positive action. . . . In the end you are a much more worthy victor because you do not seek to revenge but to implement the truth for which you have stood all along during your struggle. You were no less angry than the man who hated whites but your anger was channeled to positive action."[99]

However, within the Black Consciousness Movement one can find examples of a virulent militancy reminiscent of Cone. Biko's close colleague, Aubrey Mokoape, urged at a BPC meeting, "Brothers and sisters, I think these words have been spoken by no less authority [than the] Reverend Bartman, who felt that the White man has become subhuman, that the White man is in the way, has become a devil, that the White man has become a beast and that he can only be helped by one thing, by quite quickly removing him."[100]  Biko himself had written, "Clearly black people cannot respect white people, at least not in this country.  There is such an obvious aura of immorality and naked cruelty in all that is done in the name of white people that no black man, no matter how intimidated, can ever be made to respect white society."  Biko also wrote that underneath the black fear of whites is "a naked hatred."[101]  In fact, stated Biko, "Blacks see whiteness as a concept that warrants being despised, hated, destroyed and replaced by an aspiration with more human content in it. . . . The secret determination in the innermost minds of most Blacks . . . [is] to kick whites off those comfortable garden chairs . . . and to claim them for themselves."[102]

## LINKS TO RELIGIOUS ORGANIZATIONS

If Lutuli was viewed as a messiah to some multiracial groups, then surely Biko was that to all-black audiences.  He was for them, writes Davis, "an authentic disciple of Jesus."  But, Davis continues, this special brand of discipleship was outside the institutional Church for Biko did not find a close association with the Church helpful to his cause.  Davis states that Biko never left the Church, if the Church is defined as the community of the redeemed and faithful; the Church, by accommodating itself to the state, left him.[103]  Walshe suggests that like many of his generation, he questioned the brand of Christianity that was captive to culture rather than serving its true prophetic function.[104]  Davis argues that it was necessary for Biko to stand apart from the Church in order to prevent himself from becoming completely agnostic, so contemptuous was he of the Church's capitulation to the state.[105]  To his parish priest he admitted as much: "Christ is so conservatively interpreted at times that I find him foreign to me.  On the other hand if I accept him and ascribe to him the characteristics that flow logically from any contemplation about him and his work, then I must reject the Church almost completely."[106]  But, there was never any doubt in his priest's mind that Biko's philosophy was "at rock-bottom a fundamentally Biblical one."[107]

Although not involved personally in organized churches, Biko sought converts to his cause there.  Gerhart believes that the Black Consciousness Movement can be seen as representing a significant shift in opinion, initiating a period of reorientation among many black Christians.[108]  Of course, this reorientation had actually begun with the PAC's efforts at self-reliance, and in a very real sense, black consciousness is but a refinement of the PAC's Africanism.  But it is true that the BCM experienced greater legitimacy among black churchmen within the English-speaking churches than had the PAC.  For while the PAC had identified with the African Independent Churches (AICs), it never developed an alternative theology that could "challenge the hegemony of bourgeois Christian ideology," as Fatton puts it.[109] An "eccentric messianism" that expressed itself in "Africans' immunity to the white man's bullets" was not generally appealing to the educated black churchmen outside the African Independent Churches.[110] Yet both the educated black churchmen in the multiracial churches and their less well educated brethren in the AICs were receptive to Biko's critique of religion in South Africa.

Given the BCM's emphasis on religion, it is not surprising that links grew between SASO and the Black People's Convention, with the Interdenominational African Ministers Association (IDAMASA), and the African Independent Churches Association (AICA). A member of the latter organization, Victor Magatula, minister of the Bantu Bethlehem Christian Apostolic Church of Africa, saw a natural affinity between black theology and the African Independent Churches, since liberation was the key concern of both. In the Ethiopian churches, he says, the emphasis is on physical liberation; in the Zionist churches it is on psychological liberation.[111] Comaroff's assertion that the Zionist churches were not apolitical makes sense in the context of black theology's concern with psychological liberation from inferiority complex, slave mentality, and self-hate as a preliminary stage towards political freedom.[112] Both black theology proponents and Zionists recognized the importance of liberation not from material and political bondage alone; liberation of the mind and spirit is paramount. Biko had written, "If one is free at heart, no human-made chains can bind one to servitude."[113] Perhaps in the absence of imminent political liberation both groups had to be content with spiritual awakening.

But it was not just to the independent churches that Biko turned. Under the auspices of the Black Community Programs (BCP), launched by the Christian Institute as a black initiative with an all-black staff which included Biko, workshops for ministers of the multiracial churches were held on black theology. In 1972, Biko presented a paper at a Black Ministers of Religion Conference. Stubbs notes that Biko realized the importance of trying to "conscientize" this key section of the black community. Biko was correct in seeing that these black churchmen, paid less than their white counterparts and denied leadership opportunities, were vulnerable to politicization.[114]

Biko explained to these men that to change the church, "we have first to gain ascendance over [it] . . . and then turn [it] into one we cherish, we love, we understand, and one that is relevant to us."[115] He urged black ministers to learn the method of caucusing to put black people in control of the churches. Since 90 percent of the English-speaking church membership is black, Biko felt that by numerical strength it would be possible for their religious doctrine, black theology, to become the predominant theology in South Africa.

He urged, "It is the duty therefore of all black priests and ministers of religion to take upon themselves the duty of saving Christianity by adopting Black Theology's approach and thereby uniting once more the black man to his God."[116] In fact, under the influence of the BCM, IDAMASA, the largest and possibly oldest African church movement, had decided in 1971 to exclude white ministers from their executive committee.[117] By 1972, writes Herbstein, IDAMASA was "won over to black consciousness."[118]

SASO also found the South African Council of Churches (SACC) sympathetic to its aims. Twenty-seven churches and church organizations, including the Christian Institute, IDAMASA, and UCM, were members of the council in 1968. However, Hirson notes, the relationship between SACC and SASO was equivocal. In many respects SASO was attracted to the council, and especially the more radical Christian Institute, but at the same time it sought to be an African organization acting independently of any white body.[119] Nevertheless, Biko chose to take part in SPROCAS, the Study Project on Apartheid Society, established by the SACC in 1969, to seek alternatives to apartheid, and he served on the Christian Institute's Black Community Programs as a staff member and as editor of its publication *Black Review*, an annual survey, and *Black Viewpoint*, a quarterly journal of articles and speeches by BCM leaders. Despite Biko's links with the Christian Institute, which was undoubtedly on the cutting edge of Christian protest, that multiracial organization was nevertheless excluded from the inaugural meeting to launch the BPC in 1971.

The BCM organizations also relied on church bodies abroad to finance their projects. Thus, Hirson believes, to speak of "using black resources" or of exclusive "black identification" did not present a true account of how the organization functioned in practice.[120]

Predictably, seminary students were among the earliest proponents of black consciousness. The Federal Theological Seminary (FEDSEM) at Alice, adjacent to Fort Hare University, and founded by the Anglicans, Congregationalists, Methodists, and Presbyterians for theological training of black ministers, quickly became the center for SASO and black theology.[121] Also, the Lutheran Seminary in Mapumulo, and the Catholic Seminary in Hammanskraal were places where black theology was debated and sometimes taught. Regehr notes that black theology students were in the vanguard of the opposition to apartheid with all-black schools becoming the center of a growing Black Consciousness Movement.[122]

It was perhaps to be expected that the exclusivist nationalist position buttressed by an exclusivist black theology would come mainly from the generation educated not in the multiracial mission schools but in the ethnically segregated schools. Adams, where Lutuli had taught, was closed, and by the time Biko attended Lovedale, it had been under the control of the Bantu Education Department for ten years and was a quite different institution from the one Lutuli had attended. Students had little meaningful contact with whites, so they tended to be suspicious of all whites. The limited contact with whites no doubt had a part in shaping an exclusivist nationalism.[123] Prior writes that the aging 1960 generation of leaders schooled in the Christian liberal aspirations of becoming participants in running the South African state was being replaced with the 1976 generation socialized only in apartheid society and for whom participation was a morally unacceptable compromise.[124]

## VIOLENCE

There is no doubt a relationship between an exclusive nationalism and the advocacy of violence.  Lutuli had felt fortunate to know whites and to work alongside them in multiracial organizations, and he believed that these experiences had prevented hatred that would later explode in violence.  Biko's view on the merits of violence, however, was different.  Biko wrote, "Black theology seeks to depict Jesus as a fighting God who saw the exchange of Roman money—the oppressor's coinage—in His father's temple as so sacrilegious [sic] that it merited a violent reaction from Him—the Son of Man."[125]  Although Biko believed that God acted in history, He did so mainly through His agents on earth.  Biko reminded a group of black ministers, "God is not in the habit of coming down from heaven to solve people's problems on earth."[126]  Rather, He challenges his followers to identify with Christ, a fighting, not a passive, God who allows a lie to rest unchallenged.  Biko's acceptance of violence as a means of struggle corresponds with his belief in a transcendent God who though identifying with man's suffering empowers man to fight his own battles.

As a defense witness for the SASO-9[127] in 1976, however, Biko testified that he was not interested in armed struggle and distanced himself from those policies of the exiled ANC and PAC: "We believe that there is a way of getting across to where we want to go through peaceful means.  And the very fact that we decided to actually form an above-board Movement implies that we accepted certain legal limitations to our operations."[128]  However, SASO could hardly openly advocate violent revolution and expect to remain a legal operation in South Africa.  The fact that there was no specific rejection of violence in the documents of SASO and BPC probably means that they wanted to keep that option open.  In addresses to black audiences, Biko, like Sobukwe, emphasized the importance of revering African heroes who had fought valiantly against white conquest.[129]  His identification with both Cone and Fanon, forceful advocates of using any means to root out oppression, tends to support the view that Biko was in favor of some sort of armed struggle.

Other black-consciousness leaders, including Aubrey Mokoape, urged, "[W]e have only . . . one road, and that road is total unadulterated revolution."[130]  And South African Students' Movement (SASM), a black-consciousness oriented youth organization, developed secret cells where the question of armed struggle was debated.[131]  Jennings confirms that Biko, too, clearly saw the inevitability of violence.[132]

Biko was aware, of course, of the possible negative consequences of violence: "When there is violence, there is messiness.  Violence brings too many residues of hate into the reconstruction period. Apart from its obvious horrors, it creates too many postrevolutionary problems. *If at all possible*, we want the revolution to be peaceful and reconciliatory" (emphasis added).[133]  Biko implied that the decision to engage in violence would be determined by the government's actions.

According to Lindy Wilson, Biko's position was to *explore* the nonviolent route but that there was also the view among black-consciousness leaders "that the present Nationalist government can only be unseated by people operating a military wing."[134]  In informal sessions, the need for armed struggle was recognized, and case studies from Vietnam, Cuba, and Algeria were examined as well as contemporary struggles of the African Party for the Independence of Guinea and Cape Verde (PAIGC) and the Front for the Liberation of Mozambique (FRELIMO).[135]

Biko's position is ambiguous, but it has been suggested that his disavowal of violence was based on tactical, rather than ideological, considerations given the strength of the South African security and police forces. Gerhart concludes, "The only accurate label for Biko is revolutionary." She insists that his public rejection of violence was based on a "fine-tuned sense of what factors would best promote his cause under the conditions prevailing in South Africa."[136]  In Fatton's estimation, proponents of black theology came to envisage violence "as a regrettable and inevitable if not morally justifiable agent of revolution, given the intransigence of South Africa's white power structure."[137]  Certainly, the youth of Soweto later demonstrated that "Black Consciousness can and most probably will lead to violent confrontation."[138]

## SOWETO UPRISING

There is debate about the actual causes of the Soweto Uprising, but it is clear that the catalyst was the decision by the government in 1976 to make Afrikaans the language of instruction for social studies and mathematics in secondary schools. Students viewed the requirement not only as an attempt to force the language of the oppressor on the oppressed but also the means to cut them off from English proficiency which was the key to the better-paid jobs. The new law was but another step in the government's ongoing campaign to provide blacks an inferior education.

As early as 1953, the government had passed the Bantu Education Act, which took control of schools away from the churches and mandated that black children attend blacks-only schools under government control.[139]  Lutuli had said this about the Act:

The door has to be slammed shut hard in the faces of the younger generation, and a system devised which will recondition us to accept perpetual inferiority and perpetual isolation from Western learning and culture. To isolate us and to convince us of our permanent inferiority—these two motives lie behind much legislation from the Act of Union until now, and the Bantu Education Act is a major means to this end. . . . It is a tool in the hands of the White Master for the more effective reduction and control of the Black Servants.[140]

On June 16, 1976, students in reaction to the enforced use of Afrikaans staged a mass protest, refusing to attend classes. The boycott centered not just on the language issue but on a whole host of grievances with Bantu education: poor instruction, overcrowded schools,[141] inadequate funding for African education, and limited employment opportunities after graduation. The grievances extended even beyond complaints with education. Hirson writes, "The widespread opposition to the new regulation, which brought together conservatives and radicals, teachers and taught, indicated that the many strands of opposition—based on very different premises—were uniting against something more than on instruction over language."[142] The united stand against Afrikaans was the manifestation of deep resentment inside the townships against the entire apartheid system.

Neither SASO nor any other BCM organization was *directly* responsible for planning the boycott of schools. Like the PAC before it, the BCM took non-collaboration seriously. It planned no acts of resistance, led no defiance campaigns, offered no resolutions, sent no deputations, requested no negotiations. Motlhabi notes that on *no* occasion did the BCM attempt to make any direct demands or protest to the government regarding the black condition.[143] Biko believed that confrontation of the regime was self-destructive and that side issues become main issues.[144] Consequently, any condemnation of the regime was made in addresses to the black community, since the primary concern was with the building-up process for future action.

But, SASM, the counterpart in the high schools to SASO, helped organize the protest *after* the spontaneous uprising of the students. SASM had not originated from SASO but independently from high-school students in the Transvaal townships. Youth clubs in three Soweto high schools—Diepkloof, Orlando, and Orlando West—had formed the African Students' Movement in 1971, changing its name to South African Students' Movement the following year to indicate its national character.[145] Although autonomous from SASO, it did have direct links with SASO and BPC. By the time of the Soweto Uprising, SASM was a countrywide organization with branches in Cape Town, the Transvaal, the Eastern Cape, and Durban.

On June 13, the Naledi branch of SASM called a meeting at a church hall, where an action committee of SASM,[146] composed of two delegates from each Soweto school, was placed in charge. The 300–400 students present decided to launch the protest that became known worldwide as the Soweto Uprising. Some 20,000 children from seven Soweto schools took to the streets on June 16, and mass protest was reborn.[147] The plan was to march to Johannesburg in peaceful demonstration. Protesters carried placards: "To Hell With Afrikaans," "We Are Not Boers," and "If We Must do Afrikaans, Vorster Must do Zulu."[148] At

Orlando West, students were confronted by 300 policemen who attempted to confiscate the placards. Students began to taunt the police, who, giving no notice to disperse nor clear warning shots, opened fire into the crowd of advancing students, killing one child at Orlando West High School.

Demonstrations and police retaliation spread from Soweto to other townships on the Witwatersrand and then to black urban ghettos in Cape Town, Port Elizabeth, and East London. In Cape Town, Coloured students from both the University of the Western Cape and the secondary schools joined their African peers in demonstrations. More than 600 communities were involved and approximately 800 blacks were killed, including many children. Fierce rioting broke out as blacks, as well as some Indians and Coloureds, struck out at symbols of apartheid—government offices, beer halls, post offices, and administration-run buses—and burned collaborators' homes.[149] In August 60 percent of the labor force stayed home from work for two days in an impressive show of solidarity the likes of which had not been seen since the Defiance Campaign of 1952.[150]

Following Soweto, thousands of Africans were arrested, and hundreds of Africans were detained without trial. Four thousand young South Africans fled the country that year alone to join the ANC in exile. That decision was based less on ideological identification with the expatriate movement than on a need for an organizational base, material resources, and international connections necessary for the transition to armed violence.[151] (By this time the ANC had altered its strict nonviolent policy.)

The aftermath of the Soweto Uprising found Biko in solitary confinement for 101 days from August to October. Temporarily detained in July 1977, he was taken into custody again on August 18 and held in solitary confinement in Port Elizabeth. Biko died in detention twenty-six days later from head injuries.[152] Once when asked for proof that black consciousness was a force to be reckoned with, Biko had responded, "In one word: Soweto!"[153] The causal relationship was perhaps not that clearcut,[154] but it is widely believed that the philosophy of the Black Consciousness Movement instilled in the Soweto youth a pride and self-confidence to dare to defy the government's new educational policies. Nengwekhula does not exaggerate when he states that the uprising started in Soweto because of the diffusion of black consciousness there: "The kind of leadership . . . there [was] more radical than the leadership throughout the whole country. . . . The uprising started in Soweto, not because these people were more oppressed there but because SASM was centered there."[155] Stubbs suggests that Biko's courage in the face of hostile cross-examination at the SASO-9 trial also may have inspired the boys and girls of Soweto to face death bravely just six weeks later.[156]

The legacy of black consciousness lies not in providing any new ideological content; in many respects Biko's ideas are but a refinement of Sobukwe's. Indeed, Sobukwe was seen as one of the progenitors, one of the key thinkers, in the unfolding of black consciousness: "He was consulted. His opinion was solicited and in effect his encouragement and blessings were received."[157] Pogrund, Sobukwe's friend and biographer, revealed that when Sobukwe travelled from Kimberley to Umtata, where his mother died, and on to Graaff-Reinet for her burial, he and Biko met in King Williams Town without police knowledge. Despite the distance they managed to stay in touch, and on at least half a dozen occasions messages were exchanged between them.[158] It is known that other black-consciousness leaders as well visited Sobukwe in Kimberley for advice and direction.[159]

The contribution of the Black Consciousness Movement, then, is in its *regalvanizing* the black militancy of an earlier era following a decade-long lull in resistance politics following the bannings of the ANC and PAC. According to Pityana, it reinfused blacks "with a spiritual fibre, a mettle and a fighting spirit."[160] De Gruchy maintains, "Soweto could not have happened if the message of black dignity and protest, a message which had its greatest impact upon young black students, had not been preached and heard during the years before it took place."[161]

In the aftermath of Soweto, the black community found few friends among the whites, except for a handful of liberals and a group of committed Christians who had established ties with BCM organizations.[162] The Christian Institute in response to Soweto published *Is South Africa a Police State?*, an account of political trials, detentions, and bannings, and in the next year, *Torture in South Africa?* In March 1977, the BPC, calling for a week of mourning for those killed at Sharpeville and Soweto, had a message for the Church:

We call upon all the churches in this country to respond positively and cooperate with the spirit expressed in this message. We believe that the true Christian gospel supports the struggle for human dignity. We say the true Christian must ask himself, "What shall I tell the Lord on the day of reckoning? Shall I say I have not been able to put my hand in the effort to endorse God's image in the black man, as much as in the white man?"[163]

Also that year, SASM made its first appeal to churches, urging them to promote the black struggle.[164] This attitude on religion, deeply entrenched in the attitude of SASO and BPC, was new to SASM and probably arose out of the students' positive experiences during the uprising with pastors who counseled the protesters and offered them refuge. For while it is true that during Soweto some churches remained aloof, many increased their support to black resisters against apartheid.[165]

In October, 1977, SASO and SASM, along with seventeen other mainly black-consciousness organizations, were banned, but the black-consciousness message continued to be heard. As Bishop Tutu noted at Biko's funeral, "Steve has started something that is quite unstoppable."[166] By necessity, following the mass bannings of the late 1970s, political leadership during the next decade increasingly was provided by religious leaders. Black theologians have been in the forefront of the struggle, using biblical symbols and terminology in an effort to *conscientize* blacks and motivate them to defy apartheid. One of the most significant figures to emerge in the 1980s has been the Anglican archbishop Desmond Tutu. His leadership in the United Democratic Front's protest against the Tricameral Parliament is the subject of the next chapter.


## NOTES

1. Biko was expelled from Lovedale because of his brother's political activities in Poqo.

2. Biko was studying for a law degree by correspondence through the University of South Africa before he was banned.

3. Gail Gerhart, *Black Power in South Africa: The Evolution of an Ideology* (Berkeley: University of California Press, 1978), p. 260.

4. Mokgethi Motlhabi, *The Theory and Practice of Black Resistance to Apartheid* (Johannesburg: Ravan, 1984), p. 109.

5. UCM was formed by Basil Moore, a white minister, in 1966, the year of the birth of black theology in the United States.

6. NUSAS had been banned on black campuses in 1967. UCM was banned on black campuses in 1969 and later dissolved itself in 1972 with the statement: "We no longer believe in multiracialism as a strategy to bring about change." See David Thomas, *Councils in the Ecumenical Movement in South Africa* (Johannesburg: SACC, 1979), p. 67.

7. Millard Arnold, ed., *Steve Biko: Black Consciousness in South Africa* (New York: Random House, 1978), pp. 8–9.

8. B. A. Khoapa, *Black Review* (1972), pp. 41–42, cited in Ernie Regehr, *Perceptions of Apartheid: The Churches and Political Change in South Africa* (Scottsdale, Ariz.: Herald Press, 1979), p. 200.

9. SASO, "Black Students' Manifesto" in Hendrik van der Merwe, ed., *African Perspectives on South Africa: A Collection of Speeches, Articles and Documents* (Stanford: Hoover Institution Press, 1978), p. 97.

10. Steve Biko, "Black Consciousness and the Quest for a True Humanity," in Basil Moore, *Black Theology: The South African Voice* (London: C. Hurst & Co., 1973), p. 40.

11. Biko, "Black Consciousness and the Quest for a True Humanity," in Basil Moore, p. 40.

12. Biko, "White Racism and Black Consciousness" in Hendrik van der Merwe and David Welsh, eds., *Student Perspectives on South Africa* (Cape Town: David Philip, 1972), p. 195.

13. Biko, "White Racism and Black Consciousness," in van der Merwe and Welsh, p. 192.

14. Biko, "White Racism and Black Consciousness," in van der Merwe and Welsh, p. 194.

15. Biko, "White Racism and Black Consciousness," in van der Merwe and Welsh, p. 195.

16. Biko, "Black Consciousness and the Quest for a True Humanity," in Basil Moore,

p. 40.

17. Biko, "Black Consciousness and the Quest for a True Humanity," in Basil Moore, p. 38.

18. SASO, "Policy Manifesto," in van der Merwe, p. 100.

19. Biko, "Black Consciousness and the Quest for a True Humanity," in Basil Moore, p. 47.

20. Bennie Khoapa, "Black Consciousness," *South African Outlook* (June–July 1972), p. 101, cited in Heribert Adam, "The Rise of Black Consciousness in South Africa," *Race* 15, no. 2 (1973), p. 159.

21. Biko, "The Definition of Black Consciousness," in Steve Biko, *I Write What I Like*, ed. Aelred Stubbs (San Francisco: Harper & Row, 1978), p. 48.

22. Arnold, p. 145.

23. Biko, "Let's Talk About Bantustans," in Biko, *I Write What I Like*, pp. 80–86.

24. Biko, "Let's Talk About Bantustans," in Biko, *I Write What I Like*, p. 84.

25. *SASO Newsletter* 6, no. 1 (March–April 1976), p. 2, cited in Robert Fatton, *Black Consciousness in South Africa* (Albany: State University of New York Press, 1986), p. 93.

26. Biko, "The Definition of Black Consciousness," in Biko, *I Write What I Like*, p. 49.

27. Biko, "The Definition of Black Consciousness," in Biko, *I Write What I Like*, p. 51.

28. Biko, "Black Souls in White Skins?" in Biko, *I Write What I Like*, p. 25.

29. Biko, "Black Consciousness and the Quest for a True Humanity," in Basil Moore, p. 39.

30. Biko, "Black Souls in White Skins?" in Biko, *I Write What I Like*, p. 26.

31. Biko, "Black Consciousness and the Quest for a True Humanity," in Basil Moore, p. 40.

32. Arnold, p. 289.

33. Biko, "Black Souls in White Skins?" in Biko, *I Write What I Like*, p. 24.

34. SASO, "Policy Manifesto," in van der Merwe, pp. 99–100.

35. Biko, "The Definition of Black Consciousness," in Biko, *I Write What I Like*, p. 48.

36. Biko, "The Definition of Black Consciousness," in Biko, *I Write What I Like*, p. 49.

37. SASO, "Understanding SASO," in van der Merwe, p. 103. See also Donald Woods, *Biko* (New York: Paddington Press, 1978), p. 34.

38. Biko, "We Blacks," in Biko, *I Write What I Like*, p. 29.

39. SASO, "Policy Manifesto," in van der Merwe, p. 99.

40. Biko, "The Righteousness of Our Strength," in Biko, *I Write What I Like*, p. 123.

41. Biko, "The Definition of Black Consciousness," in Biko, *I Write What I Like*, p. 52.

42. Biko, "American Policy towards Azania," in Biko, *I Write What I Like*, p. 139.

43. Biko, "Black Consciousness and the Quest for a True Humanity," in Basil Moore, p. 47.

44. Biko, "Black Consciousness and the Quest for a True Humanity," in Basil Moore,

p. 47.

45. Biko, "The Righteousness of Our Strength," in Biko, *I Write What I Like*, p. 136.

46. Kortright Davis, "Racism and God: Steve Biko in Context," *AME Zion Quarterly Review* 97, no. 4 (January 1986), p. 21.

47. Barrington Moore, *Injustice: The Social Basis of Obedience and Revolt* (New York: M. E. Sharpe, 1978), pp. 458–459.

48. Biko, "White Racism and Black Consciousness," in van der Merwe and Welsh, p. 72.

49. Arnold, p. 116.

50. Arnold, p. 120.

51. Biko, "Our Strategy for Liberation," in Biko, *I Write What I Like*, p. 149.

52. Biko, "White Racism and Black Consciousness," in van der Merwe and Welsh, p. 69.

53. Arnold, p. 296.

54. Biko, "Black Consciousness and the Quest for a True Humanity," in Basil Moore, p. 40.

55. Fatton, p. 127.

56. Albert Lutuli, "Statement Taken from Chief Albert Lutuli," Treason Trial lawyer's brief (Carter-Karis Collection), cited in Gerhart, pp. 118–119.

57. Robert Sobukwe, "Address on Behalf of the Graduating Class at Fort Hare College, delivered at the Completers' Social," October 21, 1949, in Thomas Karis and Gwendolen Carter, *From Protest to Challenge: A Documentary History of African Politics in South Africa, 1882-1964*, vol. 2 (Stanford: Hoover Institution Press, 1972-1977), p. 334 (Document 58).

58. Baruch Hirson, *Year of Fire, Year of Ash* (London: Zed Press, 1979), p. 320.

59. "Programme of Action," Statement of Policy adopted at the ANC Annual Conference, December 17, 1949, in Karis and Carter, vol. 2, p. 338 (Document 60).

60. Biko, "Black Consciousness and the Quest for a True Humanity," in Basil Moore, p. 46.

61. Biko, "Black Consciousness and the Quest for a True Humanity," in Basil Moore, p. 36.

62. Motlhabi, *Theory and Practice*, p. 120. See also Peter Walshe, *Church versus State in South Africa: The Case of the Christian Institute* (Maryknoll, N.Y.: Orbis, 1983), p. 220.

63. Biko, "The Definition of Black Consciousness," in Biko, *I Write What I Like*, p. 50.

64. Biko's *third way* was inspired by Kaunda's *African Humanism*, Senghor's *Negritude*, and Nyerere's *African Socialism*.

65. Fatton, p. 103.

66. Biko, "Some African Cultural Concepts," in Biko, *I Write What I Like*, pp. 42–43. See also SASO, "Understanding SASO," in van der Merwe, pp. 102–103.

67. Nyamelo Pityana, "What is Black Consciousness?" in Basil Moore, p. 63.

68. Fatton, p. 126.

69. For a discussion of AZAPO's economic policies, see Fatton, pp. 130–131.

70. Biko, "Black Consciousness and the Quest for a True Humanity," in Basil Moore,

p. 41.

71. Biko, "Black Consciousness and the Quest for a True Humanity," in Basil Moore, p. 37.

72. For a detailed look at the churches' pronouncements versus actions, see Marjorie Hope and James Young, *The South African Churches in a Revolutionary Situation* (Maryknoll, N.Y.: Orbis, 1981); and Charles Villa-Vicencio, *Trapped in Apartheid* (Maryknoll, N.Y.: Orbis, 1988).

73. Villa-Vicencio, p. 115.

74. SASO, "Resolution on Black Theology," in van der Merwe, p. 309.

75. Lindy Wilson, "Bantu Stephen Biko: A Life" in N. Barney Pityana, Mamphela Ramphele, Malusi Mpumlwana, and Lindy Wilson, *Bounds of Possibility: The Legacy of Steve Biko and Black Consciousness* (Cape Town: David Philip, 1991), p. 44.

76. Cited in Lindy Wilson, "Bantu Stephen Biko: A Life," in Pityana, p. 43.

77. Biko, "We Blacks," in Biko, *I Write What I Like*, p. 31.

78. Biko, "We Blacks," in Biko, *I Write What I Like*, p. 31.

79. Biko, "The Church as seen by a Young Layman," in Biko, *I Write What I Like*, p. 56.

80. Desmond Tutu, "Whither African Theology?" in Edward Fashole-Luke, ed., *Christianity in Independent Africa* (London: Rex Collings, 1978), p. 366.

81. Biko, "The Church as seen by a Young Layman," in Biko, *I Write What I Like*, p. 59.

82. Jerry Mosala, "African Traditional Beliefs and Christianity," *Journal of Theology for Southern Africa* 43 (1983), p. 22.

83. Bonganjalo Goba, "Corporate Personality in Israel and Africa," in Basil Moore, pp. 65–73.

84. Allister Sparks, *The Mind of South Africa* (New York: Ballantine Books, 1990), p. 15.

85. Sparks, p. 14.

86. Goba, "Corporate Personality in Israel and Africa," in Basil Moore, p. 71.

87. See also Desmond Tutu, "Black Theology/African Theology—Soul Mates or Antagonists?" in Gayraud Wilmore and James Cone, eds., *Black Theology: A Documentary History 1966-1979* (Maryknoll, N.Y.: Orbis, 1979); and Kofi Appiah-Kubi and Sergio Torres, eds. *African Theology En Route* (Maryknoll, N.Y.: Orbis, 1979).

88. Biko, "The Church as seen by a Young Layman," in Biko, *I Write What I Like*, p. 56.

89. Biko, "The Church as seen by a Young  Layman," in Biko, *I Write What I Like*, p. 57.

90. Biko, "The Church as seen by a Young Layman," in Biko, *I Write What I Like*, p. 58.

91. Biko, "The Church as seen by a Young Layman," in Biko, *I Write What I Like*, p. 58.

92. Arnold, p. 118.

93. Biko, "The Church as seen by a Young Layman," in Biko, *I Write What I Like*, p. 59.

94. Biko, "We Blacks," in Biko, *I Write What I Like*, p. 31.

95. Biko, "The Church as seen by a Young Layman," in Biko, *I Write What I Like*, p. 60.

96. Besides Cone, Biko was especially influenced by Americans Cleaver, Carmichael, and Malcolm X.

97. Mokgethi Motlhabi in Gayraud Wilmore and James Cone, *Black Theology: A Documentary History 1966-1979*, p. 223.

98. James Cone, *A Black Theology of Liberation* (Philadelphia: Lippincott, 1970), p. 136.

99. SASO, "Understanding SASO," in van der Merwe, p. 103.

100. Arnold, p. 277.

101. Biko, "Fear—an Important Determinant," in Biko, *I Write What I Like*, p. 76.

102. Biko, "Fear—an Important Determinant," in Biko, *I Write What I Like*, p. 77.

103. Davis, pp. 12-14.

104. Peter Walshe, *Church versus State in South Africa*, pp. 218-219.

105. Davis, p. 14.

106. Cited in Lindy Wilson, "Bantu Steve Biko: A Life," in Pityana, p. 44.

107. David Russell, "Living in the Land of a Banned Man," *Agape* (September 1973), pp. 6-8, cited in Walshe, p. 218. See Woods, p. 69. Also, see John de Gruchy, *The Church Struggle in South Africa* (Grand Rapids, Mich.: William B. Eerdmans, 1986), p. 155.

108. Gerhart, p. 295.

109. Fatton, p. 66.

110. Gerhart, p. 204.

111. David Bosch, "Currents and Crosscurrents in South African Black Theology," *Journal of Religion in Africa* 6, no. 1 (1974), p. 11.

112. Jean Comaroff, *Body of Power, Spirit of Resistance: The Culture and History of a South African People* (Chicago: University of Chicago Press, 1985), pp. 255-263.

113. Biko, "Black Consciousness and the Quest for a True Humanity," in Basil Moore, p. 41.

114. Biko, "The Church as seen by a Young Layman," in Biko, *I Write What I Like*, p. 54. See also Louise Kretzschmar, *The Voice of Black Theology in South Africa* (Johannesburg: Ravan, 1986), p. 61.

115. Biko, "The Church as seen by a Young Layman," in Biko, *I Write What I Like*, p. 59.

116. Biko, "Black Consciousness and the Quest for a True Humanity," in Basil Moore, p. 43.

117. Hirson, p. 82. IDAMSA was founded as a Transkei institution in 1915. It went national in 1946. Its purpose was "to achieve a more effective propagation of the Gospel and create a forum through which Africans and Coloured clergymen could speak to topical ecclesiastical and political issues with a united voice." At its 1951 conference, the president, J. H. Calata, said it was sheer hypocrisy to speak of Christian brothers among blacks and whites. See Elfriede Strassberger, *Ecumenism in South Africa 1936-1960* (Johannesburg: SACC, 1974), pp. 97-98.

118. Denis Herbstein, *White Man, We Want to Talk to You* (London: Deutsch, 1978), p. 70.

119. Hirson, p. 81.

120. Hirson, pp. 85-86.

121. FEDSEM, established in 1961, was expropriated by the government for use by the adjacent Fort Hare University in 1974. The rector said the buildings could be rented by the seminary for one year on condition that students and staff refrain from provocative statements and actions. See Regehr, p. 93.

122. Regehr, p. 92.

123. See de Gruchy, p. 150.

124. Andrew Prior, "Political Culture and Violence: A Case Study of the ANC," *Politikon* 6, no. 2 (December 1984), p. 13.

125. Biko, "We Blacks," in Biko, *I Write What I Like*, pp. 31-32.

126. Biko, "The Church as seen by a Young Layman," in Biko, *I Write What I Like*, p. 60.

127. The SASO-9 were nine SASO members on trial for inculcating antiwhite feelings and encouraging racial hostilities in order to prepare for a violent revolution. In the same way that the Freedom Charter was on trial during the Treason Trial of 1956-1961, so too the ideas of black consciousness were on trial.

128. Biko, "The Righteousness of Our Strength," in Biko, *I Write What I Like*, p. 134.

129. Biko, "Black Consciousness and the Quest for a True Humanity," in Basil Moore, p. 45.

130. Arnold, p. 273.

131. Fatton, p. 100.

132. Theodore Jennings, "Steve Biko: Liberator and Martyr," *Christian Century* 94 (November 2, 1977), p. 998.

133. Woods, p. 71.

134. Biko speaking to the American Committee on Africa, August 1977, cited in Wilson, "Bantu Steve Biko: A Life," in Pityana, p. 66.

135. Keith Mokoape, Thenjiwe Mtintso, and Welile Nhlapo, "Towards the Armed Struggle," in Pityana, p. 138.

136. Gail Gerhart, cited in Arnold, p. xxv.

137. Fatton, p. 117.

138. Thomas Ranuga, "Frantz Fanon and Black Consciousness in Azania," *Phylon* 47, no. 3 (1986), p. 190.

139. Under the Act, churches could choose to continue their schools without government financial aid. Most chose not to.

140. Albert Lutuli, cited in Regehr, p. 49.

141. A change in 1975 permitted students with a pass mark over 40 percent to enter secondary schools; previously the pass mark had been 50 percent.

142. Hirson, p. 175.

143. Mokgethi Motlhabi, *The Challenge to Apartheid: Toward a Moral National Resistance* (Grand Rapids, Mich.: William B. Eerdmans, 1988), p. 61.

144. Arnold, p. 102.

145. Fatton, p. 100.

146. This committee was renamed Soweto Students Representative Council (SSRC).

147. Shaun Johnson, "Youth in the Politics of Resistance" in Shaun Johnson, ed., *South*

*Africa: No Turning Back* (Bloomington: Indiana University Press, 1989), p. 102.

148. Walshe, p. 206.

149. See Muriel Horrell, *A Survey of Race Relations, 1976* (Johannesburg: SAIRR, 1977), pp. 51–82. See also Hirson, p. 182.

150. Walshe, p. 207. There was an outbreak of violence of migrant workers against students, but it appears to have been incited by the government.

151. Fatton, p. 135. It has been estimated that over 12,000 young blacks left South Africa, 75 percent of whom joined the ANC in exile. See Prior, p. 16.

152. Biko was the forty-sixth person detained under South Africa's security legislation to die in police custody.

153. James Leatt, Theo Kneifel, and Klaus Nurnberger, eds., *Contending Ideologies in South Africa* (Grand Rapids, Mich.: William B. Eerdmans, 1986), p. 112.

154. It is known that SASO was able to keep in contact with Biko after he was banned in 1973. See Andrew Silk, "Understanding the Master: Robert Sobukwe's Legacy," *The Nation* 226, no. 12 (1978), p. 369.

155. Randwedzi Nengwekhula, "Black Consciousness Movement of South Africa," speech given to Assembly of IUEF in Geneva, November 22, 1976, p. 3, cited in Fatton, p. 101.

156. Biko, "The Righteousness of Our Strength," in Biko, *I Write What I Like*, p. 121.

157. Cited in Benjamin Pogrund, *How Can Man Die Better: Sobukwe and Apartheid* (London: Peter Halban, 1990), p. 350.

158. Pogrund, p. 350.

159. Andrew Silk, p. 369. In an interview in 1975, Sobukwe said that he still saw the need for an all-black organization but he feared SASO may have become antiwhite. See "Robert Sobukwe of the PAC," *African Report* 20, no. 3 (1975), p. 20.

160. N. Barney Pityana, "The Legacy of Steve Biko" in Pityana, P. 255.

161. De Gruchy, p. 172.

162. Hirson, p. 6.

163. Hirson, p. 270.

164. Hirson, p. 276.

165. According to Walshe, those churches that remained aloof include the Methodist, Presbyterian, and Baptist, while the Anglican, Roman Catholic, Lutheran, and Congregational churches drew closer to the protesters. Walshe, p. 207.

166. Desmond Tutu in Deane William Ferm, *Third World Liberation Theologies: An Introductory Survey* (Maryknoll, N.Y.: Orbis, 1986), p. 65.

# 4

# Bishop Desmond Tutu and the United Democratic Front

A major figure of protest in the 1980s and 1990s is the Anglican Archbishop Desmond Tutu. Tutu was born in 1931 in the Transvaal to Methodist parents and was educated at St. Anagar, a Swedish mission boarding school, and Madibane, an Anglican institution, before attending a teacher-training college in Pretoria. He taught school for four years but resigned over the Bantu Education Act, which took control of schools away from churches. After leaving the teaching profession, he received ordination training at St. Peter's Theological College in Johannesburg, a school run by the Fathers of the Community of the Resurrection for the training of Africans for the ministry.[1] Tutu saw the Church as "a likely means of service" and viewed his transition from teaching to ministry as being "grabbed by God by the scruff of the neck" in order to serve Him.[2]

## THE PRIESTHOOD

Tutu attributes his view of the interrelatedness of the spiritual and secular to his experiences at St. Peter's. It was here that he learned that religion could not be sealed off in a watertight compartment apart from the hurly-burly business of ordinary daily living. For Tutu, spirituality had to be expressed in dealing with one's neighbor, "whose keeper we must be."[3]

However, he was still not active in political protest. The Defiance Campaign of 1952 made little impact on him, living the somewhat isolated life of the student. Later, the Sharpeville Massacre, though shocking Tutu, did not draw him into politics, as he was busy finishing requirements for ordination in the Anglican Church.[4] However, his early acquaintance with Father Trevor Huddleston, an activist preacher involved in the Defiance Campaign and in the later protest against the destruction of the African township Sophiatown, made a lasting impact on Tutu. Tutu remembers how Huddleston, a favorite among the children in Sophiatown, visited him weekly in the hospital when he was recovering from tuberculosis. Tutu's strongest memory of Huddleston is the young priest's tipping his hat to Tutu's mother, a washerwoman, one day on the streets of Sophiatown—something he had never seen a white man do before. He attributes his interest in the Church to the early example of the white cleric Trevor Huddleston, whose "speaking up for the oppressed showed me what a man of the Church can do."[5]

## INTERNATIONAL EXPERIENCE

Travel abroad also gave him a chance to meet other white individuals. Tutu won a scholarship to study at King's College in England from 1962 to 1966 and described the experience of living in a nonracial society as liberating as Lutuli had found his sojourn in America. (Tutu admits that he used to seek out a policeman on his walks just to hear himself referred to as "sir" by a white man, an occurrence not likely in South Africa.)[6] At King's College and in the church he served in Great Britain, he had the opportunity to know personally many whites. He discovered, as Sobukwe and Biko had earlier, that he tended to defer to whites because he was conditioned to think more highly of whites than of himself. He explained that in South Africa the black man is brainwashed into an acquiescence of oppression and exploitation. He comes to believe what others have determined about him, filling him with self-disgust, self-contempt, and self-hatred. He allows the white person to set the standards and provide the role models.[7] Tutu understood how a sense of inferiority manifested itself among blacks: they turn on one another, treating each other as scum.[8] Although his diagnosis of the African condition was similar to the Africanists, both Sobukwe and Biko, his prescription was different. He did not withdraw from white association, but, rather, overcame his self-doubt as he learned to hold his own in interracial gatherings, in debates with white students, and in encounters with parishioners.

He credits his time in England with forestalling bitterness against whites, for he discovered his fellow students at King's College and his parishioners at St. Alban's are ordinary human beings, some good and some bad.[9] The "bad" whites, those acting like "bullies," were behaving that way because they failed to see their infinite worth. Tutu believed that whites were bent on amassing wealth to prove their worth, unaware that they have infinite worth already because they are created in God's image.[10]

He saw clearly that black liberation was the flip side of white liberation. Deep down in their hearts, he believed, whites certainly know that the security of all depends upon a population reasonably contented because they share in the good things of life.[11] He wrote, "At the present time we see our white fellow South Africans investing much of their resources to protect their so-called separate freedoms and privileges. They have little time left to enjoy them as they check the burglar proofing, the alarm system, the gun under the pillow and the viciousness of the watchdog."[12] To a group of white university students, he suggested that they too suffered from apartheid. He pointed out that they couldn't choose freely their neighbors or their spouses. Nor could they participate in open discussions because certain topics are considered subversive by the government. He concluded, "You will never be free until we blacks are free."[13]

Although Tutu believes whites are enslaved by their sinfulness, he does not consider them *irredeemable devils*. The *good news* of the Gospel for the white sinner is forgiveness. Just as many white Christians felt that Lutuli cared about them, certainly many whites who know Tutu feel the same. He prays for them—for the president, for jailers, for the police—"because they are God's children too," he explained.[14] He sympathizes with whites, realizing it would be difficult to give up so much privilege, admitting he too would need "a lot of grace" to do it if he were in their position.[15]

## CONTACT WITH BLACK CONSCIOUSNESS

Tutu returned from England to take a position at his alma mater, St. Peter's, which in the intervening years had moved from Johannesburg to Alice, and had become part of the Federal Theological Seminary (FEDSEM).[16] He arrived on campus at the time that black theology was gaining ground. During this time, he was also the chaplain at the government-controlled black university, Fort Hare, where black consciousness was surfacing. He was in total sympathy with the young students' aims, but his nonracial attitude was too firmly entrenched after four years in England for him to support them totally, for he was at odds with their racially exclusive approach and militant tone. Not surprisingly, the students at Fort Hare and FEDSEM found his views both too moderate and overly optimistic of whites' willingness to change.

Later, while dean of Johannesburg, he was encouraged by Father Aelred Stubbs, his earlier teacher, to meet with the young activists centered around Biko. Since Biko was in detention at the time, he met with others in the group, and, again, was in broad agreement with their aims. By the time of the Soweto Uprising in 1976, as dean of Johannesburg, he was thrust into politics, comforting the parents in Soweto whose children had been killed, and criticizing his own congregation for a less than whole-hearted response: "We have been really shattered by the deafening silence from the white community. You will say, what could you do? And all I would say to you is, what would you have done had they been white children? And that is all we would have wanted you to have done."[17]

Unable to meet Biko personally, Tutu nevertheless was invited to speak at his funeral in recognition of his support for the objectives of the Black Consciousness Movement.[18] Tutu said that God had called Biko to found the Black Consciousness Movement by which God "sought to awaken in the Black person a sense of his intrinsic value and worth as a child of God." He praised Biko for encouraging "blacks to glorify and praise God that he had created them black."[19]   In his oration, he emphasized what he considered his point of agreement with Biko: "Steve saw, more than most of us, how injustice and oppression can dehumanize and make us all, black and white, victim and perpetrator alike, less than God intended us to be."[20]   However, this compassion for whites is more properly what Tutu shared with Lutuli, not Biko, who was on record as hating whites.

Despite his disappointment with his parishioners' lack of response to Soweto, in general Tutu was proud of St. Mary's Cathedral parish.   A multiracial congregation, the church was a microcosm of what the future South Africa could be, Tutu believed.  He described officiating at the Eucharist with a multiracial crowd, a mixed team of clergy, and an integrated choir, servers, and sidesmen in "apartheid-mad South Africa" and "then tears sometimes streamed down my cheeks, tears of joy that . . . Jesus Christ had broken down the walls of partition and here were the first fruits of the eschatological community right in front of my eyes."[21]   Just as Lutuli believed that the oneness in Christ actualized in the Congregational Church could be a prototype of a future South Africa, so also did Tutu see that exemplified in the Anglican Church.

## SOUTH AFRICAN COUNCIL OF CHURCHES

Following his tenure as dean of Johannesburg, Tutu held the positions of bishop of Lesotho, bishop of Johannesburg, and most recently archbishop of Cape Town, heading the Anglican Church in South Africa, Namibia, Swaziland, and Lesotho.   But it is for his work with the South African Council of Churches (SACC), the umbrella group of churches critical of the government's race policies, that Tutu has become especially renowned.

SACC consists of twenty member churches and seven Christian organizations with observer status.  Among the largest members are the mainline Protestant churches: Presbyterian, Methodist, Anglican, and Congregational.   Member churches of SACC have twelve to fifteen million adherents, 80 percent of whom are black.  Following the banning of the Christian Institute in 1977, the once-moderate SACC, under Tutu's tenure as its general-secretary from 1978 to 1985, became both more Africanized, with Africans taking over positions of responsibility, and more radicalized, often being accused of being a black power base.[22]   He continued the efforts of his predecessor at SACC: appropriating funds to defend political prisoners, supporting their families and providing education for their children, aiding hard-pressed trade unionists, and assisting refugees fleeing to neighboring countries.   Perhaps his most important accomplishment was strengthening SACC's contacts with the exiled liberation groups, including the ANC.

Underpinning the efforts of the SACC is a theology of opposition to apartheid articulated by Tutu. His disavowal of apartheid rests on twin doctrines: man as the image of God, and reconciliation through Christ's redemption. Tutu regards man's creation in the image of God as his most important attribute; the Bible makes no reference to racial, ethnic, or biological characteristics.[23] But apartheid says some are more like God than others. "Skin colour and race become salvation principles, since in many cases they determine which people can participate in which church services—which are believed to be of saving significance." In short, apartheid "can make a child of God doubt that he is a child of God."[24]

Secondly, apartheid denies the central act of reconciliation which the New Testament declares was achieved by God in His Son, Jesus Christ. For Tutu, the heart of the Christian message is that Christ's work on the cross has restored human brotherhood which sin had destroyed. Whereas the Bible says that God's intention for humankind is harmony, peace, justice, wholeness, and fellowship, "apartheid says that human beings fundamentally are created for separation, disunity, and alienation."[25] Apartheid says that Christ has *not* in fact broken down the dividing wall of partition that used to divide Jew from Gentile, rich from poor, slave from free. Apartheid denies the unity of the family of God. But for Tutu, there is neither black, white, Indian, or Coloured, but a brother, a sister—one family, God's family.

Tutu also condemns apartheid for the suffering it causes its victims. He believes that God is concerned with the whole man, not just his spirit, and that the Gospel accordingly preaches total liberation. Responding to the Marxist charge that religion is an opiate of the people, Tutu writes that Christ never used religion that way, promising them pie-in-the-sky-when-you-die. He "knew that people want their pie here and now, and not in some future tomorrow." The prophets, too, emphasized this world, condemning as worthless religiosity a concern with offering God worship unmindful of the sociopolitical implications of religion.[26] Tutu writes, "If we are to say that religion cannot be concerned with politics then we are really saying that there is a substantial part of human life in which God's writ does not run."[27]

Tutu's exposure to Latin American liberation theology when he was on staff with the World Council of Churches' Theological Education Fund is evident in his assertion that God's interest in the whole man translates into His desire to secure justice for the oppressed:

We must proclaim that in a country of injustice and oppression, where Blacks receive an inferior education, are forced to live in matchbox houses, cannot move freely from place to place, and have to leave their wives and families behind them when they want to work in town—we must declare that this is God's world. He is on the side of the oppressed, of the poor, of the despised ones. We must say these things even if they make us suffer. It is not politics. It is the Gospel of Jesus Christ the liberator who will set us free.[28]

## IF GOD BE FOR US

In setting His children free, God has chosen to enlist us in His service as coworkers.[29] Therefore, the Church cannot be neutral:

If certain laws are not in line with the imperatives of the Gospel then the Christian must agitate for their repeal by all peaceful means. Christianity can never be a merely personal matter. It has public consequences and we must make public choices. Many people think Christians should be neutral, or that the Church must be neutral. But in a situation of injustice and oppression such as we have in South Africa, not to choose to oppose, is in fact to have chosen to side with the powerful, with the exploiter, with the oppressor.[30]

The Church, according to Tutu, must sustain the hope of a people tempted to grow despondent by taking the side of the oppressed. If it does not do this, then when liberation does come, the Church will be consigned to the outer darkness for having retarded the liberation struggle.[31]

Tutu believed that liberation was inevitable: "Injustice and evil and oppression will not last for ever. They have been overcome by God in the cross of Jesus Our Lord. As we protest the evil . . . we must do so knowing that victory is ours already. The authorities will ultimately fail because what they're doing is evil and against God's law."[32]

He had hope in the future because "Our cause is a just cause. . . . Our freedom is an inalienable right bestowed on us by God."[33] The government, he wrote, will end up as "mere marks on the pages of history, part of its flotsam and jetsam."[34] Even when the situation looks dismal, Tutu urges faith because "He is a God of surprises."[35] His sense of being held up and buoyed by prayers of Christians throughout the world also encouraged him: "What hope has the government got of defeating us when we are being prayed for every day in Arizona?" he queried.[36] His Christian faith is a source of courage, too. The worst thing that can happen, he often says, is for them to kill us, but "death," he insists, "is not the worst thing that can happen to a Christian."[37] Receiving the Nobel Peace Prize in 1984 was a source of hope, a boost to morale. "Hey, we're winning!" Tutu exclaimed.[38]

Tutu's assurance of ultimate victory derives from the parallels he sees between South African blacks and the Israelite slaves in the Exodus story. He points out that at times it must have seemed to the slaves that God did not care but in time they did reach the Promised Land: "This God did not just talk—he acted. He showed himself to be a doing God. Perhaps we might add another point—He takes sides. He is not a neutral God. He took the side of the slaves, the oppressed, the victims. He is still the same even today, he sides with the poor, the hungry, the oppressed, the victims of injustice."[39]

God later confirmed his preferential option for the oppressed by sending Hebrew prophets to denounce injustices perpetuated by the powerful against the powerless—the widows and orphans.[40] He again showed his siding with the poor in his decision to come to earth as one of the oppressed, a man acquainted with sorrows. Tutu places great store in the fact that in becoming human in Christ, God was not born into sumptuous surroundings but in a stable. God chose to empty the Godhead of divine glory to take on the form of a servant. In doing so, God chose to identify with and to share human suffering and pain. Like black South Africans, Tutu points out, Jesus was numbered among those rejected by society. He identified in the manner of his birth, life, and death with the marginalized. He deliberately chose as his friends not the mighty, the Bothas, but the "scum of society."[41]

While some black-theology proponents associated with Biko believed blacks were morally superior to whites, Tutu was quick to denounce this notion. He wrote that God is on the side of the oppressed not because they are better or more deserving than their oppressors, but simply because they were oppressed. We say that God is on our side, wrote Tutu, "not as some jingoistic nationalist deity who says 'my people right or wrong' but as one who saves and yet ultimately judges those whom he saves."[42]

One gets the impression that Biko and the black theologians supporting his movement felt that suffering had made blacks more moral than whites, and hence the political order following black majority rule would be a Golden Age of justice and compassion. Tutu warns against this notion: "[We] have too much evidence that the removal of one oppressor means the replacement by another; yesterday's victim quite rapidly becomes today's dictator. [We] know only too well the recalcitrance of human nature and so accept the traditional doctrines of the fall and original sin."[43] Tutu has refused to preach a liberation which excludes whites and fails to criticize blacks. In this respect, Tutu's thinking is closer to the Christianity proclaimed by Lutuli than that of Biko and Sobukwe.

## MULTIRACIAL MODERATION

Tutu states that he is determined to work alongside all concerned individuals—both black and white—for a nonracial democratic society. This includes the communists in South Africa. Though he rejects communism as too materialistic and atheistic to satisfy the deep spiritual aspirations of Africans, like Lutuli he is grateful for any assistance from whatever source. He wrote, "I hate Communism with every fibre of my body, as I believe most blacks do—but when you are in a danger and a hand is stretched out to help you, you do not ask the pedigree of its owner."[44] He does not include among those with whom he will work the homeland leaders, such as Chief Mangosuthu Buthelezi of KwaZulu. Like Biko, he denounces them as "corrupt men looking after their own interests, lining their pockets . . . [and] lacking integrity."[45]

Like Lutuli, Tutu advocates nonviolent methods in the pursuance of multiracialism. Because our cause is just, he writes, "we cannot afford to use methods of which we will be ashamed when we look back."[46] He has supported the aims of the exiled leaders of the African National Congress (ANC), whom he made a point to visit when he was overseas, but has condemned their methods: "We as a Council deplore all forms of violence, and have said so times without number. We deplore structural and legalized violence that maintains an unjust socio-political dispensation, and the violence of those who would overthrow the State."[47] But he knows that many ANC members, such as Nelson Mandela, are Christians who took up arms when peaceful methods failed. In fact, in recent years, his criticism of the ANC's methods have been muted. He explains that although he will never tell someone to pick up a gun, he will "pray for the man who picks up the gun, pray that he will be less cruel than he might otherwise have been."[48]

He has consistently warned that oppressed people will become desperate, and desperate people will use desperate methods. He clarified his position in an interview: "I am a man of peace, but not a pacifist. Clearly, the Christian Church is not entirely pacifist—I need only refer to the position of Western Christendom during the struggle against Nazism. The idea of a 'just war' is very much alive. How could I commend nonviolence to Blacks who know that resistance movements in Europe were praised to the skies, and who hear similar movements condemned because they are black?"[49]

While Tutu is uncomfortable with advocating violence, he recognizes that "those of us who still speak 'peace' and 'reconciliation' belong to a rapidly diminishing minority"[50] and writes that "it is a miracle of God's grace that Blacks can still say they are committed to a ministry of justice and reconciliation and that they want to avert . . . [a] bloodbath."[51]

## THE NEW CONSTITUTION

On May 5, 1983, President P. W. Botha introduced to Parliament the new constitution bill which extended the franchise to Indians and Coloureds. The government stated that blacks were not given a chamber because they already had their own constitutional path to follow in the homelands and in black local government structures. The new framework mandated three separate chambers of Parliament for Coloureds, Indians, and whites, whose members would be selected on separate voters rolls in separate elections. There would be 178 seats in the white House of Assembly, eighty-five in the Coloured House of Represen-tatives, and forty-five in the Indian House of Delegates. Coloureds and Indians would have control over matters that pertain to them alone, such as education and housing, with the president deciding which issues were their *own* matters and which were of *general* concern.[52]

Issues of general concern would be voted on in the three chambers, and differences in the bills between the three chambers would be hammered out by the President's Council, consisting of sixty members, twenty elected in the white chambers, ten in the Coloured chamber, and five in the Indian chamber. Twenty-five would be appointed proportionately by the president from opposition members in the three chambers. The decision of the President's Council would be final.[53] Heading the system would be an executive state-president who, in addition to the power to appoint many members of the President's Council, could bypass the legislature, select his cabinet from the three houses as he wished, and suspend Parliament for up to thirteen months. Because of the supremacy of the white chamber, the dominant party in it was assured of always electing the state-president. As long as the National Party kept winning white elections, the state-president would always be an Afrikaner Nationalist.[54]

Tutu was vociferous in his rejection of the proposal. He saw it as a refinement rather than a refutation of apartheid. Tutu accused it of co-opting a segment of the oppressed as junior partners in order to add their numbers to the white oppressors. He told a meeting of the Natal Indian Congress that Indians and Coloureds were being included in the system because whites couldn't defend the system alone any longer. Whites were finding total repression too costly internally as well as internationally in terms of legitimacy. If they accepted the Tricameral Parliament, Africans would regard them as traitors in the liberation struggle, he warned.[55]

At the same time, divide-and-rule strategies were implemented to co-opt middle-class urban blacks from their less well off rural brethren. The Koornhoff Bills set up black municipal councils for the townships, and replaced the old influx control system with a new system, to be administered by the black councils, that granted urban status only to those who had jobs and *approved* accommodations, which excluded shanties or leased rooms. Furthermore, it was decreed that the townships would become financially self-supporting now that they had their own councils.[56]

Tutu issued a statement from the SACC noting that since the new Parliament would exclude 73 percent of the population from sharing political power, and it effectively ensured whites would get their parliamentary majority (with four whites to every two Coloureds and one Indian in the President's Council), fundamental change would be blocked. He urged SACC's member churches to reject the new constitution and to urge their parishioners to boycott the upcoming elections to the two new chambers.[57] Despite Tutu's plea, white voters approved the new constitution with 66 percent of votes voting in favor of it in a landslide victory.[58]

## THE UNITED DEMOCRATIC FRONT

The United Democratic Front (UDF) was inaugurated in Cape Town on August 20, 1983, as an umbrella group of 600-700 student, community, religious, professional, and trade union organizations to oppose the new constitution.

Although Tutu was a patron of the United Democratic Front, he could not be present at its Cape Town launching, and so Dr. Allan Boesak, a minister in the Coloured Dutch Reformed Church,[59] gave the keynote address. Boesak appealed for unity of all opponents of apartheid, including whites, for the struggle could not be "by one's skin color but rather by one's commitment to justice, peace, and human liberation."[60] He spoke of apartheid as a "thoroughly evil system, and, as such, it [could] not be modified, modernized or streamlined. It [had] to be eradicated irrevocably."[61]

The highlights of Boesak's speech were adopted in the *UDF Declaration* which stressed the goal of a single, nonracial South Africa free of bantustans and group areas in which all individuals would have the vote. The UDF adopted the slogan, "Apartheid Divides—UDF Unites."[62] Just as the ANC associated with white groups through the Congress Alliance, the UDF also permitted affiliation of white organizations in the belief that "all the oppressed sections of the community had an over-riding interest in the destruction of apartheid."[63] The UDF believes that the strategy of closing ranks had achieved its purpose of consciousness-raising envisaged by Sobukwe and Biko, and that now is the time for all enemies of apartheid—black and white—to join forces. Committed to multiracialism, the UDF also endorses the ANC's Freedom Charter as its guiding document.

From the launching of the UDF until the first elections under the new constitution in 1984, campaigns were instigated throughout the country to discredit the upcoming elections under the banner of *One Million Signatures*. The UDF's boycott of the elections was wildly successful: only 17.5 percent of eligible Coloureds and 15.5 percent of Indians participated.[64] Likewise, elections held in the townships for the black municipal councils were boycotted. Turnout was 5 percent in Soweto, 11 percent at Port Elizabeth, 15 percent in the Vaal Triangle, 19 percent in Durban, and 20 percent on the Eastern Rand.[65] At the same time that the multiracial UDF was inaugurated, the National Forum (NF) was also being formed as an umbrella group whose all-black affiliates include the Azanian People's Organization (AZAPO),[66] ex-PAC members, and black-consciousness groups. In the 1980s we witness the historical competition between the two approaches fought out between the earlier organizations. Meredith writes, "The nationalist movement was still affected by the same split which had prevailed since the 1940s, between the ANC/Charterist camp and the Afri-canist/black consciousness camp."[67] The groups affiliated with the National Forum accept no part for whites in the struggle against apartheid but allow for their inclusion in a postapartheid society. Like the PAC and BCM before them, the NF excludes whites because "however well-intentioned [whites] cannot identify with the class interests of the oppressed Black Masses."[68]

The political document of the National Forum, the *Manifesto of the People of Azania*, calls for the black working class to lead the struggle toward a "democratic antiracist and socialist Azania."[69] The land must be "wholly owned and controlled by the Azanian people."[70] The National Forum is critical of the UDF's support of the Freedom Charter, because it preserves racial groups and recognizes minority rights. But, despite their different tactics, the NF and the UDF have the same goal: a nonracial society based on the principle of one-man-one-vote within a socialist economic framework.[71]

Although Tutu was an executive member of the NF Committee, helping to prepare for its inaugural in 1983, his dual commitment to it and the UDF could not be maintained.[72] His profound commitment to multiracialism, which earlier kept him from wholeheartedly embracing Biko and his movement, likewise kept him from close contact with the NF. But his initial interest shows, as Sparks puts it, a streak of militancy within moderation.[73]

Indeed, a statement in a letter to Prime Minister John Vorster in 1976 clearly shows an amalgam of the inclusive liberalism of Lutuli and the exclusive Africanism of Biko: "Blacks are grateful for all that has been done for them, but now they claim *an inalienable right to do things for themselves*, in co-operation with their fellow South Africans of all races."[74] Likewise, he has adopted the black-theology approach associated with the Africanist-inspired Black Consciousness Movement, but employs it differently than Biko to stress the unity of the family of God. Perhaps Tutu, who admits to abhorring capitalism, based as it is on the survival of the fittest and on man's lower instincts,[75] admired AZAPO's forceful stand against capitalism, and so was drawn to the National Forum. What Tutu's equivocation may represent is a cross-fertilization of ideas between the two approaches.

In any event, multiracialism has re-emerged and replaced Africanism as the *dominant* element in black politics. A movement away from black-consciousness ideology to a commitment to the Charterist philosophy occurred around 1980, and by mid-1987 the dominance of the Charterist position was complete. To be sure, several former black-consciousness advocates have found a political home in the UDF.[76] Terror Lekota, a leading figure in the BCM, has become active in the UDF, which he attributes to the influence of Mandela upon him while imprisoned with the ANC leader on Robben Island.[77] One explanation of the popularity of the multiracial UDF is that the ANC's intensification of the struggle against military installations, security force personnel, and economic targets have given it prestige that legitimates the *internal* organization that most closely reflects its ideology. It was probably the assimilation of black youths following Soweto, brutalized and radicalized by their encounter with the police, into the ranks of the ANC in exile which is responsible for the intensification of the armed struggle.

Tutu is quick to state that the UDF does not purport to be a substitute for the ANC. It was conceived as a transitional front, not a political party, and certainly not as a rival but as a supplement to the then-exiled ANC.[78] Its acceptance of former ANC members within its ranks means, writes McKean, that the relationship between the UDF and the ANC goes beyond mere symbolism and similarity.[79]

But, if it served as the internal wing of the then-exiled ANC, it nevertheless lacked the experienced political leadership of the ANC. Tutu is clear on that point. He says that Nelson Mandela, Oliver Tambo, and Walter Sisulu of the ANC are the true political leaders of black South Africans, not clerics like himself and Boesak.[80] He is primarily a priest who happens to see the connection between "our Father in heaven" and "our brothers on earth." With the mass bannings in 1977, the government effectively decimated African political leadership, and Tutu stepped in to fill the void. He points out that his meetings with de Klerk were "talks about talks" and that the real negotiations for a new political settlement would have to be between the government and the ANC leaders. He sees himself not as a politician but as a prophet, a modern-day Jeremiah, speaking under "the influence of God's hand."[81] Likewise, du Boulay sees him as a Moses figure, but not in the sense of doing the leading, which he defers to the ANC, but in sharing the vision.[82] True to his word, upon the release of Nelson Mandela from prison, he told reporters, "I can now get on with the work of the Church."[83]

The UDF did not cease to exist after the Coloured and Indian elections. Rather, the campaigns opened a new chapter of resistance, and the UDF initiated the longest sustained period of agitation in the history of black resistance since 1960.[84] For three years, protests raged throughout the country as the UDF employed a variety of strategies: work stay-aways; rent, consumer, and bus boycotts; antisports campaigns; and campaigns for the unbanning of the ANC. The flurry of activity is reminiscent of the ANC's activities in the 1950s, and like the ANC, the UDF has come under a wide array of security provisions including preventive detentions of key figures, treason charges against leaders, and bans on meetings and key affiliates.


## THE VIOLENCE/NONVIOLENCE DEBATE

Like the BCM organizations of the 1970s, the UDF realized that to operate legally above ground it had no other option but to commit itself publicly to nonviolence. However, despite its own nonviolence stance, the UDF has found its leading spokesman, Bishop Tutu, at times too moderate and has stated its doubts especially about Tutu's doctrine of reconciliation. UDF members feel that changes have to be made to political structures before reconciliation can take place.

But Tutu, like Lutuli before him, is convinced that the Gospel can change the hearts of white Christians, and that black South Africans must continually try to persuade whites. Du Boulay explains that his instincts are to negotiate rather than to confront, to reconcile rather than to attack. Although aware that militant blacks would see him as politically naive, Tutu persisted in this view and attempted to meet with President Botha time and time again. He has remarked that Moses went to see Pharaoh not once but several times and in spite of Botha's hardened heart, he would try again.[85] Tutu explains, "Whether I like it or not,

Mr. P. W. Botha and I are brothers, members of the same family. I cannot write him off. I cannot give up on him because God, our common Father, does not give up on anyone."[86] Of President F. W. de Klerk, Tutu believes he has witnessed a change of heart: "Give him credit, man. Do give him credit. I do."[87]

It is not surprising that the black theology espoused by Tutu has come under increasing attack from radical township youths. The *Washington Post* suggests that the "relative moderation and restraining influence" of Tutu is "in danger of being swamped by the rising tide of anger in the townships."[88] A group of mainly black theologians, following the state of emergency in 1985, published the *Kairos Document*, which expresses the sentiments of the young township militants and their growing differences with Tutu.

The *Kairos Document* states that it is wrong for the established churches to preach "reconciliation" in the present circumstances of South Africa. There can be no reconciliation between justice and injustice, good and evil. To be reconciled to the intolerable crimes committed against black South Africans is nothing short of sinful. It is to become accomplices in our own oppression.[89]

For the *Kairos Document* theologians, reconciliation and negotiation can only *follow* white repentance and a clear commitment to fundamental change. But true repentance on the part of the government is belied by the state of emergency, military repression in the townships, and jailing of political opponents. Until some evidence of true repentance is seen, negotiation is a waste of time; premature negotiation only prolongs African bondage.[90]

Rather than preach negotiation and reconciliation, it advises churches to urge confrontation until the state indicates it is willing to undergo fundamental change. Instead of trying to convince those in power to change, the churches should commit themselves to the struggle of the oppressed against unjust structures.

The *Kairos Document* attacks the multiracial churches for pleading with those in power to act justly. Justice that is determined from above, by the oppressor, necessarily is a justice of reformism—a justice of concessions that leaves untouched the basic structural injustice of apartheid. What is required instead is church support for those who are below, the oppressed, in their efforts to rid the country of unjust structures. Churches should not merely pray for a change of government but actively aid those seeking to remove it.[91]

The *Kairos Document*, while not explicitly advocating violence in the struggle for liberation, is very critical of the way non-violence has been absolutized by the churches. "Non-violence has been made into an absolute principle without regard for who is using it, which side they are on or what purpose they have in mind." Violence becomes associated in peoples' minds with the actions of those seeking to overthrow unjust structures, but not with the violence of the structures themselves, or the violence used by the state to maintain those structures.[92]

Tacitly, the *Kairos Document* legitimates the use of violence. It supports the notion of *just revolution* which is part of the Christian tradition of *just war*,[93] stressing the principles of *last resort* and *lesser of two evils*. Perhaps the *Kairos*

*Document* inadequately deals with the principle of *probability of success*. It can be argued, as Inkatha's Buthelezi has, that the state's power is such that the probability of a successful revolution is minimal.[94]  Clearly, the *Kairos Document* is not a directive to revolution but an analysis of the possibilities open to black South Africans.  It argues that black South Africans have a right to defend themselves against the violence of the state, because the government is tyrannical, "an enemy of the common good" that relies on terrorism to maintain its power.[95]

Although the state is tyrannical, the document makes clear that that is no excuse for hatred, since the Bible calls us to love our enemies.  But to love does not mean to sit back and wait for our enemies to see the light.  The present crisis is proof of the ineffectiveness of "years and years of Christian moralising about the need for love."[96]  Sometimes the most loving thing we can do for both the oppressed and our enemies the oppressors is "to eliminate oppression, remove the tyrants from power, and establish a just government for the common good of all the people."[97]

In the aftermath of the *Kairos Document*, the World Council of Churches sponsored conferences in Harare in 1986 and in Lusaka in 1987, bringing together leading churchmen in South Africa with the leaders of the exiled liberation movements.  In effect the conferences endorsed the conclusions of the *Kairos Document*: it was the institutional violence of the state that had spawned the counterviolence of the oppressed.  The *Lusaka Statement* recognized that the South African regime by waging war on its inhabitants had ceased to be *legitimate* government, and thus compels the resistance movement to use force in defense against the violence of the state in order to end oppression.  Like the *Kairos Document*, the *Lusaka* and *Harare* statements encourage churches to strengthen their commitment to the freedom fighters and to stand in solidarity with them.[98]  It argues that the institutional Church cannot dictate to the victims of violence, or pass moral judgments on a revolution of *last resort*.

The acceptance of violence to counter the violence of the state rests on a radical interpretation of Christianity.  Perhaps only a radical gospel is sufficient for the times, if resistance is not to be severed totally from its religious roots.  In fact, the radical message of the *Kairos Document* has met with great response among the township youth.  Mayson describes how instead of asking, "Is it in the Bible?" as an earlier generation would have, today's youth ask, "Is it in the *Kairos Document*?"[99]  Conversely, a day of prayer to end violence that was called for by Tutu and other church leaders[100] on July 16, 1985, the ninth anniversary of the Soweto Uprising, was received unenthusiastically by blacks.  In Tutu's call for prayer, the Church's efforts, compared to the *Kairos Document*'s prescriptions, sound remarkably timid:

We have prayed for our own rulers, as is demanded of us in the Scriptures.  We have entered into consultation with them as is required by our faith.  We have taken the reluctant and drastic step of declaring apartheid to be contrary to the declared will of God, and . . . have declared it . . . a heresy.  We now pray that God will replace the present structures of oppression with ones that are just, and remove from power those who persist in defying his laws, installing in their place leaders who will govern with justice and mercy.[101]

The feeling that the Church is too timorous is voiced not only by township youths and the black theologians associated with the *Kairos Document*, but increasingly by the once-moderate South African Council of Churches. The *Christian Science Monitor* reported in July 1987 that the SACC "inched a step closer toward accepting the use of violence to overthrow the current system." At its annual meeting, the SACC by a large majority adopted for urgent reaction from its member churches a statement drawn up earlier that year by the exiled ANC. "The statement," writes the *Monitor*, "while not directly associating the SACC with political violence, would in effect accept the use of violence by the ANC."[102] The action reflects perhaps the impact of the *Kairos Document* on the Council.

Tutu himself, while not a signatory, has admitted that he is in "general agreement" with the *Kairos Document* but wishes the tone were not so strident.[103] Like Lutuli, he prefers to employ moderate language perhaps to allay white fears and to prevent further repression. For instance, he is careful to say he is for *majority* not *black rule*—although in the South African context where blacks comprise the majority of the population, this means one and the same thing.

Following the publication of the *Kairos Document*, Tutu's view of reconciliation underwent some modification. Reconciliation, Tutu later wrote, does not rule out confrontation. Just as there can be no cheap grace for the Christian, neither can there be cheap reconciliation. That reconciliation is costly is demonstrated by our reconciliation with God which cost God the life of Jesus.[104]

Tutu has said he fears "time may be running out for a peaceful resolution" and that he could envisage a time in which he would endorse violence as the only way of ensuring a just society.[105] He increasingly expresses sympathy with those who call for a violent response against a violent regime. He told an audience, "There may be a time when we have to take up arms and defend ourselves." In June 1986, to a crowd in Toronto, he said that if sanctions failed, "The Church would have no alternative but to say it would be justifiable to use violence and force to overthrow an unjust regime."[106] By 1992 Tutu was insisting that reconciliation means confronting people with their sin, including structural, or political, sin. Reconciliation, Tutu came to believe, means calling to repentance and restitution those who have benefitted from apartheid.[107] For Tutu, violence may be the lesser of two evils, the greater evil being unyielding oppression.

The violence traditionally associated with the Africanists has now been legitimized by the Charterists who endorse multilateral collaboration. The chasm separating the Africanists and Charterists on the propriety of violent means has narrowed, as violence became an acceptable option not only to the PAC-BC-NF wing but to the ANC as well. (And while the UDF chose not to employ force itself, it remained uncritical of the ANC's position.) The major contribution of

Africanist thinking on the Charterists has been to infuse the Charterists with a militancy and determination to use whatever means necessary to achieve liberation. Mandela's release from prison in February 1990 was not contingent upon his disavowal of violence because he and the ANC were unequivocal on their position, and despite the government's efforts to persuade the ANC to dissolve its military wing, Umkhonto we Sizwe, the ANC in the *Pretoria Minute* of August 1990 agreed only to *suspend*, not to *terminate*, the armed struggle.

A new dimension to the violence debate in South African politics is the black-on-black violence between ANC *comrades* and Inkatha *collaborators* that is endemic in the townships. Since Mandela's release, 10,000 Africans have been killed in clashes between the ANC and the Inkatha Freedom Party (IFP).[108] The phenomenon of "necklacing"—placing gasoline-soaked tires around the necks and shoulders of alleged collaborators—has become increasingly commonplace. Despite its formal opposition to acts of undisciplined violence, many UDF and ANC members are sympathetic with the young perpetrators and believe necklacing serves a useful purpose in safeguarding the organization from informers. Predictably, the first to speak out against it were church leaders including Tutu who on at least two occasions has thrown himself across a suspected informer, telling the mob he would have to be killed first. Some leaders have feared taking too great a stand against it, lest they lose influence with the militant youth they want to restrain.[109] Tutu has never held this position and in fact was instrumental in arranging the historic meeting in September 1991 between Mandela and Buthelezi in an effort to quell the mounting political violence which was killing eight people a day and threatening to render a negotiated settlement unworkable.[110]

Despite the National Peace Accord, signed by both sides, one of the worst incidents of black-on-black violence occurred in June 1992 at Boipatong, a township south of Johannesburg. Forty-six pro-ANC Xhosas were hacked and speared to death in their beds by pro-Inkhata Zulus. SACC General-Secretary Frank Chikane and Bishop Tutu led a delegation of church leaders to the government forty-eight hours after the massacre and accused the government's security forces of collusion with the attackers. Three months later, at Bisho in the nominally independent homeland of Ciskei, twenty-four ANC and Communist Party supporters were killed by the defense forces of Oupo Gqozo, Ciskei's military leader, who fired on 50,000 protesting marchers. Again, the South African government came under attack from Tutu and other religious leaders for supporting the attackers and not doing enough to prevent the massacre.

If the black-on-black rivalries have been incited by the government with direct support given to opponents of the ANC, as is claimed by the ANC and many outside observers,[111] then attacks by township youths loyal to the ANC against migrant workers committed to Buthelezi's Inkatha are merely an extension of the violent struggle waged against the government. The *Kairos Document* had argued that there could be no reconciliation without true repentance on the part of the government. Despite the release of Mandela, the unbanning of the ANC, and the repeal of much apartheid legislation (including the Group Areas, Population Registration, and Land Acts), the government's complicity in township violence, along with its blanket denials in the face of mounting evidence to the contrary, suggested to many that there was no true change of heart. In fact, the ANC accused the government of fueling the violence in order to stop the negotiations altogether.[112]

A new element in the cycle of violence has been the escalation of attacks against white civilians. In the worst act of indiscriminate terrorism against white civilians since the legalization of the black resistance movements in 1990, ten whites were killed and at least fifty-three injured while worshipping at St. James Church in Kenilworth, a suburb of Cape Town. The attack bore the hallmarks of three previous attacks against whites by the Azanian People's Liberation Army (APLA), the military wing of the PAC, but the PAC denied responsibility. Coming the day before black and white parties negotiating an end to apartheid were to unveil a preliminary draft of a nonracial constitution, the massacre was denounced by Tutu as "the most despicable thing imaginable."[113]

According to the *Christian Science Monitor*, with the escalation of violence, the angry, violent rhetoric of the PAC is striking more of a chord with black youths than the more moderate stance of the ANC.[114] The Azanian People's Liberation Army's slogan, "One bullet, one settler," has enticed its followers to pursue terrorism, murder white farmers, and shoot white motorists, thereby fueling similar action from the right-wing Afrikaner Resistance Movement (AWB).[115] The murder of Communist Party leader Chris Hani in April 1993 is an example of the spiraling violence unleashed by right-wing extremists in a last-ditch effort to stop the negotiations that would lead to multiracial elections the following year. Looking back at the dark period preceding national elections, Tutu admitted that he had underestimated the level of violence that would threaten the transition to democracy in South Africa.[116]

## NOTES

1. Tutu was baptized a Methodist, later became a member of the AME Church, and finally in 1943 became an Anglican. The changes did not reflect changing religious beliefs but rather changes in circumstances. His parents would switch denominations depending upon which church-sponsored school their children were attending or where Tutu's father was teaching.

2. Shirley du Boulay, *Tutu: Voice of the Voiceless* (Grand Rapids, Mich.: William B. Eerdmans, 1988), p. 46.

3. "Evidence to the Eloff Commission," *Ecunews* (June 1983), cited in du Boulay, p. 48.

4. du Boulay, p. 54.

5. Marjorie Hope and James Young, *The South African Churches in a Revolutionary*

*Situation* (Maryknoll, N.Y.: Orbis, 1981), p. 112.

6. Dennis Wepman, *Desmond Tutu* (New York: Franklin Watts, 1989), p. 45.

7. "A Vision for Humanity," address given on the award of the Martin Luther King, Jr. Peace Prize, January 1986, cited in du Boulay, p. 22.

8. Desmond Tutu, *Hope and Suffering* (Grand Rapids, Mich.: William B. Eerdmans, 1984), p. 52.

9. Comment, King's College Newsletter (December 1984), cited in du Boulay, p. 60.

10. *Argus* (March 5, 1981), cited in du Boulay, p. 140.

11. Desmond Tutu, *Crying in the Wilderness: The Struggle for Justice in South Africa* (Grand Rapids, Mich.: William B. Eerdmans, 1982), p. 87.

12. Tutu, *Crying in the Wilderness*, p. 87.

13. Tutu, *Crying in the Wilderness*, p. 43.

14. du Boulay, p. 140.

15. du Boulay, p. 163.

16. The buildings and property of FEDSEM were confiscated by the government in 1974.

17. du Boulay, pp. 106–107.

18. Tutu also spoke at Sobukwe's funeral six months after Biko's funeral, calling him a "holy man, devoted to Jesus Christ his Lord and Master." See Tutu, *Crying in the Wilderness*, p. 66.

19. Tutu, *Crying in the Wilderness*, p. 62.

20. Tutu, *Crying in the Wilderness*, p. 63.

21. Tutu, *Hope and Suffering*, p. 135.

22. See David Thomas, *Councils in the Ecumenical Movement in South Africa* (Johannesburg: SACC, 1979), p. 63.

23. Desmond Tutu, "Christianity and Apartheid," in John W. de Gruchy and Charles Villa-Vicencio, eds., *Apartheid is a Heresy* (Grand Rapids, Mich.: William B. Eerdmans, 1983), p. 40.

24. Tutu, "Christianity and Apartheid," in de Gruchy and Villa-Vicencio, pp. 45–46.

25. Tutu, "Christianity and Apartheid," in de Gruchy and Villa-Vicencio, pp. 41–42.

26. Tutu, *Crying in the Wilderness*, pp. 28–29.

27. Tutu, *Hope and Suffering*, p. 170.

28. Tutu, *Crying in the Wilderness*, pp. 31–32.

29. Tutu, *Hope and Suffering*, p. 60.

30. Tutu, *Crying in the Wilderness*, p. 34.

31. Tutu, *Hope and Suffering*, p. 87.

32. Tutu, *Hope and Suffering*, p. 42.

33. Tutu, *Crying in the Wilderness*, p. 89.

34. du Boulay, p. 179.

35. Desmond Tutu, cited in Bonganjalo Goba, "A Theological Tribute to Archbishop Tutu," in Buti Tlhagale and Itumeleng Mosala, eds., *Hammering Swords into Ploughshares: Essays in Honour of Archbishop Mpilo Desmond Tutu* (Johannesburg: Skotaville, 1986), p. 63.

36. du Boulay, p. 140.

37. Tutu, *Hope and Suffering*, p. 18.

38. du Boulay, p. 201.

39. Tutu, Hope and Suffering, p. 51.

40. Desmond Tutu, cited in Simon Maimela, "Archbishop Desmond Mpilo Tutu, a Revolutionary Political Priest or Man of Peace?" in Tlhagale and Mosala, p. 47.

41. "General Secretary's Report, 1984," p. 5, cited in Maimela, "Archbishop Desmond Mpilo Tutu, a Revolutionary Political Priest or Man of Peace?" in Tlhagale and Mosala, p. 47.

42. Desmond Tutu, "The Theology of Liberation in Africa," in Kofi Appiah-Kubi and Sergio Torres, eds., *African Theology En Route* (Maryknoll, N.Y.: Orbis, 1979), p. 166.

43. Tutu, "The Theology of Liberation in Africa," in Kofi Appiah-Kubi and Sergio Torres, p. 167.

44. Peter Godwin, *Sunday Times* (1985), cited in du Boulay, p. 237.

45. *Citizen* (June 30, 1982), cited in du Boulay, p. 168.

46. Desmond Tutu, *The Words of Desmond Tutu,* ed. Naomi Tutu (New York: Newmarket Press, 1989), p. 48.

47. Tutu, *Hope and Suffering*, p. 181.

48. Tutu, in Naomi Tutu, p. 51.

49. Hope and Young, p. 111.

50. Desmond Tutu, "Black South African Perspectives and the Reagan Administration," *TransAfrica Forum* 1, no. 1 (Summer 1982), p. 15.

51. Tutu, *Hope and Suffering*, p. 99.

52. Black affairs were defined as a *general* affair.

53. See Muriel Horrell, *A Survey of Race Relations, 1983* (Johannesburg: SAIRR, 1984), pp. 71-77.

54. Allister Sparks, *The Mind of South Africa* (New York: Ballantine Books, 1990), p. 319.

55. du Boulay, p. 165.

56. Sparks, pp. 331-332.

57. du Boulay, pp. 165-166.

58. Sparks, p. 330.

59. Boesak is a pastor in the Coloured Nederduitse Gereformeerde Sendingkerk (NGK) and past president of the World Alliance of Reformed Churches.

60. Mokgethi Motlhabi, *Challenge to Apartheid: Toward a Moral National Resistance* (Grand Rapids, Mich.: William B. Eerdmans, 1988), p. 84.

61. Motlhabi, pp. 89-90.

62. Motlhabi, p. 93.

63. Howard Barrell, "The United Democratic Front and the National Forum: Their Emergence, Composition, and Trends," *South African Review* 2 (1984), p. 8.

64. Jo-Anne Collinge, "The United Democratic Front," *South African Review* 3 (1986), p. 253. The official results were 30 percent for Coloureds and 20 percent for Indians.

65. Sparks, p. 332.

66. AZAPO, founded in 1978, is the leading black-consciousness organization. It sees the problem as racial capitalism which benefits the minority of whites and their

allies, white workers and the reactionary section of the black working class.

67. Martin Meredith, "The Black Opposition," in Jesmond Blumenfeld, ed., *South Africa in Crisis* (London: Croom Helm, 1987), pp. 79–80.

68. Motlhabi, p. 83.

69. Francis Meli, *South Africa Belongs to Us: A History of the ANC* (Bloomington: Indiana University Press, 1989), p. 198.

70. See Tom Lodge, "The UDF: Leadership and Ideology," in John Brewer, *Can South Africa Survive?: Five Minutes to Midnight* (London: Macmillan, 1989), p. 214.

71. The economic policies they advance are reminiscent of Biko's *communalism*. All the resistance movements reflect tinges of socialism.

72. One explanation for Tutu's distancing himself from the NF is that AZAPO boycotted the visit of Senator Edward Kennedy, whom Tutu had invited to South Africa. The explanations for the boycott are that Kennedy also planned to meet with Mongosuthu Gatsha Buthelezi, and Kennedy represented an imperialist country that helped to buttress apartheid. In any event, Tutu was disturbed by the boycott.

73. du Boulay, p. 198.

74. Tutu, *Hope and Suffering*, p. 31.

75. Tutu, *Crying in the Wilderness*, pp. 100 and 112.

76. Shaun Johnson, "Youth in the Politics of Resistance," in Shaun Johnson, ed., *South Africa: No Turning Back* (Bloomington: Indiana University Press, 1989), p. 140.

77. John Brewer, "Internal Black Protest," in Brewer, p. 193.

78. William Claiborne, "de Klerk, Tutu Group to Meet," *Washington Post* (October 7, 1989), p. A25.

79. David McKean, "The UDF and the Anti-Apartheid Struggle," *TransAfrica Forum* 4, no. 1 (Fall 1986), p. 39.

80. du Boulay, p. 220.

81. Tutu, *Hope and Suffering*, p. 22.

82. du Boulay, p. 264.

83. Charles Villa-Vicencio, "To Be Servant of the People: The Church and Change in South Africa," *Sojourners* (December 1992), p. 27.

84. In 1985, the UDF became the third South African organization to be declared an *affected organization* which meant it could not receive funds from abroad. The Christian Institute and NUSAS are the other two organizations in South African history that have been declared affected.

85. du Boulay, p. 168.

86. Tutu, "Spirituality: Christian and African," in John de Gruchy and Charles Villa-Vicencio, eds., *Resistance and Hope: South African Essays in Honour of Beyers Naude* (Grand Rapids, Mich.: William B. Eerdmans, 1985), p. 163.

87. Charles Villa-Vicencio, "The Conditions for Freedom: Mandela's Release Marks Decisive Moment in South Africa," *Sojourners* (April 1990), p. 31.

88. Allister Sparks, "South African Protagonists Invoke Christianity," *Washington Post* (October 2, 1985), p. A21.

89. *Kairos Document: The Challenge to the Churches* (Grand Rapids, Mich.: William B. Eerdmans, 1986), p. 10.

90. *Kairos Document*, p. 11.

91. *Kairos Document*, p. 12.

92. *Kairos Document*, p. 13.

93. These are the recognized criteria of just war: all other possibilities of nonviolent change have been exhausted; the cause must be just; the methods used must involve no unnecessary or excessive violence; there must be reasonable prospect that the ends will be attained.

94. John Brewer, "Inkatha in South African Politics," in Johnson, pp. 365–366.

95. *Kairos Document*, p. 24.

96. *Kairos Document*, p. 12.

97. *Kairos Document*, pp. 24–25.

98. Charles Villa-Vicencio, *Trapped in Apartheid* (Maryknoll, N.Y.: Orbis, 1988), p. 115.

99. Cedric Mayson, "Christianity and Revolution," *Sechaba* (October 1987), p. 14.

100. Ironically, some of these church leaders were signatories of the *Kairos Document*.

101. *Journal of Theology for Southern Africa* 52 (September 1985), p. 58, cited in John de Gruchy, "The Church and the Struggle for South Africa," in Tlhagale and Mosala, pp. 196–197.

102. Ned Temko, "Shift to Left by Key South African Church Council Taken as Sign that Change is too Slow Coming," *Christian Science Monitor* (July 7, 1987), p. 1.

103. Margaret Novicki, Interview with Bishop Tutu, *Africa Report* 31, 2 (March–April 1986), p. 53.

104. Tutu, *Hope and Suffering*, p. 38.

105. Temko, p. 32.

106. *Cape Times* (June 2, 1986), cited in du Boulay, p. 244.

107. "A Prisoner of Hope," *Christianity Today* 36 (October 5, 1992), p. 41.

108. Robert Rotberg, "South Africa's Political Transformation," *Christian Science Monitor* (July 27, 1993), p. 19.

109. Steven Mufson, *Fighting Years: Black Resistance and the Struggle for a New South Africa* (Boston: Beacon Press, 1990), pp. 97–98.

110. "Church Leaders Broker South African Meeting," *Christian Century* (July 14–21, 1993), p. 708.

111. "Southern Africa in the 90s," a special issue of *Washington Notes on Africa*, p. 3. See also Allister Sparks, "I Despair for My Country," *Washington Post* (June 28, 1992), p. C7.

112. Hannes Siebert, "The Painful Liberation of South Africa: The Church Assumes Role as Mediator," *Sojourners* (December 1991), p. 31.

113. Eric Miller, "Ten Whites Killed in South African Attack," *Washington Post* (July 26, 1993), p. A18.

114. John Battersby, "South African Democracy Talks Foundering Over Election Date," *Christian Science Monitor* (July 26, 1993), p. 4.

115. Walter Kansteiner, "Medals' Moral for South Africa," *Christian Science Monitor* (July 7, 1993), p. 19.

116. Desmond Tutu, "We Are Going to Make It," *Los Angeles Times* (March 30, 1994), p. B7.

# Conclusion

As South Africans went to the polls in the first all-race elections in the nation's history, there was some fear that violence, sanctioned by both white and black extremists, could unravel the process and lead to civil war. That this did not happen has been called by many observers a "miracle."

"Woo-hoo! It's a transformation. We are free today. We are free." These were the words spoken by Bishop Tutu as Nelson Mandela was inaugurated president of a democratic South Africa and the world witnessed the end of 342 years of white rule. "Measured against the challenge we faced in 1990, what we have achieved is nothing less than a miracle," Tutu told the *Los Angeles Times*.[1]

The words, "a miracle," were heard on many lips, as the realization sank in that this was an unprecedented case of a ruling group relinquishing its monopoly of power without imminent military threat to its continued rule. Many see this historic election of April 1994 as a vindication of faith in the impossible. Tutu attributed the successful transition not only to the international community's pressure through sanctions but also to the power of prayer.

There is no doubt that Christianity shaped the struggle against apartheid; Christian ideals served as an ethical critique of apartheid, as a source of righteous anger that inspired action, and as a wellspring of confidence in eventual victory. Christian values of resistance leaders inspired and shaped black political protest over the twentieth century and in no small measure were instrumental in ushering in a new democratic era.

## THE CONTINUING RELEVANCE OF RELIGION

What role remains for religion to play in a postapartheid society? Forgiveness of enemies is one of the fruits of religion vital to any possible reconciliation of the races in South Africa. The world has witnessed some remarkable events in recent months that point to the reality of forgiveness on the part of black South Africans. Mandela, for instance, chose to include and embrace his former jailers at inaugural events in a spirit of forgiveness that bodes well for national reconciliation. Observers have been impressed with Mandela's complete lack of bitterness against his former oppressors despite being imprisoned for twenty-seven years, more than a third of his adult life. In a postelection celebration on May 2, 1994 in Johannesburg, Mandela set the tone for the incoming government: "Let us stretch out our hands to those who have beaten us and say to them that we are all South Africans. We had a good fight, but now this is the time to heal the old wounds and to build a new South Africa."[2]

Forgiveness, however, is two-sided. It requires not only mercy on the part of the persecuted but it also demands repentance on the side of the oppressor. Beyers Naude, head of the former Christian Institute and one of the leading Afrikaners to oppose apartheid, sees a merciful attitude on the part of the ANC leadership: "[I]n some incredible way God has sown the seeds of a gracious attitude, of the spirit of ubuntu, in the hearts and minds of the whole African community." Yet, he fails to see the admission of guilt on the part of the oppressors: "As for as I know, none of the leaders of the National Party ever said they were sorry about the system they created."[3]

For Tutu, repentance means not only expressing regret to those wronged under apartheid but also offering restitution:

Those who have wronged must be ready to make what amends they can. They must be ready to make restitution and reparation. If I have stolen your pen, I can't really be contrite when I say, "Please forgive me," if at the same time I still keep your pen. If I am truly repentant, then I will demonstate this genuine repentance by returning your pen.[4]

Genuine repentance requires making amends by accepting policies that empower blacks economically, which will inevitably occur at the expense of white South Africans. A serious constraint on white renunciation of economic privilege is that many South Africans do not consider themselves as belonging to one community. Christianity, which is the predominant religion of the majority of blacks and whites in South Africa, may be able to provide that sense of oneness that can make self-sacrifice possible. Though sinful, man is not entirely sinful, or there would be no hope for the future South Africa. Niebuhr writes that the fact that various conceptions of a just solution to a problem can be synthesized into a common solution disproves the idea that groups are consistently egoistic. If that were so, society would be an anarchy of rival interests. The ability of communities to synthesize divergent approaches to arrive at "tolerably just solutions" proves man's capacity to consider interests other than his own.[5] Christianity may contribute to a democratic South Africa in helping to forge a just compromise by synthesizing conflicting interests.

Still, the ANC in power may be tempted as the National Party did to rationalize its own interests in terms of religious truth. It would not be surprising to see the resistance movement's theology of "prophetic criticism" that railed against the illegitimacy of government replaced by one that emphasizes the "priestly sanctification" of government, which renders blanket approval of the actions of government. Niebuhr notes that the oppressed who rise up against an unjust government may be the executor of divine judgment in history, but they are not themselves immune to divine judgment.[6] Tutu affirms the Niebuhrian understanding of man's obstinacy in insisting he has a monopoly on truth or virtue, that his viewpoint is ipso facto God's viewpoint. "We are all created in the image of God. The problem is that we have returned the compliment by creating God in our own image," he explained in an interview.[7] It would behoove the new government to guard against self-righteousness, keeping in mind that political conflicts are between sinners, not between sinners and saints, and that yesterday's oppressed, upon gaining power, are likely to exhibit the same will to power which they abhorred in their opponents.

If religion is to continue to play a vital, constructive role in postapartheid South Africa, it will be important that it raise up those "prophetic minorities" of which Niebuhr speaks to hold the government accountable. A model for this kind of activity is Bishop Donal Lamont of Zimbabwe, who continued to speak against abuses of power in government after white rule in Rhodesia was turned over to the black majority in an independent Zimbabwe. A prophetic faith will eschew the role of court chaplain that sanctifies uncritically state action. We see evidence of church leaders serving that function already. Bishop Tutu was one of the first critics to speak out against the ANC's failure to take strong action against individuals within that organization guilty of human rights violations in the period leading up to national elections.[8] And recently he has attacked officials of the ANC government for riding a "gravy train" of opulence. Cabinet members in their chauffeur-driven Mercedes are a disturbing sight to the masses who have neither basic transportation, housing, nor jobs, he has warned.[9]

## CHALLENGES AHEAD

The tasks facing the new government are formidable. Reducing unemployment and poverty are the main challenges for the ANC. Fifty-three percent of black South Africans live below the poverty line (compared to just 2 percent of whites), and 50 percent of black South Africans are unemployed. For those who are employed, comparisons with white workers are stark: white salaries are 7.5 times more than black wages. And despite the lifting of trade and investment sanctions, only a handful of the U.S. companies which disinvested have returned.[10]

There is reason for concern also over the education system for blacks. Only 38.3 percent of black students who took the exam for a diploma in 1993 passed, and only 8.1 percent passed with scores high enough to continue at the university level. Conversely, 98 percent of white students passed the exam, 43 percent of whom qualified for university admission.[11] These results can be explained not only by higher funding of white schools over black ones but also by the fact that between 5 and 15 percent of six-to-fifteen-year-old blacks are out of school at any time. Mass resistance of the 1980s meant making South Africa ungovernable, and many township youths believed the political struggle took precedence over getting an education.

Clearly, South Africa embraces two distinct worlds: one that allows its white population to gain higher education at rates that occur in richer industrialized countries and the other that limits Africans to levels found in developing countries.[12] Two economies exist side-by-side: one which offers a developed country's wages and lifestyle against one that like other less developed countries can barely provide a subsistence. No government can possibly meet the expectations of both white and black South Africans, whose goals—losing as little privilege as possible for whites and gaining the good life for blacks—may seem mutually exclusive.

Another trend deserves attention. Almost as great as the income disparity between blacks and whites is the growing gap among blacks. Of the wealthiest 20 percent of South African households, about a fourth are black. Their incomes are rising faster than any other sector in South Africa. At the same time, the incomes of the 40% of the poorest blacks have been declining for the last twenty years. The growing black middle class is a key constituency of the ANC, and the ANC will have to choose between this more conservative middle-class support and a radical mass constituency.

There are signs that the ANC is leaning toward a more moderate economic agenda than it had espoused as a liberation movement. Although Mandela reiterated his commitment to the Freedom Charter and its socialist economic policies upon his release from Robben Island, with the demise of the Soviet Union and socialism in worldwide disrepute, he has come to reject a key tenet of the Freedom Charter: the nationalization of banks and mining. In addition, *sunset clauses*, protecting for several years 1.2 million white civil servants' jobs in a bloated bureaucracy that had been maintained by the Nationalists to provide jobs for Afrikaners, have been accepted by the ANC. This promise will go far in allaying white fears of imminent loss of privilege, but will necessarily mean less funds for jobs, housing, and education that blacks have come to expect under a new black-controlled government. The government says it is committed to the Reconstruction and Development Program and pledges the construction of a million homes, electrification and telephones for 2.5 million homes, free and compulsory schooling through age ten, free infant health clinics, land redistribution, and the creation of 2.5 million jobs over the next five years. It is not clear how these projects can be paid for without reducing the standard of living for white South Africans, who already pay among the highest income taxes in the world. The ANC, therefore, may be tempted to do less than promised for the black masses to appease the middle class.[13]

Even if a concerted effort is made to balance the conflicting interests of social classes, some critics warn that given projected low growth rates of 2.5 percent in the coming years, it will take at least ten years for parity to be achieved between standards of living in black and white communities.[14] If black South Africans see little economic improvement in this transitional period, the possibility of violence erupting is great. Township youth are impatient for Mandela to produce the goods, even though he has warned, "You must not expect dramatic changes [the day after the election], or in the first year, or even in the first several years. These things take time."[15] The militant Pan-Africanist Congress (PAC) has potential to gain support if disillusionment with economic progress sets in among poor blacks. The PAC, although faring poorly in elections with a mere 1.25 percent of the vote, nonetheless holds celebrity status in the townships because of attacks by its armed wing, the Azanian People's Liberation Army (APLA), against white farmers. The inability of the ANC to prevent youth in its organization from chanting, "Kill the Boer, kill the farmer" at pre-election demonstrations points to the possible switching of loyalties from the ANC to the PAC by young people, who comprise the largest sector of the African population.[16]

Both the PAC and Black Consciousness Movement (BCM) under Sobukwe and Biko had attempted to tap into the African Independent Churches (AICs) as a source of political support given their compatible visions of exclusive African nationalism. The fact that the AICs are the largest and fastest growing religious group in South Africa may signify the ascendancy of the nationalist approach over the Charterist vision in the future. Although these groups have been viewed by most observers as apolitical or conservative—eschewing violence and respecting authority—[17]there has been some indication that turmoil in the townships over recent years has politicized them. Their numbers alone[18] could make them a potentially important political force in the future, and it is to be expected that the PAC-BCM-NF wing will attempt to draw upon the AICs for political support.

Given the culture of violence that permeates South African society, it would not be surprising to see notions of *just revolution* used against an unresponsive government. Even Mandela, when he is not cautioning patience, has been known to urge his activist audiences to "overthrow the government" if the ANC does not improve their lot.[19] Liberation theology which condoned the use of violence against an unjust regime inspired much political protest over the last two decades. If the new government chooses to appease the middle class and to ignore the poor, one might expect liberation theology again to come to the forefront and resonate among township youth. To meet the new situation of poor blacks fighting a ruling class comprised of both blacks and whites, these righteous rebels will necessarily borrow more heavily from the Latin America school with its emphasis on *class* conflict than from the American school of liberation theology that stressed the *race* struggle.

Black South Africans became politically free in 1994 but economic liberty in any real sense has yet to be attained. To the delegates attending the World Council of Churches conference in South Africa, Tutu remarked that elections would mean the legal death blow of apartheid but the "pernicious consequences would almost certainly remain for many a long year."[20]

Christianity can make a contribution to the continuing struggle for justice in South Africa. It can inspire white South Africans to repent for their past complicity in maintaining an evil system, foster forgiveness on the part of black South Africans, invoke a sense of unity among the races, and assist in the search for a balanced compromise of interests. It can challenge South Africans not to lose sight of the importance of the poor in any scheme of justice, and, most important, provide hope that somehow all of this is indeed possible.

The world is watching events in South Africa with more than a passing interest. As Bishop Tutu noted on the occasion of the joint awarding of the Nobel Peace Prize to Mandela and de Klerk in 1993, South Africa is a microcosm of the world, embodying all the global issues of white and black, rich and poor, of developed and underdeveloped peoples. "Once we have got it right," Tutu said, "South Africa will be the paradigm for the rest of the world."[21]

## NOTES

1. Desmond Tutu, "We Are Going to Make It," *Los Angeles Times* (March 30, 1994), p. B7.

2. John Battersby, "South Africa Takes Final Steps Toward Long-Sought Democracy," *Christian Science Monitor* (May 4, 1994), p. 1.

3. "South Africa: The Spirit of Reconciliation," *Sojourners* (July 1994), p. 9.

4. Desmond Tutu, "We Forgive You," in Desmond Tutu, *The Rainbow People of God: The Making of a Peaceful Revolution*, ed. John Allen (New York: Doubleday, 1994), p. 222.

5. Reinhold Niebuhr, *The Nature and Destiny of Man*, vol. 2 (New York: Charles Scribner's Sons, 1964), p. 249.

6. See Reinhold Niebuhr, *The Nature and Destiny of Man*, vol. 1, (New York: Charles Scribner's Sons, 1955), p. 226; *The Nature and Destiny of Man*, vol. 2, p. 239; *Beyond Tragedy: Essays on the Christian Interpretation of History* (New York: Charles Scribner's Sons, 1937), p. 247; and *Christianity and Power Politics* (New York: Charles Scribner's Sons, 1940), p. 22, p. 139.

7. Cited in Charles Villa-Vicencio, "To Be Servant of the People: The Church and Change in South Africa," *Sojourners* (December 1992), p. 29.

8. "Doing Business in South Africa," *Christian Century* (September 22–29, 1993), p. 891.

9. Tutu Joins Attack on "Gravy Train," *Guardian* (September 28, 1994), pp. 1, 24.

10. Economic data comes from "South Africa II: Dividends from Democracy," *Africa Confidential* 35, no. 9 (May 6, 1994).

11. Lynda I. Loxton, "Fewer Black South Africans Pass Key Examination," *Chronicle of Higher Education* (March 16, 1994), p. A42.

12. Schools are integrating slowly; very few white schools have become more than 15 or 20 percent black in a country where 90 percent of the country's 11 million school-age children are nonwhite.

13. One year after the elections only one thousand of the million houses planned have been built in a country where eight million people are homeless.

14. M. John Lamola, "Change is Pain: A Projective Reflection on the Mission of the Church in South Africa Beyond 1994," *International Review of Mission* 83, no. 328 (January 1994), p. 39.

15. Cited in Paul Taylor, "Father of His Country," *Washington Post Magazine* (February 13, 1994), p. 14.

16. Forty percent of black South Africans are under age fifteen. See Shaun Johnson, "Youth in the Politics of Resistance," in Shaun Johnson, *South Africa: No Turning Back* (Bloomington: Indiana University Press, 1989), p. 96.

17. Bill Keller, "A Surprising Silent Majority in South Africa," *New York Times Magazine* (April 17, 1994), pp. 35ff.

18. One estimate is that 40 percent of African Christians are members of AICs. Marks and Trapido believe that the *vast majority* of black Christians belong to the AICs. See Shula Marks and Stanley Trapido, "South Africa Since 1976: An Historical Perspective," in Johnson, p. 35.

19. Taylor, p. 14.

20. Desmond Tutu, "To the Participants in the Meeting of the CC/WCC: A Word of Welcome," *International Review of Mission* 83, no. 328 (January 1994), p. 9.

21. Cited in Allister Sparks, "The Secret Revolution," *The New Yorker* (April 11, 1994), p. 59.

# Select Bibliography

Adam, Heribert. "The Rise of Black Consciousness in South Africa." *Race* 15, no. 2 (1973), pp. 149–165.

Africa Watch. *No Neutral Ground: South Africa's Confrontation with the Activist Churches*. New York: Human Rights Watch, 1989.

Appiah-Kubi, Kofi, and Sergio Torres, eds. *African Theology En Route*. Maryknoll, N.Y.: Orbis, 1979.

Arnold, Millard, ed. *Steve Biko: Black Consciousness in South Africa*. New York: Random House, 1978.

———. *Steve Biko: No Fears Expressed*. Johannesburg: Skotaville, 1987.

Baartman, Ernest, "Black Consciousness." *Pro Veritate* (March 1973), pp. 4–6.

———. "The Significance of the Development of Black Consciousness for the Church." *Journal of Theology for Southern Africa* 2 (1973), pp. 18–22.

Barkat, Ankar M. "Churches Combating Racism in South Africa." *Journal of International Affairs* 36, no. 2 (Fall-Winter 1982–1983), pp. 297–305.

Barrell, Howard. "The United Democratic Front and the National Forum: Their Emergence, Composition, and Trends." *South African Review* 2 (1984), pp. 6–20.

Becken, Hans Jergen, ed. *Relevant Theology for Africa*. Durban: Lutheran Publishing House, 1973.

Beinart, William. *Twentieth-Century South Africa*. London: Oxford University Press, 1994.

Benson, Mary. *The African Patriots*. London: Faber and Faber, 1963.

———. *Chief Albert Lutuli of South Africa*. London: Oxford University Press, 1963.

———. *Nelson Mandela*. London: Panaf, 1980.

———. *South Africa: The Struggle for a Birthright*. New York: Funk and Wagnalls, 1969.

———. "The Struggle in South Africa Has United All Races." *Notes and Documents* (August 1984), United Nations Centre Against Apartheid.

———. *The Sun Will Rise: Statements from the Dock by South African Political Prisoners*. London: International Defence and Aid Fund, 1974.

Bentley, Judith. *Archbishop Tutu*. Milwaukee: G. Stevens, 1988.

Bernstein, Hilda. *No. 46. Steve Biko*. London: International Defence and Aid Fund, 1978.

Biko, Steve. *I Write What I Like*. Ed. Aelred Stubbs. San Francisco: Harper & Row, 1978.

Birt, Robert E. "An Examination of James Cone's Concept of God and its Role in Black Liberation." *Philosophical Forum* 9, no. 2-3 (Winter-Spring 1977–1978), pp. 339–349.

Blumberg, Myrna. "Durban Explodes." *Africa South in Exile* (October-December 1959), pp. 9–18.

Boesak, Allan. *Black and Reformed*. Maryknoll, N.Y.: Orbis, 1986.

———. *A Call For an End to Unjust Rule*. Edinburgh: St. Andrew's Press, 1986.

———. *A Farewell to Innocence*. Maryknoll, N.Y.: Orbis, 1977.

———. *The Finger of God*. Maryknoll, N.Y.: Orbis, 1982.

———. "Liberation and Theology in South Africa." In Appiah-Kubi, Kofi, and Sergio Torres, eds. *African Theology En Route*. Maryknoll, N.Y.: Orbis, 1979.

———. *Walking on Thorns*. Grand Rapids, Mich.: William B. Eerdmans, 1984.

———. *When Prayer Makes News*. Philadelphia: Westminster Press, 1986.

Bosch, David. "Currents and Crosscurrents in South African Black Theology." *Journal of Religion in Africa* 6, no. 1 (1974), pp. 1–22.

Brewer, John D. *After Soweto: An Unfinished Journey*. Oxford: Clarendon Press, 1986.

———, ed. *Can South Africa Survive?: Five Minutes to Midnight*. London: Macmillan, 1989.

Briggs, D. Roy, and Joseph Wing. *The Harvest and the Hope: The Story of Congregationalism in Southern Africa*. Johannesburg: United Congregationalist Church of Southern Africa, 1970.

Brooks, Alan, and Jeremy Brickhill. *The Whirlwind Before the Storm*. London: International Defence and Aid Fund, 1980.

Bunting, Brian. "Chief Luthuli and the Treason Trial." In *Moses Kotane, South African Revolutionary*. London: International Defence and Aid Fund, 1975, pp. 223–233.

Buthelezi, Manas. "Black Theology and the Le-Grange Commission." *Pro Veritate* 13, no. 6 (October 1975), pp. 4–6.

Callaghy, Thomas. *South Africa in Southern Africa*. New York: Praeger, 1983.

Callan, Edward. *Albert John Luthuli and the South African Race Conflict*. Kalamazoo: Western Michigan University Press, 1962.

Carr, Cannon Burgess. "The Black Consciousness Movement in South Africa and Namibia." *Objective: Justice* 7, no. 3 (July-August-September 1975), pp. 17–23.

Carter, Gwendolen. "African Nationalist Movements." In Davis, John A., and James K. Baker. *Southern Africa in Transition*. New York: Praeger, 1965, pp. 14–16.

———. "African Nationalist Movements in South Africa." *Massachusetts Review* (Autumn 1963), pp. 147–64.

Cawood, Lesley. *The Churches and Race Relations in South Africa*. Johannesburg: SAIRR, 1964.

Chidester, David. *Shots in the Street: Violence and Religion in South Africa*. Boston: Beacon Press, 1991.

"Chief Albert John Luthuli, 1898–1967." *African Communist* 31 (1967), pp. 38–44.

Chikane, Frank. "Church and State in Apartheid South Africa." *Sechaba* 22, no. 6 (June 1988), pp. 2–6.

Choonoo, R. Neville. "Parallel Lives: Black Autobiography in South Africa and the United States." (Ph.D. dissertation, New York: Columbia University, 1982).

"Church and Liberation." *Sechaba* (May 1980), pp. 15–18.

"The Church and Violence: Who Stands Where." *Clarion Call* 3 (1986).

"Church, State Square Off." *Africa News* 30, no. 15 (April 11, 1983), pp. 3–4.

Cochrane, James. *Servants of Power: The Role of English-Speaking Churches, 1903–1930: Towards a Critical Theology Via an Historical Analysis of the Anglican and Methodist Churches*. Johannesburg: Ravan, 1987.

Collinge, Jo-Anne. "The United Democratic Front." *South African Review* 3 (1986), pp. 248–266.

Comaroff, Jean. *Body of Power, Spirit of Resistance: The Culture and History of a South African People*. Chicago: University of Chicago Press, 1985.

"Communists and Christians in the South African Revolution." *African Communist* 110 (1987), pp. 52–71.

Cone, James. *Black Theology and Black Power*. New York: Seabury Press, 1969.

———. *A Black Theology of Liberation*. Philadelphia: Lippincott, 1970.

———. *Speaking the Truth*. Grand Rapids, Mich.: William B. Eerdmans, 1986.

Cramer, Christopher. "Rebuilding South Africa." *Current History* 93, no. 583 (May 1994), pp. 208–212.

Daniel, John. "Radical Resistance to Minority Rule in South Africa: 1906–1965." (Ph.D. dissertation, Buffalo: State University of New York, 1975).

Davenport, T. R. H. *South Africa: A Modern History*. New York: Macmillan, 1991.

Davey, Cyril. *Fifty Lives for God*. London: Oliphants, 1973, pp. 108–110.

Davidson, Basil. "Questions about Nationalism." *African Affairs* 76, no. 302 (January 1977), pp. 39–46.

Davies, Robert, Dan O'Meara, and Sipho Dlamini. *The Struggle for South Africa: A Reference Guide to Movements, Organizations and Institutions*. London: Zed Books, 1984.

Davis, John, and James Baker. *Southern Africa in Transition*. New York: Praeger, 1966.

Davis, Kortright. "Racism and God: Steve Biko in Context." *AME Zion Quarterly Review* 97, no. 4 (January 1986), pp. 2–19.

Davis, Stephen. *Apartheid's Rebels: Inside South Africa's Hidden War*. New Haven: Yale University Press, 1987.

de Klerk, William A. *The Puritans in Africa: The History of Afrikanerdom*. London: Rex Collings, 1975.

Desmond, Cosmas. *Christians or Capitalists? Christianity and Politics in South Africa*. London: Bowerdean Press, 1978.

Dibble, Ernest F. *Young Prophet Niebuhr: Reinhold Niebuhr's Early Search for Social Justice*. Washington, D.C.: University Press of America, 1979.

"Doing Business in South Africa." *Christian Century* (September 22–29, 1993), pp. 890–891.

Dollie, Na-Iem, "The National Forum." *South African Review* 3 (1986), pp. 267–277.

du Boulay, Shirley. *Tutu: Voice of the Voiceless*. Grand Rapids, Mich.: William B. Eerdmans, 1988.

Dubb, A. A., and A. G. Schutte, eds. "Black Religion in South Africa." *African Studies* 33, no. 2 (1974).

Duggan, William R. "Three Men of Peace." *Crisis* 81 (1974), pp. 331–338.

El-Khawas, Mohamed A. "The Liberation Struggle in South Africa: Will the 1980s Be Decisive?" *TransAfrica Forum* 3, no. 2 (Fall 1983), pp. 79–91.

Fanon, Frantz. *The Wretched of the Earth*. New York: Grove Press, 1967.

Fatton, Robert. "The ANC of South Africa: The Limitations of a Revolutionary Strategy." *Canadian Journal of African Studies* 18, no. 3 (1984), pp. 593–608.

———. *Black Consciousness in South Africa*. Albany: State University of New York Press,

1986.

Feit, Edward. *African Opposition in South Africa: The Failure of Passive Resistance.* Stanford: Hoover Institution Press, 1967.

―――. *South Africa: The Dynamics of the ANC.* London: Oxford University Press, 1962.

Ferm, Deane William. *Third World Liberation Theologies: An Introductory Survey.* Maryknoll, N.Y.: Orbis, 1986.

―――. *Third World Liberation Theologies: A Reader.* Maryknoll, N.Y.: Orbis, 1986.

Forman, Lionel, and E. S. Sachs. *The South African Treason Trial.* London: John Calder, 1957.

Franklin, Raymond S. "The Political Economy of Black Power." *Social Problems* 16, no. 3 (Winter 1969), pp. 286–301.

Frederikse, Julie. *South Africa: A Different Kind of War.* Johannesburg: Ravan, 1986.

―――. *The Unbreakable Thread: Non-racialism in South Africa.* Johannesburg: Ravan, 1990.

Gerhart, Gail. *Black Power in South Africa: The Evolution of an Ideology.* Berkeley: University of California Press, 1978.

Gibson, Richard. *African Liberation Movements: Contemporary Struggles Against White Minority Rule.* London: Oxford University Press, 1972.

Gordimer, Nadine. "Chief Luthuli." *Atlantic Monthly* (April 1959), pp. 34–39.

Gqubule, Simon. "What is Black Theology?" *Journal of Theology for Southern Africa* 8 (1974), pp. 16–23.

Graham, Paul. "Policies for Peace." *IDS Bulletin* 25, no. 1 (January 1994), pp. 62–68.

Gray, Tony. *Champions of Peace: The Story of Alfred Nobel, the Peace Prize and the Laureates.* New York: Praeger, 1976.

Grobler, Jackie. *A Decisive Clash? A Short History of Black Protest Politics in South Africa 1875-1976.* Pretoria: Acacia, 1988.

Gruchy, John W. de. *The Church Struggle in South Africa.* Grand Rapids, Mich.: William B. Eerdmans, 1986.

―――. *Cry Justice! Prayers, Meditations and Readings from South Africa.* Maryknoll, N.Y.: Orbis, 1986.

Gruchy, John W. de, and Charles Villa-Vicencio, eds. *Apartheid is a Heresy.* Grand Rapids, Mich.: William B. Eerdmans, 1983.

―――, eds. *Resistance and Hope: South African Essays in Honour of Beyers Naude.* Grand Rapids, Mich.: William B. Eerdmans, 1985.

Grundy, Kenneth W. "South Africa: The Combatants Regroup." *Current History* 87, no. 529 (May 1988), pp. 205–207, 226.

Guma, Alex La, ed. *Apartheid: A Collection of Writings on South African Racism by South Africans.* New York: International Publishers, 1985.

Harcourt, Melville. "Albert Lutuli." In *Portraits of Destiny.* New York: Sheed and Worrel, 1966, pp. 99–173.

Harland, Gordon. *The Thought of Reinhold Niebuhr.* New York: Oxford University Press, 1960.

Hastings, Adrian. "The Christian Churches and Liberation Movements in Southern Africa." *African Affairs* 80, no. 320 (July 1981), pp. 345–354.

―――. *A History of African Christianity 1950–1975.* London: Cambridge University Press, 1979.

Hein, David. "Religion and Politics in South Africa." *Modern Age* 31, no. 1 (Winter 1987), pp. 21–38.

Herbst, Jeffrey. "Creating a New South Africa." *Foreign Policy* 94 (Spring 1994), pp. 120–133.

Herbstein, Denis. *White Man, We Want To Talk to You.* London: Deutsch, 1978.

Hewson, Leslie. *An Introduction to South African Methodists.* Cape Town: Methodist Publishing House, 1951.

Hinchliff, Peter. *The Church in South Africa.* London: SPCK, 1968.

———. "The English-Speaking Churches and South Africa in the Nineteenth Century." *Journal of Theology for Southern Africa* (December 1979), pp. 28–38.

Hindson, D. C., ed. *Working Papers in South African Studies* 3 (1983).

Hirson, Baruch. *Year of Fire, Year of Ash.* London: Zed Books, 1979.

Hoekema, David A. "Is Reconciliation Possible?" An Interview with Allan Boesak. *Christian Century* (May 23, 1984), pp. 546–550.

Hooper, Charles. "Chief Luthuli: He Knows the Woes of the Landless Squatters." *Fighting Talk* 16 (February 1962), unpaged.

Hope, Marjorie, and James Young. *The South African Churches in a Revolutionary Situation.* Maryknoll, N.Y.: Orbis, 1981.

Horrell, Muriel, ed. *A Survey of Race Relations.* (Yearbooks: 1952, 1960, 1976, 1983) Johannesburg: SAIRR 1953–1984.

Hughes, John. "Apartheid's Compassionate Antagonist." *Saturday Review* 45 (June 16, 1962), p. 22.

Jennnings, Theodore. "Steve Biko: Liberator and Martyr." *Christian Century* 94 (November 2, 1977), pp. 997–999.

Johanson, Brian. *Church and State in South Africa.* Johannesburg: Ravan, 1973.

Johnson, Shaun, ed. *South Africa: No Turning Back.* Bloomington: Indiana University Press, 1989.

Joseph, Helen. *If This Be Treason.* London: Deutsch, 1963.

*Kairos Document: The Challenge to the Churches.* Grand Rapids, Mich.: William B. Eerdmans, 1986.

Kane-Berman, John. *South Africa: The Method in the Madness.* London: Pluto Press, 1979.

Karis, Thomas, and Gwendolen Carter. *From Protest to Challenge: A Documentary History of African Politics in South Africa, 1882–1964.* 4 Vol. Stanford: Hoover Institution Press, 1972–1977.

Karis, Thomas. "The Resurgent ANC." In Callagy, Thomas. *South Africa in Southern Africa.* New York: Praeger, 1983, pp. 191–236.

———. "Revolution in the Making." *Foreign Affairs* 62, no. 2 (Winter 1983–1984), pp. 378–406.

———. "South African Liberation: The Communist Factor." *Foreign Affairs* (Winter 1986–1987), pp. 267–287.

Keller, Bill. "A Surprising Silent Majority in South Africa." *New York Times Magazine* (April 17, 1994), pp. 34–41.

Kerr, Alexander. *Fort Hare, 1915–48: The Evolution of the African College.* London: C. Hurst & Co., 1968.

Kiernan, J. P. "Where Zionists Draw the Line: A Study of Religious Exclusiveness in an African Township." *African Studies* 33, no. 2 (1974), pp. 79–90.

Kotze, D. A. *African Politics in South Africa 1964–1974: Parties and Issues.* London: C. Hurst & Co., 1975.

Kretzschmar, Louise. *The Voice of Black Theology in South Africa.* Johannesburg: Ravan,

1986.

Kuper, Leo. *Passive Resistance in South Africa*. New Haven: Yale University Press, 1957.

Lamola, M. John. "Change is Pain: A Projective Reflection on the Mission of the Church in South Africa Beyond 1994." *International Review of Mission* 83, no. 328 (January 1994), pp. 37–44.

———. "Does the Church Lead the Struggle?" *Sechaba* 22 no. 6 (June 1988), pp. 7–11.

Leatt, James, Theo Kneifel, and Klaus Nurnberger, eds. *Contending Ideologies in South Africa*. Grand Rapids, Mich.: William B. Eerdmans, 1986.

Legum, Colin, and Margaret Legum. *The Bitter Choice: Eight South Africans' Resistance to Tyranny*. New York: World Publishing Co., 1968, pp. 49–69, 103–117.

Lodge, Tom. "The ANC, 1982." *South African Review* 1 (1983), pp. 50–54.

———. "The ANC, 1983." *South African Review* 2 (1984), pp. 21–25.

———. *Black Politics in South Africa Since 1945*. New York: Longman, 1983.

———. "The United Democratic Front: Leadership and Ideology." In Brewer, John. *Can South Africa Survive?: Five Minutes to Midnight*. New York: Macmillan, 1989, pp. 206–230.

Loewen, Jacob A. "Mission Churches, Independent Churches, and Felt Needs in Africa." *Missionalia* 4, no. 4 (1976), pp. 404–425.

Luthuli, Albert. "Africa and Freedom." *Vital Speeches* 28 (February 1962), pp. 267–271.

———. "Boycott Us." *Spectator* 204 (1960), p. 208.

———. "Change Sweeps Over Zululand." *Rotarian* 68 (June 1946), pp. 40–42.

———. "The Effect of Minority Rule on Nonwhites." In Spottiswoode, Hildegarde. *South Africa: The Road Ahead*. London: Bailey Bros. and Swinfen Ltd., 1960, pp. 109–118.

———. "Foreword" to Rubin, Leslie, and Neville Rubin. *This Is Apartheid*. London: Christian Action, 1966.

———. "Freedom Front in the Congress." *Listener* 15 (September 20, 1956), pp. 422–423.

———. *Let My People Go*. London: Collins, 1962.

———. "Let Us Speak Together of Freedom." *Fighting Talk* 10 (1956), pp. 4–5.

———. "Luthuli Speaks on Liquor Rights and Bantu Authorities." *Race Relations News* 23 (August 1961), pp. 106–107.

———. "No Arms for South Africa." In *Statements and Addresses: Notes and Documents*. New York: United Nations Centre Against Apartheid, 1969, pp. 30–33.

———. "On the Rivonia Trial." In *Statements and Addresses: Notes and Documents*. New York: United Nations Centre Against Apartheid, 1969, pp. 34–35.

———. "A Program for a New South Africa." *Saturday Night* 77 (January 20, 1962), pp. 9–18.

——— [Lutuli]. *The Road to Freedom is Via the Cross*. London: The ANC, n.d.

———. "South Africa Shall Have Its Freedom." *Africa Today* 3, no. 5 (September-October 1956), pp. 2–5.

———. *Statements and Addresses: Notes and Documents*. New York: United Nations Centre Against Apartheid, 1969.

———. "The Vision of Democracy in South Africa." *Fellowship* 25, no. 9 (1959), pp. 5–9.

———. "We are Bound to Struggle." *Dissent* 3 (1956), p. 7.

———. "What I Would Do If I Were Prime Minister." *Ebony* 17 (February 1962), pp. 20–29.

Mafeje, Archie. "Soweto and Its Aftermath." In Murray, Martin, ed. *South African Capitalism and Black Political Opposition*. Cambridge: Schenkeman, 1982, pp. 739–759.

Magubane, Bernard. "Soweto: Ten Years After." *TransAfrica Forum* 4, no. 1 (Fall 1986), pp. 63–75.

Mahabane, Zaccheus. *The Good Fight: Selected Speeches of Rev. Zaccheus R. Mahabane.* Evanston: Program of African Studies, Northwestern University, 1966.

Maimela, Simon. *Proclaim Freedom to My People.* Johannesburg: Skotaville, 1987.

Mandela, Nelson. *The Struggle is My Life.* New York: Pathfinder Press, 1986.

Marx, Anthony. *Lessons of Struggle: South African Internal Opposition, 1960–1990.* New York: Oxford University Press, 1992.

Matthews, Z. K. *Freedom for My People.* London: R. Collings, 1981.

Mayson, Cedric. "Christianity and Revolution." *Sechaba* (October 1987), pp. 12–15.

———. "The Liberation of Christians." *Sechaba* (November 1983), pp. 22–25.

Mbali, Zolile. *The Churches and Racism: A Black South African Perspective.* London: SCM Press, 1987.

McKean, David. "The UDF and the Anti-Apartheid Struggle." *TransAfrica Forum* 4, no. 1 (Fall 1986), pp. 31–46.

Mdlalore, Thoko. "The Place of the Church in Our Liberation Struggle." *African Communist* 104 (1986), pp. 18–27.

Meli, Francis. *South Africa Belongs to Us: A History of the ANC.* Bloomington: Indiana University Press, 1989.

Merwe, van der, Hendrik, ed. *African Perspectives on South Africa: A Collection of Speeches, Articles, and Documents.* Stanford: Hoover Institution Press, 1978.

Merwe, van der, Hendrik, and David Welsh, eds. *Student Perspectives on South Africa.* Cape Town: David Philip, 1972.

"The Missing Man." *New Commonwealth* 39 (April 1961), p. 211.

Mitchell, Louis. "Steve Biko: South Africa's Modern Symbol." *Crisis* 85, no. 4 (1978), pp. 123–135.

Molteno, Frank. "South Africa 1976: A View From Within the Liberation Movement." *Social Dynamics* 5, no. 2 (1975), pp. 66–74.

Moodie, T. Dunbar. *The Rise of Afrikanerdom: Power, Apartheid and the Afrikaner Civil Religion.* Berkeley: University of California Press, 1975.

Moore, Basil, ed., *Black Theology: The South African Voice.* London: C. Hurst & Co., 1973.

Mosala, Jerry. "African Traditional Beliefs and Christianity." *Journal of Theology for Southern Africa* 43 (1983), pp. 15–24.

Mosala, Jerry, and Buti Tlhagale, eds. *The Unquestionable Right to Be Free: Essays on Black Theology.* Johannesburg: Skotaville, 1986.

Motlhabi, Mokgethi. *Challenge to Apartheid: Toward a Moral National Resistance.* Grand Rapids, Mich.: William B. Eerdmans, 1988.

———, ed. *Essays on Black Theology.* Johannesburg: University Christian Movement, 1972.

———. *The Theory and Practice of Black Resistance to Apartheid.* Johannesburg: Ravan, 1984.

Mphahlele, Ezekiel. "Albert Luthuli: The End of Nonviolence." *Africa Today* 14 (August 1967), pp. 1–3.

Mufson, Steven. *Fighting Years: Black Resistance and the Struggle for a New South Africa.* Boston: Beacon Press, 1990.

Murray, Martin. *South Africa: Time of Agony, Time of Destiny: The Upsurge of Popular Protest.* London: Verso, 1987.

————, ed. *South African Capitalism and Black Political Opposition*. Cambridge: Schenkeman, 1982.

Muzorewa, Gwinyai H. *The Origins and Development of African Theology*. Maryknoll, N.Y.: Orbis, 1985, pp. 101–24.

Nash, Margaret. *Ecumenical Movements in the 1960s*. Johannesburg: Ravan, 1975.

Ngcokovane, Cecil Mzingisi. *Apartheid in South Africa: Challenge to Christian Churches*. New York: Vantage Press, 1984.

Ngubane, Jordan. *An African Explains Apartheid*. London: Pall Mall, 1963.

————. "Albert Luthuli: President of Congress." *Drum* (February 1953), p. 21.

Niebuhr, Reinhold. *Beyond Tragedy: Essays on the Christian Interpretation of History*. New York: Charles Scribner's Sons, 1937.

————. *The Children of Light and the Children of Darkness: A Vindication of Democracy and a Critique of Its Traditional Defense*. New York: Charles Scribner's Sons, 1944.

————. *Christian Realism and Political Problems*. Fairfield, N.J.: Augustus M. Kelley Publishers, 1977.

————. *Christianity and Power Politics*. New York: Charles Scribner's Sons, 1940.

————. *The Irony of American History*. New York: Charles Scribner's Sons, 1962.

————. *Moral Man and Immoral Society*. New York: Charles Scribner's Sons, 1932.

————. *The Nature and Destiny of Man*. Vol. 1. New York: Charles Scribner's Sons, 1955.

————. *The Nature and Destiny of Man*. Vol. 2. New York: Charles Scribner's Sons, 1964.

Nkosi, Robert, "Robert Soboukwe: An Assessment." *Africa Report* 7, no. 4 (April 1962), pp. 7–9.

Nkosi, Z. "The Lessons of Soweto." *African Communist* 68 (1977), pp. 18–33.

Nolan, Albert. *God in South Africa: The Challenge of the Gospel*. Grand Rapids, Mich.: William B. Eerdmans, 1988.

Norman, Edward. *Christianity in the Southern Hemisphere: The Churches in Latin America and South Africa*. New York: Oxford University Press, 1981.

Novicki, Margaret. "Interview with Bishop Tutu." *Africa Report* 31, no. 2 (March-April 1986), pp. 53–54.

Nurnberger, Klaus, *Ideologies of Change in South Africa and the Power of the Gospel*. Durban: Lutheran Publishing House, 1979.

Nyameko, R. S. and G. Singh. "The Role of Black Consciousness in the South African Revolution." *African Communist* 68 (1977), pp. 34–47.

Ojo-Ade, Femi. "Stephen Biko: Black Consciousness, Black Struggle, Black Survival." *Journal of Modern African Studies* (Great Britain) 3 (1981), pp. 539–546.

PAC. *PAC in Perspective*. London: PAC, 1973.

PAC. *Time for Azania*. Toronto: Norman Bethune Institute, 1976.

Paton, Alan. "Chief Albert Luthuli: His Crime is Loyalty." In Callan, Edward, ed. *The Long View*. New York: Twayne Publishers, 1968, pp. 201–03.

————. "In Memorium: Albert Luthuli." *Christianity and Crisis* 27 (1967), pp. 206–207.

Pillay, Gerald J. *Voices of Liberation: Albert Lutuli*. Pretoria: HSRC Publishers, 1993.

Pityana, N. Barney, Mamphela Ramphele, Malusi Mpumlwana, and Lindy Wilson, eds. *Bounds of Possibility: The Legacy of Steve Biko and Black Consciousness*. Cape Town: David Philip, 1991.

Pogrund, Benjamin. *How Can Man Die Better: Sobukwe and Apartheid*. London: Peter Halban, 1990.

"Portrait of a Traitor." *Africa Today* (January-February 1957), pp. 2-5.

Prior, Andrew. "Political Culture and Violence: A Case Study of the ANC." *Politikon* 6, no. 2 (December 1984), pp. 12-20.

"A Prisoner of Hope." *Christianity Today* 36 (October 5, 1992), pp. 39-41.

Prozesky, Martin, ed. *Christianity in South Africa*. Bergvlei, South Africa: Southern Book Publishers Ltd., 1990.

Randall, Peter. *A Taste of Power*. Johannesburg: Ravan, 1973.

Ranuga, Thomas. "Frantz Fanon and Black Consciousness in Azania." *Phylon* 47, no. 3 (1986), pp. 182-191.

Rathbone, Richard. "The People and Soweto." *Journal of Southern African Studies* 6, no. 1 (October 1979), pp. 124-132.

Reeves, Ambrose. *Shooting at Sharpeville: The Agony of South Africa*. Boston: Houghton Mifflin, 1969.

Regehr, Ernie. *Perceptions of Apartheid: The Churches and Political Change in South Africa*. Scottsdale, Ariz.: Herald Press, 1979.

Republic of South Africa. *Report of the Commission of Inquiry into South African Council of Churches*. Pretoria: Government Printing Office, 1983.

Ritner, Peter. *The Death of Africa*. New York: Macmillan, 1960, pp. 69-74.

"Robert Sobukwe of the PAC." *Africa Report* 20, no. 3 (1975), pp. 18-20.

Robertson, Janet. *Liberalism in South Africa*. Oxford: Clarendon Press, 1971.

"The Role of Chief Luthuli." *African Communist* 70 (Fall 1977), pp. 14-19.

Roux, Edward. *Time Longer Than Rope: The Black Man's Struggle for Freedom in South Africa*. Madison: University of Wisconsin Press, 1964.

St. Laurent, Philip. "The Negro in World History." *Tuesday Magazine* 3 (July 1968), pp. 14-15, 21, 30.

Sampson, Anthony. *The Treason Cage: The Opposition on Trial in South Africa*. London: Heinemann, 1958.

*Sechaba*. ANC 70th Anniversary (January 1982), pp. 3-7.

Shephard, Robert. *Lovedale, South Africa: The Story of a Century, 1845-1945*. Lovedale: Lovedale Press, n.d.

Shultz, George. "The Church as a Force for Peaceful Change in South Africa." *Bulletin*. Washington, D.C.: United States Department of State (August 1986), pp. 30-32.

Siebert, Hannes. "The Painful Liberation of South Africa: The Church Assumes Role as Mediator." *Sojourners* (December 1991), pp. 30, 31, 34.

Sikakane, Enos. "The Need for Black Theology." *Pro Veritate* (April 1974), pp. 20-23.

Silk, Andrew. "Understanding the Master: Robert Sobukwe's Legacy." *The Nation* 226, no. 12 (1978), pp. 368-370.

Simons, Jack, and Ray Simons. *Class and Colour in South Africa, 1850-1950*. London: International Defence Aid Fund for South Africa, 1983.

Simpson, Theodore. "Black Theology—And White." *Pro Veritate* (March 1974), pp. 16-20.

Sobukwe, Mangaliso Robert. *Speeches of Mangaliso Sobukwe, 1949-1959*. No publishing information available.

Sparks, Allister. *The Mind of South Africa*. New York: Ballantine Books, 1990.

———. "The Secret Revolution." *The New Yorker* 70 (April 11, 1994), pp. 56-78.

Spottiswoode, Hildegarde. *South Africa: The Road Ahead*. London: Bailey Bros. and Swinfen Ltd., 1960.

Stone, Ronald. *Reinhold Niebuhr: Prophet to Politicians*. Nashville, N.Y.: Abingdon

Press, 1972.

Strassberger, Elfriede. *Ecumenism in South Africa, 1936-1960*. Johannesburg: SACC, 1974.

Study Commission on U.S. Policy Toward Southern Africa. *South Africa: Time Running Out*. Berkeley: University of California Press, 1981.

Sullivan, Michael. "Total Power: The Evolution of Apartheid." *TransAfrica Forum* 4, no. 1 (Fall 1986), pp. 47-62.

Sundermeier, Theo, ed. *Church and Nationalism in South Africa*. Johannesburg: Ravan, 1975.

Sundkler, Bengt G. M. *Bantu Prophets in South Africa*. New York: Oxford University Press, 1961.

Tambo, Oliver. "The Black Reaction." *Issue* 4, no. 3 (1974), pp. 3-5.

———. *Prepare for Power*. New York: G. Braziller, 1988.

Tatum, Lyle, ed. *South Africa: Challenge and Hope*. New York: Hill & Wang, 1987.

Templin, J. Alton. *Ideology on a Frontier: The Theological Foundation of Afrikaner Nationalism, 1652-1910*. Westport, Conn.: Greenwood Press, 1984.

Thomas, David. "Church-State Relations in South Africa: Uncomfortable Bedfellows." *South Africa International* 13, no. 1 (July 1982), pp. 49-61.

———. *Councils in the Ecumenical Movement in South Africa*. Johannesburg: SACC, 1979.

Thompson, Leonard. *A History of South Africa*. New Haven: Yale University Press, 1990.

"Three African Freedom Movements." *Freedomways* 2, no. 1 (Winter 1962), pp. 75-87.

Tthhagale, Buti, and Itumzleng Mosala, eds. *Hammering Swords into Ploughshares*. Johannesburg: Skotaville, 1986.

Turner, Harold W. "African Religious Research—New Studies of New Movements." *Journal of Religion in Africa* 11, no. 2 (1980), pp. 137-153.

———. "The Place of Independent Religious Movements in the Modernization of Africa." *Journal of Religion in Africa* 2, no. 1 (1969), pp. 43-63.

Turner, Ruth. "Violence and Non-violence in Confrontation: A Comparative Study of Ideologies. Six Historical Cases. Paine, Lenin, Hitler, Gandhi, Luthuli, and King." (Ph.D. dissertation, Amherst: University of Massachusetts, 1979).

Turok, Ben. *Revolutionary Thought in the Twentieth Century*. London: Zed Books, 1980.

Tutu, Desmond. "Afterword: A Christian Vision of the Future of South Africa." In Prozesky, Martin, ed. *Christianity in South Africa*. Bergvlei, South Africa: Southern Book Publishers Ltd., 1990, pp. 233-240.

———. "Black South African Perspectives and the Reagan Administration." *TransAfrica Forum* 1, no. 1 (Summer 1982), pp. 7-15.

———. "Black Theology/African Theology—Soul Mates or Antagonists?" In Wilmore, Gayraud, and James Cone. *Black Theology: A Documentary History, 1966-1979*. Maryknoll, N.Y.: Orbis, 1979, pp. 483-491.

———. "Christianity and Apartheid" in Gruchy, John W. de, and Charles Villa-Vicencio, eds. *Apartheid is a Heresy*. Grand Rapids, Mich.: William B. Eerdmans, 1983.

———. *Crying in the Wilderness: The Struggle for Justice in South Africa*. Grand Rapids, Mich.: William B. Eerdmans, 1982.

———. "Deeper Into God: Spirituality for the Struggle." An Interview with Desmond Tutu in Wallis, Jim, and Joyce Hollyday. *Crucible of Fire: The Church Confronts Apartheid*. Maryknoll, N.Y.: Orbis, 1989, pp. 63-69.

———. "Freedom Fighters or Terrorists?" In Villa-Vicencio, Charles, ed. *Theology and*

*Violence: The South African Debate.* Johannesburg: Skotaville, 1987.

———. "God and Nation in the Perspective of Black Theology." *Journal of Theology for Southern Africa* 15 (1976), pp. 5–11.

———. "God Intervening in Human Affairs." *Missionalia* 5, no. 2 (1977), pp. 111–117.

———. *Hope and Suffering.* Grand Rapids, Mich.: William B. Eerdmans, 1984.

———. *Nobel Peace Prize Lecture.* New York: Phelps-Stokes Fund, 1986.

———. *The Rainbow People of God.* Ed. Allen, John. New York: Doubleday, 1994.

———. "Some African Insights and the Old Testament." *Journal of Theology for Southern Africa* 1 (1972), pp. 16–22.

———. "Spirituality: Christian and African." In Gruchy, John W. de, and Charles Villa-Vicencio, eds. *Resistance and Hope: South African Essays in Honour of Beyers Naude.* Grand Rapids, Mich.: William B. Eerdmans, 1985, pp. 159–164.

———. "The Theology of Liberation in Africa." In Appiah-Kubi, Kofi and Sergio Torres, eds. *African Theology En Route.* Maryknoll, N.Y.: Orbis, 1979, pp. 162–168.

———. "To the Participants in the Meeting of the CC/WCC: A Word of Welcome." *International Review of Missions* 83, no. 328 (January 1994), pp. 9–10.

———. "Viability." In Becken, Hans-Jergen. *Relevant Theology for Africa.* Durban: Lutheran Publishing House, 1973, pp. 34–39.

———. "Whither African Theology?" In Fashole-Luke, Edward, ed. *Christianity in Independent Africa.* London: Rex Collings, 1978, pp. 364–369.

———. *The Words of Desmond Tutu.* Ed. Tutu, Naomi. New York: Newmarket Press, 1989.

Villa-Vicencio, Charles. "The Church: Discordant and Divided." *Africa Report* 28, no. 4 (July-August 1983), pp. 13–16.

———. "The Conditions of Freedom: Mandela's Release Marks Decisive Moment in South Africa." *Sojourners* (April 1990), pp. 30–34.

———. *The Spirit of Hope: Conversations on Politics, Religion, and Values.* Johannesburg: Skotaville, 1994.

———, ed. *Theology and Violence: The South African Debate.* Johannesburg: Skotaville, 1987.

———. "To Be Servant of the People: The Church and Change in South Africa." *Sojourners* (December 1992), pp. 27–29.

———. *Trapped in Apartheid.* Maryknoll, N.Y.: Orbis, 1988.

Wallis, Jim. "The Miracle of South Africa." *Sojourners* (July 1994), pp. 4–5, 40.

Wallis, Jim and Hollyday, Joyce. *Crucible of Fire: The Church Confronts Apartheid.* Maryknoll, N.Y.: Orbis Books, 1989.

Walls, Andrew. "The Challenge of African Independent Churches," *Evangelical Review of Theology* 4, vol. 2 (1980), pp. 225–234.

Walshe, Peter. *Black Nationalism in South Africa.* Johannesburg: Ravan, 1973.

———. *Church Versus State in South Africa: The Case of the Christian Institute.* Maryknoll, N.Y.: Orbis, 1983.

———. "Church versus State in South Africa: The Christian Institute and the Resurgence of African Nationalism." *Journal of Church and State* 19, 3 (Autumn 1977), pp. 457–479.

———. *The Rise of African Nationalism in South Africa: The ANC 1912-1952.* Berkeley: University of California Press, 1971.

———. "South Africa: Prophetic Christianity and the Liberation Movement." *The Journal of Modern African Studies* 29 (1991), pp. 27–60.

Washington Office on Africa, "Apartheid's Legacy: Southern Africa in the 90s." *A Special Issue of the Washington Notes on Africa*. No publishing information.

Webster, John, ed. *Bishop Desmond Tutu, The Voice of One Crying in the Wilderness*. London: Mowbray, 1982.

Weissman, Stephen. "Dateline South Africa: The Opposition Speaks." *Foreign Policy* 58 (Spring 1985), pp. 151–170.

Welsh, David. "The 1983 Constitutional Referendum and the Future of South Africa: View One." *South Africa International* 14, no. 3 (January 1984), pp. 427–434.

Wepman, Dennis. *Desmond Tutu*. New York: Franklin Watts, 1989.

West, Martin. *Bishops and Prophets in a Black City*. Cape Town: David Philip, 1975.

———. "Independence and Unity: Problems of Cooperation Between African Independent Church Leaders in Soweto." *African Studies* 33, no. 2 (1974), pp. 121–129.

Wiechers, Marinus. "The 1983 Constitutional Referendum and the Future of South Africa: View Two." *South Africa International* 14, no. 3 (January 1984), pp. 435–439.

Wilmore, Gayraud. *Black Religion and Black Radicalism*. Maryknoll, N.Y.: Orbis, 1972.

———. "Steve Biko, Martyr." *Christianity and Crisis* 37 (October 17, 1977), pp. 239–240.

Wilmore, Gayraud, and James Cone. *Black Theology: A Documentary History, 1966–1979*. Maryknoll, N.Y.: Orbis, 1979.

Wilson, Francis. *Outlook on a Century: South Africa, 1870–1970*. Transvaal: Lovedale Press, 1973.

Wilson, Monica, and Leonard Thompson, eds. *A History of South Africa to 1870*. Cape Town: David Philip, 1982.

———, eds. *The Oxford History of South Africa: 1870–1966*, vol. 2. Oxford: Clarendon Press, 1971.

Witvliet, Theo. *A Place in the Sun: An Introduction to Liberation Theology in the Third World*. Maryknoll, N.Y.: Orbis, 1985.

Wolterstorff, Nicholas. "South African Crucible: Two Prophetic Voices in a Land of Racial Pain." *Sojourners* 9 (March 1980), pp. 30–33.

Woods, Donald. *Biko*. New York: Paddington Press, 1978.

Woodson, Dorothy. "Albert Luthuli and the African National Congress: A Bio-Bibliography." *History in Africa* 13 (1986), pp. 345–362.

———. "The Speeches of Albert J. Luthuli." *Africana Journal* 13, no. 1–4, pp. 41–49.

Young, James. "South African Churches: Agents of Change." *Christian Century* (November 24, 1982), pp. 1199–1201.

Zulu, Alphaeus. "Whither Black Theology?" *Pro Veritate* (March, 1973), pp. 11–13.

Zulu, Lawrence B. "Nineteenth Century Missionaries: Their Significance for Black South Africa." In Motlhabi, Mokgethi, ed. *Essays on Black Theology*. Johannesburg: University Christian Movement, 1972, pp. 85–90.

# Index

**About the Author**

LYN S. GRAYBILL currently teaches African Politics in the Department of Government and Foreign Affairs at the University of Virginia. She holds degrees from the College of William and Mary and the University of Virginia.

ISBN 0-275-95141-3

EAN

HARDCOVER BAR CODE